Format Matters

Format Matters: Standards, Practices, and Politics in Media Cultures

edited by Marek Jancovic, Axel Volmar,
and Alexandra Schneider

μ meson press

Bibliographical Information of the German National Library
The German National Library lists this publication in the Deutsche
Nationalbibliografie (German National Bibliography); detailed
bibliographic information is available online at http://dnb.d-nb.de

Published in 2020 by meson press, Lüneburg
www.meson.press

Design concept: Torsten Köchlin, Silke Krieg
Cover image: Photograph by Jessica Ruscello
Copy editing: Kyle Stine

The print edition of this book is printed by Books on
Demand, Norderstedt.

ISBN (Print): 978-3-95796-155-6
ISBN (PDF):   978-3-95796-156-3
ISBN (EPUB): 978-3-95796-157-0
DOI: 10.14619/1556

The digital editions of this publication can be downloaded freely at:
www.meson.press.

Contents

Format Matters: An Introduction to Format Studies

Axel Volmar, Marek Jancovic, and Alexandra Schneider

Wherever there are media, there are also formats. Lisa Parks and Nicole Starosielski recently argued that "our current mediascapes would not exist without our current media infrastructures" (Parks and Starosielski 2015, 1). The same is true for formats. If infrastructures represent the sine qua non of media content in the final instance, then formats represent the necessary forms of structuring and delivering media that coordinate between infrastructures and users. Formats typically consist of specific sets of descriptions and requirements of how to arrange and present information—from simple specifications of geometrical dimensions or aspect ratios through the dramaturgical structure of TV shows and radio stations to the morphologies of digital file formats. These descriptions affect the aesthetic and perceptual qualities of media and instruct human users and technological devices how media content should be handled.

One basic effect of media formats is to determine how medial artifacts and information can pass through vast media infrastructures and ensure interoperability over diverse industries and ecologies of media devices. A standardized paper format, such as A4 or US letter, for instance, ensures that the paper you buy fits the printer you own, that the letter you print will fit the envelopes you keep in your drawer, and that whoever receives your letter will be able to file it by fitting it neatly in a folder or filing cabinet. Formats both reflect and stimulate specific media practices, workflows, and other forms of cooperation. Not incidentally, the oldest use of "format" as a technical term stems from the early modern printing industry where it indicated the way a book was folded and the number of pages produced from one paper sheet (Volmar 2017, 15–16; Jancovic in this volume).

In short, formats represent critical nodes of media culture because they mediate between the content and the material constraints of media, the local and the translocal, individuals and collectives, artifacts and practices, and intended and unintended use. Formats can hence be regarded as specific sets of designed and negotiated features and functions that determine the aesthetic configurations of a medium, produce and reflect diverse relations of cooperation, and refer to different domains of application and models of monetization. Despite their considerable implications for both the appearance and use of media, formats have long remained neglected in media studies. By bringing together a wide range of case studies on the standards, practices, and politics of formats in media culture tied to photography, film, radio, television, and the web, in both professional and amateur uses, *Format Matters* seeks to lay the foundations for the research field of *format studies*.

What Is a Format and Why Does It Matter?

Discussions of the term "format" are troubled by a semantic indeterminacy. It seems to refer to certain material characteristics of media objects, such as shape and dimension, but can also describe structural or programmatic relationships between individual elements and their organizational logic. It is used to name perceptible formal properties of mediated content and information but can also mean their erasure, as in the verb "to format," which, in computing, denotes the preparation of an inscription surface or storage medium for writing. Literary scholar Michael Niehaus postulates that "the format stands . . . at the 'interface' between medium and form" (Niehaus 2018, 43, our translation). This observation closely resembles Jonathan Sterne's (2012, 8) tentative definition: "format is what specifies the protocols by which a medium will operate." It seems that these analytical entities—medium, format, protocol, interface—form a circular field in which concepts can be explained in terms of each other, but nonetheless remain elusive individually. Protocols are intricately connected to practices of formatting. Not far behind their remarkable resurrection in computer science lies their semantic history as media of law and diplomacy: a protocol is the first sheet of a manuscript, and closely related to "codec" (a coder-decoder program) with its origin in literal books, *codices*. To encode or decode something means to translate information from one format into another, for example, from a format in which a video file is stored on a carrier to one understood by the graphics stack of an operating system. The carried information might, in turn, be exchanged via a series of protocols, such as BitTorrent or UDP, which are also standardized descriptions of how two systems can communicate with each other.

But unlike the terms codec, protocol, or interface, the notion of format possesses a strange definitory pliability, seemingly refusing any conclusive *definiens*. Niehaus compares formats with genres—and indeed, in radio broadcasting, format denotes what might colloquially be called the music genre. In the United Kingdom, Ofcom, the regulatory authority of the broadcasting industry, issues broadcast licenses to stations for a specific format, for example, blues or country. A format change—a reformatting, as it were—requires Ofcom's approval and is a question of "purchasing a new library of CDs, hiring new disc jockeys, and undertaking an advertising campaign" (Romeo and Dick 2005, 59). Speaking about radio formats of a different kind, cultural critic Gilbert Seldes wrote in 1950:

> To make individual programs forgettable, yet hold the audience, means that the format must be the link between one program and another. . . . Drama and the big popular comedy programs are in the upper reaches of radio; lower down, format is purely a matter of packaging, wrapping other people's goods in new paper. (Seldes 1950, 112)

This understanding of format as a structural link, some kind of packaging or container, is also at play in television. In this area, format denotes a central premise on top of which a number of screenplays can be developed, a standardized dramaturgical armature that can be filled with "content." In 1966, the Writers Guild of America defined "format" in its basic agreement as a written document with a fixed minimum price of US\$1,120 that sketches out the central characters, themes, or storylines of a serial or episodic narration (Meadow 1970). This sense of the word has entered Europe with some delay, after the gradual introduction of a dual radio and television system in which public and private broadcasters coexist and compete for audiences beginning in the 1980s. It was followed by an expansion of format program television: the organization of broadcasting into repeated, structurally and functionally well-differentiated, thematically similar and increasingly franchised elements, a process that has also been called "formatting" (Meckel 2002).

The metaphor of formats as vessels harkens back to the notion that they are something incidental to the essence, something that is not *the thing proper,* such as a fungible film can that houses an invaluable negative. In computing, this seeming peripherality manifests as the file extension, which is hidden from end users by default like an insignificant appendage. The format of digital files is a syntactic interpretation aid that describes how information contained in the file is encoded and allows it to be used for a specific application or purpose. We also speak of container formats: WARC and MP4 are receptacles that can carry variously encoded audio, video, and subtitle streams and metadata in a single file. The distinction is not always clear, however: television transmission standards like PAL and DVB are often called formats, sometimes protocols, and they are also video encoding methods. Thanks to the informal but practically universally implemented ID3 tagging format, MP3, too, became both codec and container, capable of carrying multimedia information besides audio.

Finally, format is also a common word for aspect ratio. German telecommunication law knows what is often called the "format protection clause."[1] It prevents operators of public broadcasting networks from tampering with the "format" of television signals in the widescreen aspect ratio. Historically, such practices of reformatting have been central to the theorization of formats in art history, as we will discuss in a moment. In the sense of "aspect ratio," the word has been in common use for paintings and photographs, as well as for cinema and television, since their early days.

In an effort to make the term general enough to be conceptually useful, some German studies on media formats have explicitly distanced themselves from its usage in broadcasting, where it primarily denotes a commercial market strategy, as well as from its use as a technical descriptor, such as VHS or MP3. Hans-Jürgen Bucher, Thomas Gloning, and Katrin Lehnen (2010) are interested in "format" purely as an intermediate analytical tier between macro-scale media and micro-scale communicative forms that can encompass both intentional and unintentional communicative structures. But perhaps we must do the opposite, addressing formats precisely at the points where the many dissonant and incommensurable meanings we attach to this term become apparent and thus where, as Susanne Müller (2014, 261) has argued, formats become analytically productive.

Situating Formats

Despite their definitory fuzziness, formats as cultural objects and formatting as a cultural practice are supposed to serve specific purposes. Formats matter because they have been designed to do so. Unlike media, formats—as their etymology as something that has been given a specific form suggests—are the results of conscious decisions. In our everyday experience, we usually encounter formats as specific formal and aesthetic configurations of media with respect to parameters such as size, aspect ratio, and resolution (see Somaini in this volume). Behind the look and feel of a medium like film, which can be captured in different formats, such as 16mm, VHS, and MP4, however, are hidden not only aesthetic but economic and other strategic considerations that balance the desire for a certain quality with the cost of providing the necessary definition of a medium

---

1   *Telekommunikationsgesetz* §49.

(see Sterne 2012, 4–5). As mentioned above, formats are also designed to enable (or obstruct) interoperability between devices, often to facilitate task-specific processes. In such cases, the purpose of format is to support tasks and workflows, both professional and domestic, often by means of specially formatted "work media" (Schüttpelz 2017, 37), such as temporary production prints used in film editing or forms and paper files that circulate within administrative institutions as part of bureaucratic procedures (Vismann 2008; also Volmar in this volume).

Next to regulating the properties of technical media, formats can also consist in sets of rules and formal elements that determine the common ground for how social and political interaction and competition can unfold. These can be, for instance, formats for games or sports (see Stauff in this volume), TV shows, discussions, workshops, auctions, or even the course of scholarly discourse (see Michell in this volume) and the preservation of cultural memory (see Jancovic in this volume). Formats can hence be regarded as operative cultural metadata: as pro-grams or "scripts" in the sense of Madeleine Akrich (1992). The potential for enabling playing fields for diverse forms of cultural practice and the production of collective meaning on the basis of comparatively simple grammatical structures makes formats powerful anchor points for the study of social and cultural phenomena in general. Formats further point to specific communities of practice, which can form around one or a series of interrelated formats and which can be addressed as what we want to call *format cultures*. As such, formats pave the way to rich ethnographies of media: some media formats are associated with children, others are favored by experts in their given fields, and yet others are revered by amateurs, collectors, or artists.

Due to their ability to stabilize practices and forge collectives, formats may unfold considerable cultural effects. In a media-saturated world, format specifications represent sites of condensed power, power struggles, and valuable commodities. Format is not an issue to be taken lightly. Entire "wars" have been fought over the economic supremacy of formats. Some of the defeated quickly disappeared into oblivion, while others may enjoy latent but surprisingly long afterlives: one could think of the Betamax tape, whose production only stopped very recently, or the sudden and unexpected comeback of compact cassettes, now more of a collector's item than a music reproduction format, whose sales have surged in the last year. Therefore, it is important to keep in mind that many formats are collectively and cooperatively designed by private corporations and public organizations according to distinct strategies. These strategies are often directed at governing the flows of information and capital and controlling acceptable and unacceptable uses of technology and infrastructure (see Hoof in this volume).

One of the first attempts to address formats in the humanities was undertaken by Swiss art historian Jacob Burckhardt. In 1886, Burckhardt discussed the notion of "format" in his lecture "Format und Bild" (format and image). His interest in formats arose from an irritation or even nuisance. The lecture begins with the observation that we become aware of the format of images primarily through reproductions, particularly etchings, because copper engravers and publishers often violate the original aspect ratio of artworks when transforming them into copperplates for printing, and paintings are sometimes cropped so as to fit into a particular spaces. Burckhardt's criticism of this reformatting leads art historian Stefanie Stallschus to ask: "Does speaking about the format inevitably also mean speaking about media use and viewing habits?" (2013, 74, our translation).

Burckhardt's stance on formats is ambivalent. He embraces a normative perspective on the history of art: once set by the artist, the format of a painting and all of its reproductions should remain constant. At the same time, he develops an argument that anticipates Derrida's thoughts regarding the frame by almost a century and makes, moreover, the genuinely media-theoretical claim that "the format provides the separation of the beautiful from all the rest of the room . . . The format is not the work of art, but a condition of its existence" (translated by Freyermuth 2015, 180) because the format "protects art from dissolving into endlessness" (Burckhardt 1919, 254, our translation).

In a similar fashion, art historian David Joselit used the notion of format in his book *After Art* (2013) to describe the relation between works of art and the socio-political, economic, and physical environments that make up the contemporary art world and art market. "The rest of the room," or the physical space in which an artwork is situated, has been substituted in this approach by the discursive and infrastructural space that surrounds it. In an interview, Joselit states that he regards "format" as

> a strategy for activating the space between what an image shows and what an image does. . . . The artwork almost always contains vestiges of what might be called the roots—or infrastructural extensions—of its entanglements in the world. These might include the means of production of the image, the human effort that brought it into being, its mode of circulation, the historical events that condition it, etc. The artwork's format solidifies and makes visible that connective tissue,

> reinforcing the idea that the work of art encompasses both an image
> and its extensions. (Joselit 2015, n.p.)

Consequently, Joselit is less concerned with the hermeneutics of artworks
than with their place, meaning, and circulation within a global system
or infrastructure. Sterne (2012) takes a similar perspective on the development of MP3, using one of the most commonly circulated forms of
recorded sound as a starting point for a history of digital audio with a focus
on the compression and circulation of musical recordings. Like Burckhardt
and Joselit, Sterne emphasizes the close relation of formats to their cultural
surroundings and infrastructural contexts when he states that "all formats
presuppose particular formations of infrastructure with their own codes,
protocols, limits, and affordances" (15). It is through their embeddedness
and entanglement in infrastructural contexts that formats can unfold their
power so effectively. Formats act as gates through which media must pass.
Just as format was the condition of existence of art for Burckhardt, it is,
for Sterne, what defines a medium's operation, and therefore the medium
itself. Sterne recognizes that formats have "a contractual and conventional
nature" since "most crucial dimensions of a format are codified in some
way—sometimes through policy, sometimes through the technology's construction and sometimes through sedimented habit" (15).

The two definitions have similarities, but there is also an important
difference between Burckhardt's approach, which is ultimately normative
and prescriptive, and Sterne's descriptive stance. In her 2015 article "Formatting Film Studies," Haidee Wasson discusses the usefulness of Sterne's
format theory for film studies. Wasson (2015, 58) argues that the idea
of a format offers "a productive instrument to move beyond an ahistorical, unchanging, and thus rather expansive, concept of a medium."
For example, as scholars of nontheatrical, industrial, amateur, and other
"useful cinemas" (see Acland and Wasson 2011) have shown, small-gauge
film formats have been crucial for the circulation of film beyond movie
theatres. Or to put it differently, "format theory is an invitation to continue the project of interrogating what seems natural about our mediated
worlds" (Wasson 2015, 59). As Wasson argues, "one of the most productive
and compelling shifts in film studies today is that our previously prescriptive definitions of cinema are thankfully giving way to fulsome
descriptions of cinema through time and across diverse and complex
geographies" (58).

Since formats may still exist independently of the infrastructures they were
designed for, such histories and geographies are often obliquely inscribed

in them as residual traces of long-gone standards, business decisions, rivalries, and compromises. The logo of the SD memory card, which superseded disc-based consumer storage media, paradoxically shows an optical disc. This is a lingering reference to its ancestral roots in the Super Density disc format, a precursor of the DVD. This innocuous logo emblematizes how formats are simultaneously receptive to the industrial impulses toward innovation, and yet also reflect institutional indolence. Sterne (2012, 15) maintains that studying these sedimentations of "old infrastructural context," of culture, knowledge, and practice, can open up new pathways into media history.

In the digital domain, archivists and artists alike have long been concerned with the intricacies of computer file formats and the power they exert over networked visual culture. Works such as photographer Thomas Ruff's *JPEGs* series (2007) and Ted Davis's *Codec* (2009) explore the materiality and circulation of digital image formats and compression schemes. Artist and media theorist Rosa Menkman's 2010 visual compendium of glitches, *A Vernacular of File Formats*, was perhaps the most comprehensive artistic inquiry into the mechanisms of digital still image and video formats. Formats, as both artists and scholars thus recognize, offer productive opportunities for media studies to move past unwieldy conceptual constructs and obsolete periodizations. Instead, they shed light on the neglected capillary threads of media cultures beyond individual media.

A Plea for Format Studies

In a most general sense, we can summarize by saying that we use the term "format" to describe a coherent pattern of order and composition—a standardized template for the organization of space, time or information according to some rhythmical, structural, aesthetic or volumetric rules. But how can such a warren of meanings satisfy the terminological requirements of so many disciplines and industries? And how can it function as a meaningful instrument of classification? After decades of scattered usage in fields ranging from fine arts through broadcasting to media and consumer electronics industries, for things and practices as dissimilar as TIFF files and TED talks, book sizes and blues radio stations, what technological and epistemic displacements have led to formats now appearing as a field of scholarly interest useful enough to potentially challenge media as the operative unit of media studies?

Friedrich Kittler once predicted that "a total media assemblage based on the digital will eliminate the very concept of medium" (Kittler 1986, 8, our translation). Sure enough, it took less than 30 years for media theorists (in Germany, at least) to begin diagnosing a crisis of media, and of media studies (Pias 2011; Hagener 2012). Perhaps media research indeed sees itself facing the obsolescence of its conceptual raison d'être and is testing other units of analysis to replace it. Or could it simply be that the technological conditions of contemporary academic labor made encounters with formats much more ubiquitous and disruptive than they had been in the past? After all, when a troublesome PDF file or a dataset refuses to be "opened" or a video file resists being embedded in a slideshow, oftentimes it is the format that is the defiant culprit. Many a manuscript has been rejected over improper formatting. Perhaps format matters simply get noticed more.

Whatever the reason, Sterne's pioneering study on the MP3; Wasson's urge for "formatting" film studies; Niehaus's observations on formats, programs, and genres; and a handful of other reflections on formatting by media scholars and art historians (e.g., Joselit 2013; Stallschus 2013; Müller 2014) are part of an increasing number of recent attempts to address questions of format. Among the numerous academic conferences and publications of the last years are the French journal *Pli—revue: Architecture & édition* (2016), which devoted its second issue to "Format(s)," and the conferences *"Vom Medium zum Format"* (From Medium to Format) and *"Bilder trimmen: Politiken des Formats seit 1960"* (Trimming Images: Format Politics Since 1960), which took place in September 2017 at the Ruhr University Bochum and the University of Bern, respectively. An international workshop that led up to the present publication was held shortly after, in December 2017, at the University of Mainz. Given this growing interest, we think it is time for more concerted research efforts that establish format studies as a new interdisciplinary field.

Format studies is not a replacement of media studies or its successor. What we do argue, however, is that a focus on format might indeed provide methodological remedies against the pitfalls of essentialist views and definitions of "media." Since formats represent "particular historical instantiations" of media (Sterne 2012, 11), format studies might offer ways to grasp large and oversimplified categories, such as analog/digital, in a more differentiated manner and make them appear less as oppositions than as interactions or different and often superimposed configurations of formats. We believe that inscribed in formats we find both radical innovations that transform media technologies and continuities that endure historical ruptures.

Moreover, format studies brings media practices and the strategies for controlling them to the fore, and thus also points to the political and economic dimensions of the often collective creation and ownership of formats. Format studies seems to be particularly suitable for investigating digitally networked media because, as discussed above, it draws attention to infrastructural constellations. This places format studies in proximity to what Lisa Parks and Nicole Starosielski (2015) call "critical infrastructure studies." Lastly, format studies is timely because the steady increase in new digital formats has been accompanied by an increasing tendency to hide them from users. While an earlier generation of computer users was familiar with a plethora of formats and file extensions, as a consequence of the rise of cloud computing-based business models, few smartphone users today might know which formats the apps, streamed music or video on their device are stored in. This black-boxing should be taken as an imperative for format scholars to begin unpacking formats and their politics. Formats are, after all, one of the main weapons with which media industries conduct their wars and battles. Apart from pragmatic considerations of functionality and use, formats are oftentimes developed tactically and serve to lock users into particular hardware or software environments, or utilized to reinforce geopolitical borders and interests. As such, they demand a critical questioning of the political processes of legitimation that the standardization of a particular format represents.

About the Volume and Its Contributions

This volume is the result of a sustained collaborative exchange between media scholars representing a diverse array of research interests. Sterne emphasizes that the value of format theory lies not in replacing media studies, but in modulating the questions it asks and in learning to ask them with finer precision. Inaugurating a format studies, then, should not be seen as a bid to establish another insular colony in an increasingly fragmented landscape of humanities and social sciences research. Rather, it is an attempt at discovering new means of travel across this landscape. From the philosophical deliberation of aesthetics to rummaging through dusty boxes in archives, the chapters collected in this volume explore, combine, and experiment with a range of scholarly perspectives and methodological approaches to formats. Included are both highly focused case studies that investigate single formats overlooked by previous research, as well as larger theoretical and historical surveys that seek to identify and understand broader cultural mechanisms of formatting and format-making across history. While the focus remains on audiovisual media broadly conceived, the variety of approaches results in engaging and, as we believe, productive exchanges between film studies, digital studies, infrastructure studies, production studies, cultural techniques research, media archaeology, bibliography and archival studies, and other fields. Taken together, the contributions collectively chart the various ways in which formats shape and are shaped by past and present media cultures.

Format Matters is divided into three sections. The first, "Control, Access, Infrastructure," examines the way formats function as instruments of both interoperability and gatekeeping. In the opening chapter of the volume, "Reformatting Media Studies," Axel Volmar collates some methodological and theoretical building blocks for format studies and explores how contemporary media studies may benefit from the study of formats. Volmar opens by developing a heuristic taxonomy of formats from which he deduces a couple of common functions and affordances of formats. He lays out three methodological and theoretical entry points into the study of format that consider how formats relate to or originate from practices, how they facilitate and enforce forms and conditions of cooperation, and how they can be used for conceptualizing media-historical change by situating them within broader media-historical dynamics of specialization and generalization.

Wanda Strauven's chapter "Let's Dance: GIF 1.0 versus GIF 2.0" studies how the Graphics Interchange Format (GIF), a defining features of the recent World Wide Web, became actively used in a large variety of applications: from time-lapse weather maps to grassroots net design, from communicative strategies on social media to genetics and DNA storage. By tracing these multiple archaeologies through time, Strauven discusses how the GIF can best be understood as the active counterpart of a container, that is, as a tool.

In "Formats and Formalization in Internet Advertising," Ramon Lobato and Julian Thomas carry on the thread of web-specific formats. The chapter discusses the outcomes and prospects of attempts to stabilize formats in internet advertising, a media sector characterized by increasing automation, fragmentation, and internal conflict. From the flashing banner ads of the 1990s to today's auto-playing videos, internet advertising has long been seen as disorganized, highly fluid, and sometimes unconscionably exploitative. One response has been the ongoing work of industry bodies on standardizing internet advertising formats, a project that promises greater interoperability and consumer protection.

Florian Hoof's chapter "Liveness Formats: A Historical Perspective on Live Sports Broadcasting" investigates strategies to control the circulation of cultural goods that emerge out of economic necessities to standardize and control the distribution of live broadcasting. It traces the history of liveness format control, starting at the end of the 19th century with early sports bulletin boards, fight films, and theatre television, and continuing with the shift to pay TV, pay-per-view, and contemporary forms of over-the-top streaming services. Drawing, in particular, on the history of sports broadcasting, Hoof defines and lays out two concepts of control. The first, "fortifying," tries to control live broadcasts by protecting the medium that stores the signal; the second, "infrastructuring," tries to dominate the distribution network used to circulate or distribute live broadcasts.

The second section, "Archaeologies of Success and Failure," centers on the circulation of compression formats in television, film, and photography. Some of these formats, such as the sports highlight, have been so historically successful that they are hardly recognized as formats that once had to be established, whereas others have long been forgotten. Markus Stauff's contribution on "Formatting Cross-Media Circulation" takes sports highlights as an example to discuss how formats and formatting enable the circulation of content across different media. The chapter argues that the "spreadability" of selected moments from sports events, one of the most consistent elements of cross-media culture for over a century, results from the modularity and scalability of the highlight format. Sport allows for and even systematically triggers various representations of the original event. As a format, the sports highlight is highly constrained through copyright claims and regulatory policies, and yet it still offers flexibility: it can be adapted to different technical infrastructures, a number of industrial strategies and, of course, fan activities. Conceptually, this chapter uses the sports highlight to question a rigid, materialist understanding of formats and formatting. Taking its lead from the television industry's global trade in formats as local adaptations of content, Stauff argues that formats matter because of the continuous formatting processes at the intersection of technical, economic, and aesthetic dynamics.

Alexandra Schneider's chapter "Viewer's Digest: Small Gauge and Reduction Prints as Liminal Compression Formats" uses format studies as a framework to discuss reduction prints as a historical practice for the distribution of films. Similar to contemporary compression formats, small-gauge reduction prints had a key purpose in facilitating the circulation of moving images in nontheatrical venues. Rather than treating reduction prints as a mere oddity in the history of cinema, Schneider proposes to consider them as a "liminal format": liminal in the sense of being not there yet or transitional, a kind of *format de passage*. The chapter aims to further our understanding of the complex historical dynamics of formats and particularly of the continuities and discontinuities between analog, electronic, and digital media.

In "Formatting Faces: Standards of Production, Networks of Circulation, and the Operationalization of the Photographic Portrait," Roland Meyer asks how formatting as a repeatable and standardizable pictorial practice became productive in the field of visual culture. Focusing on three "primal scenes" of formatting images of human faces, from early popular portrait photography and standardized police photography to the beginnings of Facebook as a platform of image circulation, he shows how the introduction of new pictorial formats not only changed the conditions of pictorial production but also helped to establish new practices of distributing and connecting pictures, thus fostering new logistics of images.

The section concludes with Erika Balsom's "Instant Failure: Polaroid's Polavision, 1977–1980," an excavation of the Polavision format. In 1977, at the dawn of the home video era, Polaroid Corporation introduced this proprietary film format and apparatus promising instant development and playback. The system was a devastating commercial failure and caused Polaroid major financial losses before its discontinuation in 1980, but during its brief existence it was used by prominent figures such as Charles and Ray Eames, Andy Warhol, and Stan Brakhage. Polavision was a social medium avant la lettre in that it was a system grounded in prosumer activity, relationality, and feedback rather than in the quality of the films it yielded. And yet, this emphasis ran up against significant limitations. In line with the archaeological interest in failed media, this chapter recovers the curious episode of Polavision's instant movies, finding in this largely forgotten enterprise a way to insist on photochemical film as a family of formats rather than a single medium.

The third section, "Formats in Transition," looks into the malleability, inertia, and dynamism of media formats and investigates moments of irritation between them. In "Fold, Format, Fault: On Reformatting and Loss," Marek Jancovic examines how format standardization and cultural practices of reformatting produce conflicting relationships with history, memory, and loss. By addressing examples of reformatting across a number of historical contexts and industries—the folding of books, the microfilming of secret state documents, and the format migrations routinely performed by audiovisual archives—the chapter contemplates the political dimension of formats. Grounding a theory of formats in the study of paper and bookmaking, Jancovic argues that formats need to be understood not as stable and self-evident properties of things, but as dynamic practices rife with loss, friction, and incompatibility.

Antonio Somaini's "The Screen as 'Battleground': Eisenstein's 'Dynamic Square' and the Plasticity of the Projection Format" deals with three different meanings of "format": the size of the photosensitive area of a frame on celluloid film, the aspect ratio of a projected image, and the way in which a digital moving image file is encoded for storage, processing, transmission, and display. The chapter presents a close analysis of Sergei Eisenstein's seminal essay advocating the plasticity of the film format, referring to a series of examples from Eisenstein's own films and from artists and film directors such as László Moholy-Nagy and Fritz Lang.

In their chapter "HD's Invention of Continuity and SD's Resistance? A Historiography of Cinema and Film to (Be)come and Formats to Overcome," Oliver Fahle and Elisa Linseisen assume a post-cinematic perspective to reflect on media change and its limits. Taking into account cinema's genuine ability to develop and transform, Fahle and Linseisen advocate for a concretizing, historiographical distinction between the persistence and resistance of cinema, delineated by the two concepts of "medium" and "format." Because formats rely on specific media-technical surroundings, the persistence of a medium is based on the resistance of its formats. By closely examining the intersection of two digital formats—high-definition digital imagery and standard-definition digital formats—Fahle and Linseisen propose to write a history of cinema and film to come, in correlation with a history of formats to overcome.

Kalani Michell's chapter "Pod Fictions" concludes the volume with a rich and multifaceted analysis of the academic podcast *Aca-Media*, sponsored by the Society for Cinema and Media Studies and its official publication, the *Journal of Cinema and Media Studies*. Michell uses this case study to consider how media studies as a discipline values and creates hierarchies between various academic formats. Ultimately, the close examination of this particular online outgrowth of the organization's scholarly journal within the context of recent radio, podcast, interface, and institutional branding scholarship reveals not only the meaning of a new media format but also a portrait of a discipline in transition—media studies at a time when it is itself in the process of reformatting.

Acknowledgements

A majority of the chapters in this volume have evolved out of papers presented at the interdisciplinary conference "Format Matters," held at the Johannes Gutenberg University Mainz in December 2017, under the auspices of the German Research Foundation and the Johannes Gutenberg University Mainz Internal Research Fund. A number of additional papers were first presented at "Vom Medium zum Format" in September 2017 at the University of Bochum. We thank all the participants at these conferences for the inspiring and engaging discussions and suggestions.

We thank our copy editor, Kyle Stine, whose critical commentary and background in film and media studies contributed greatly to the volume. Simone Nowicki and Nicole Braida both supported the project, as did all the students who discussed format matters with us in seminars and beyond. We also express our gratitude to meson press for its vision and commitment to think scholarly publishing differently, beyond corporate logics.

This publication has been partly funded by a project of the Collaborative Research Center "Media of Cooperation" (SFB 1187 *Medien der Kooperation*, project A01) at the University of Siegen.

References

Acland, Charles R., and Haidee Wasson, eds. 2011. *Useful Cinema*. Durham, NC: Duke University Press.

Akrich, Madeleine. 1992. "The De-Scription of Technical Objects." In *Shaping Technology/ Building Society: Studies in Sociotechnical Change*, edited by Wiebe E. Bijker and John Law, 205–24. Cambridge, MA: MIT Press.

Bucher, Hans-Jürgen, Thomas Gloning, and Katrin Lehnen. 2010. *Neue Medien – neue Formate: Ausdifferenzierung und Konvergenz in der Medienkommunikation*. Frankfurt am Main: Campus Verlag.

Burckhardt, Jacob. 1919. *Vorträge 1844–1887*. Edited by Emil Dürr. Basel: Schwabe.

Freyermuth, Gundolf S. 2015. "From Analog to Digital Image Space: Toward a Historical Theory of Immersion." In *Immersion in the Visual Arts and Media*, edited by Fabienne Liptay and Burcu Dogramaci, 165–203. Leiden: Brill.

Hagener, Malte. 2012. "Das Medium in der Krise: Der Film, das Kinematographische und der Wert von instabilem Wissen." *AugenBlick: Marburger Hefte zur Medienwissenschaft*, no. 52: 30–46. doi:http://dx.doi.org/10.25969/mediarep/2514.

Joselit, David. 2013. *After Art*. Princeton, NJ: Princeton University Press.

———. 2015. "Against Representation." Interview by David Andrew Tasman. *DIS Magazine*. http://dismagazine.com/blog/75654/david-joselit-against-representation/.

Kittler, Friedrich A. 1986. *Grammophon, Film, Typewriter*. Berlin: Brinkmann & Bose.

Meadow, Robin. 1970. "Television Formats: The Search for Protection." *California Law Review* 58 (5): 1169–97.

Meckel, Miriam. 2002. "Programmstrukturen des Fernsehens." In *Medienwissenschaft: ein Handbuch zur Entwicklung der Medien und Kommunikationsformen*, edited by Joachim-Felix Leonhard, Hans-Werner Ludwig, Dietrich Schwarze, and Erich Straßner, 2269–79. Handbücher zur Sprach- und Kommunikationswissenschaft [HSK], 15.3. Berlin: Walter de Gruyter.

Müller, Susanne. 2014. "Formatieren." In *Historisches Wörterbuch des Mediengebrauchs*, edited by Heiko Christians, Matthias Bickenbach, and Nikolaus Wegmann, 253–67. Cologne: Böhlau.

Niehaus, Michael. 2018. *Was ist ein Format?* Hannover: Wehrhahn Verlag.

Parks, Lisa, and Nicole Starosielski. 2015. "Introduction." In *Signal Traffic: Critical Studies of Media Infrastructures*, edited by Lisa Parks and Nicole Starosielski, 1–30. Urbana: University of Illinois Press.

Pias, Claus. 2011. "Was waren Medien-Wissenschaften? Stichworte zu einer Standortbestimmung." In *Was waren Medien?*, edited by Claus Pias, 7–30. Zürich: Diaphanes.

Romeo, Charles J., and Andrew R. Dick. 2005. "The Effect of Format Changes and Ownership Consolidation on Radio Station Outcomes." *Review of Industrial Organization* 27 (4): 351–86.

Schüttpelz, Erhard. 2017. "Infrastructural Media and Public Media." *Media in Action* 1 (1): 13–61.

Seldes, Gilbert. 1950. "Oracle: Radio." In *The Great Audience*, 105–216. New York: Viking.

Stallschus, Stefanie. 2013. "Format." In *Kunst-Begriffe der Gegenwart. Von Allegorie bis Zip*, edited by Jörn Schafaff, Nina Schallenberg, and Tobias Vogt, 73–77. Cologne: Walther König.

Sterne, Jonathan. 2012. *MP3: The Meaning of a Format*. Durham, NC: Duke University Press.

Vismann, Cornelia. 2008. *Files: Law and Media Technology*. Translated by Geoffrey Winthrop-Young. Stanford, CA: Stanford University Press.

Volmar, Axel. 2017. "Formats as Media of Cooperation." *Media in Action* 1 (2): 9–28. https://www001.zimt.uni-siegen.de/ojs/index.php/mia/article/view/19/23.

Wasson, Haidee. 2015. "Formatting Film Studies." *Film Studies* 12 (1): 57–61.

CONTROL, ACCESS, INFRASTRUCTURE

1

Reformatting Media Studies: Toward a Theoretical Framework for Format Studies

Axel Volmar

From Medium to Format

Following Marshall McLuhan's dictum that the medium is the message, media theorists since the 1980s have conceptualized media not as mere mediators, or neutral conveyors of messages, but as formations that come in between processes of perception, expressions of knowledge, and uses of language that add something to the transmission without being consciously perceived or reflected upon by those involved. This insight brought mediality or a medium's supposedly intrinsic quality, obstinacy, or resistance (*Eigensinn*; see Hoffmann 2002, 153–54; Krämer 1998, 75; Anders 1956, 2) into the focus of media theory and has subsequently stimulated the writing of a plethora of media histories and ontologies of all kinds (see Engemann, Heilmann, and Sprenger 2019). And yet, in many of the media-theoretical works oriented toward the elaboration of a certain media specificity and the idea of media as being material or technical *in-betweens*, there often remains a certain uncertainty about whether mediality should be understood as ontologically determined by the nature, structure, or functioning of the medium itself or as socially constructed by particular decisions made in the course of the design, provision, or commodification of a media technology. Media-theoretical distinctions between analog and digital appear to be similarly precarious in this respect. Although work on analog–digital differentiation since the 1990s has provided media scholars with important points of reference, the broad oppositions that defined this differentiation, such as continuous versus discreet (Schröter and Böhnke 2004), have lost a great deal of their significance for defining and elucidating media in view of a world increasingly saturated with digitally networked technologies, infrastructures, and services. On account of this growing ambiguity, media scholars have directed attention away from media as isolated research objects toward consideration of their surrounding environments, histories and cultures, such as, for instance, toward the infrastructures that connect media artifacts, people, and devices. In this regard, infrastructure studies has gained considerable currency in recent years (Parks and Starosielski 2015; Edwards et al. 2009); and yet, format studies has not received the same attention or been pursued in the same way until now.

Although formats are closely related and often intrinsic to specific media, they are, as we have shown in the introduction to this volume, not necessarily congruent with them. Both deeply connected to and independent from media, formats follow their own logics, which may result in formats being responsible for the particular characteristics of a medium rather than its overall qualities. The fact that some formats are able to migrate from one medium to another or spread across different media already suggests that formats point to other aspects of media formation, production, distribution, and reception than a focus on, for instance, a single medium would. The study of formats can thus, as media scholar Jonathan Sterne argues in his book *MP3: The Meaning of a Format*, contribute to seeing media history in a new light that illuminates more the interconnections between media rather than their individual evolvement or histories:

> Cross-media formats like MP3 operate like catacombs under the conceptual, practical, and institutional edifices of media. Formats do not set us free of constraints or literature from the histories that have already been written. They only offer a different route through the city of mediality. . . . If they have enough depth, breadth, and reach, some formats may offer completely different inroads into media history and may well show us subterranean connections among media that we previously thought separate. The study of formats does not mean forgetting what we've learned from the study of media or, more broadly, communication technologies. It is simply to consider the embedded ideas and routines that cut across them. (Sterne 2012, 16)[1]

1   Sterne uses the term mediality "to evoke *a quality of or pertaining to media* and the complex ways in which communication technologies refer to one another in form or content" (2012, 9).

The study of formats thus promises to answer media-theoretical questions in new ways that reveal connections that previously went unnoticed. One could argue that, more generally speaking, format studies would then have the task of contextualizing, historicizing, and theorizing such connections that connect or "cut across" media. In light of the increasing conversion of analog media into the universal medium of binary code (see Linseisen and Fahle in this volume), histories of formats are likely to tell us more about the process of digitalization than do, for instance, general histories of *the* computer or *the* Internet. Let us take an often posed question as an example: Why did media studies not foresee the emergence of social media despite its being so close to the development of digital computing and networking? I think it is fair to say that one of the main reasons lies in the field's wrong assumptions about the presumed specificity of digitally networked media. The cybertheories and associated artistic and technical projects of the 1980s and 1990s imagined the future of networked computing either in the form of primarily discursive, text-based spaces directed at the users' communicative and imaginative capacities (see, for instance, Turkle 1995) or as immersive sensory environments based on generative computer graphics and technological interactivity. Both visions conceived of digitally networked media as a part of reality that was thought to be isolated and radically independent from the rest of the world, mostly because assumptions regarding the nature of cyberspace were based on supposedly intrinsic properties of digital computers and the medium of binary code. A consideration of new digital multimedia formats, such as JPEG, MPEG, and MP3, which emerged around 1990, might have painted a different picture and fostered the conviction that it would not be human-ity's destiny to migrate into unknown, immaterial cyberworlds but that, conversely, *the world*—captured and manifested in the manifold forms of digital audiovisual data—would sooner or later take over and ultimately oust both the idea and the technical reality of what was considered to be cyberspace. As I will show below, formats tend to shift scholarly attention from questions of mediation to those regarding the interoperability of technologies, media-related practices, labor chains, and exploitation chains as well as collective forms of technological innovation.

Starting from general distinctions between media and formats, I ask in this chapter why and how formats matter, what contemporary media studies may gain from the study of formats, and how format studies could be framed methodologically and theoretically. To answer these questions, I present some building blocks for a preliminary theoretical and methodological framework that can help to determine what can be considered significant about formats and how to study them. In section two, I briefly survey the subject matter of format studies and develop a heuristic taxonomy of formats from which derive a couple of common functions and affordances of formats, which I elaborate on in section three. In section four, I discuss three methodological and theoretical entry points into the study of formats, namely, how formats originate from practices, how formats facilitate and enforce forms and conditions of cooperation, and how formats can be used for conceptualizing media-historical change by situating them within broader media-historical dynamics of spe-cialization and generalization.

A Brief Taxonomy of Formats

What exactly do we mean when we talk of formats? Formats can obviously be as different as the size of stationery, the way of storing a sound on a recording medium, or the narrative structure of a television show. As I have elaborated elsewhere in greater detail (see Volmar 2017), we can, for the sake of simplicity, heuristically distinguish five types of formats, although this typology by no means claims to be exhaustive:

Size-and-Shape Formats

Originating from book, paper, and picture formats, size-and-shape formats frame and dimension the display and presentation of—usually visual—con-tent by means of limitation, orientation, and alignment. This is probably the most common type of format. Two-dimensional size-and-shape formats determine standardized and unstandardized sizes of inscription and dis-play surfaces and indicate the physical properties of the involved materials and storage media, most commonly in conjunction with forms of mass production and reproduction. Moreover, formats often also specify the orientation and aspect ratios of the presented information, such as in por-trait and landscape orientations. Different denominations relative to size, such as small gauge, pocket book, or large size further suggest that formats are closely linked to use practices, in the realms of both media production and media consumption.

Diagrammatic and Structural Formats

By specifying dimensions and setting boundaries, formats provide a general framing of information or content. Apart from that, formats can also determine the spatial, temporal, or logical structures in which content is stored, transmitted, and presented. In that sense, the notion bears relation to the evolutionary term "formation" and is further reminiscent of the fact that the word "information" literally refers to symbolic content, or data, that have been brought *in formation*, or arranged into a specific form. This entails, in particular, the spatial, diagrammatic division and ordering of information surfaces, e.g., in the form of lists, tables, and especially forms and other previously structured, preformatted documents (Gitelman 2014; Young 2017), all of which evoke saturated histories of bureaucratic practices, e.g., for registration, inventory, and bookkeeping. Moreover, inscription surfaces demand specific practices of preparation and care before they can be used as symbolic media. Such practices of formatting are among the oldest cultural techniques we know. Formatting practices are generally thought to have originated with the preparation of paper sheets and wood blocks in the early modern printing industry. Formatting is, of course, also one of the key concepts in typesetting and graphic design, used in conjunction with rules and practices of text and image layout (see Müller 2014). However, the emergence of formatting can be considered to have started much earlier. As Jacques Derrida (1997, 287) argues in *Of Grammatology*, we can already read the ploughing of land to prepare the soil for proper cultivation as a practice of formatting meant to enable a form of writing.

Encoding and Data Formats

Another frequent type of format involves techniques of encoding information and data streams. This type entails formats used for displaying numbers, dates, and time as well as newer ones conceived to store and reproduce audio and video information, from musical recordings to digital file formats. Such formats are usually characterized by the introduction of additional data, or metadata, into the content or signal flow, such as information about how to render the content into a usable or consumable form. Tailored primarily but not exclusively to enable and coordinate automated forms of reading, writing, and processing, these metadata—such as the playback speeds of vinyl records, line and page breaks in analog TV signals, or information in the headers and structure of digital file formats—regulate how information and data flows are expected to be handled (e.g., stored, transmitted, displayed, or processed) by people and especially technological apparatuses. These formats not only *represent* but also *do* things, as they contain commands or control code and often demand action on behalf of the user.

Metaphorical Formats

In certain contexts, the term format has crossed over into other cultural uses, with metaphors deriving presumably from large book and image formats. Around 1900, for instance, the noun *Format* became fashionable in German-speaking countries, where it came to be used as a denomination to distinguish individuals of extraordinary capabilities, achievements, or character. A person may be, for instance, credited as having format (*Format haben*) if they are deemed capable—thanks to exceptional leadership, athletic talent, or financial success—of filling an imaginary frame of expectation. This frame of reference usually corresponded to the values of the bourgeois class and their attempts to secure moral superiority (see also Niehaus 2018, 18–24). In turn, individuals may also demonstrate format (*Format zeigen*) in situations that call for great courage or present difficult choices, such as between the individual and the greater good.

Narrative and Processual-Event Formats

Finally, in the second half of the 20th century, the notion of format has increasingly come to denote strongly structured events that follow predefined sequences, rules, or schemes, such as trading, sports, or auction formats. First and foremost, however, this group of formats pertains to mass media, as they entail the many event and narrative formats for news, music, talk, or game shows, which were conceived in the broadcasting industry. Knut Hickethier calls such media formats "media-industrially optimizable genres," a definition that emphasizes the often highly serialized, commodified, and industrial character of media formats (Hickethier 2010, 152, my translation). In this signification, formats usually refer to the overall concept, trademarking, and branding of (generally copyrighted) media programs or even entire stations, as becomes apparent in the notion "format radio," an industry term for commercial stations that are limited to a narrow range of content and tailored to cater to specific target audiences in order to maximize ad revenue. More broadly, processual formats can also be understood as the requirements used to govern the form of public discourses, for instance, by means of the peer-reviewed scientific journal or arbitrary decisions such as limiting Twitter posts to 140 characters (see also the chapter by Kalani Michell on academic podcasts in this volume).

Common Features and Functions of Formats

It merits questioning whether the distinct types of formats listed above share common characteristics. Presumably the most fundamental tasks of formats consist in framing, limiting, and confining physical media and their content. Formats set boundaries as they frame content and otherwise determine the spatial dimensions and aspect ratios of inscription and display surfaces; they regulate and limit the volume, length, and quality of technical media and artistic forms; and they structure the diagrammatical (spatial) or sequential (temporal) dimensions of content, information, or data. The British linguist Roy Harris emphasized this last point in crediting Valentin Haüy (1745–1822), the founder of the Royal Institution for Blind Youth in Paris, with discovering that "the underlying formal substratum of writing is not visual but spatial" (Harris 1995, 45; cf. Schmidt and Wagner 2018)—an insight that led Haüy's student Louis Braille to invent the tactile writing system for the visually impaired that bears his name. The spatial quality of information becomes evident in documents, such as, for instance, forms or lists (see Young 2017), in which spatial layout is used to prescribe what kinds of information are expected in bureaucratic procedures, from filing tax reports to registering for an app or online site. In the temporal domain, formats are used to determine essential narrative or sequential elements on various scales, from the segmentation of a TV show to the microtemporal organization of information flows in technical media, such as television signals or digital transmission standards.

Through limiting and structuring content, formats also shape—directly or indirectly—the ratio between the amount of information or content and the physical conditions, qualities, and capacities of a given medium or surrounding infrastructure, be it in terms of resolution, storage space, transmission bandwidth, or processing power of a technological system, network, or labor chain. With the introduction of optical sound on film in the late 1920s, for example, the image frames on 35mm film stock had to be slightly reduced in size (while preserving the aspect ratio) to make physical space for the soundtrack. Then with the introduction of digital sound in the 1990s, the analog film stock became even more crowded with information stemming from the Dolby Digital, DTS, or SDDS soundtracks and sync codes. The digital soundtracks nicely show how deeply data processing is rooted in material realities. Digital formats similarly depend on material conditions, such as the availability and cost of storage space or transmission bandwidth. Hence, another vital function of formats consists in reconciling differing demands regarding the conveyance and presentation of content with the material and economic constraints of a given medium. Therefore, media formats often do not represent the technologically feasible but rather the economically reasonable.

Since cost factors play a major role in extending infrastructures and including more participants, techniques of compression represent a recurring feature of many formats. Sterne (2012, 4–6) describes the trade-off between the ideals of verisimilitude and compression as fundamentally defining a given medium. In this sense, formatting can be conceived as a specific cultural—and often collaborative—practice of reconciling abstract, semiotic content with material conditions and constraints. Once a new format becomes accepted as a tolerable trade-off between different demands, it sooner or later tends to fade out of sight into the invisible "background" of infrastructure (Star and Ruhleder 1996) and can prove to remain stable over relatively long periods of time. By virtue of their power to harmonize media artefacts with infrastructures and (labor) practices, formats assume fundamental logistic and economic functions within media systems. Or to put it differently, formats determine how easily and in which form media artifacts, or more generally, media content, can travel. The study of formats therefore demands a gradual shift in scholarly attention from the content of media—including their qualities and effects—to media artefacts and the associated logics and conditions of circulation. This in turn includes close consideration of the ecological and infrastructural configurations, such as transmission networks and hard- and software infrastructures, that make these circulations possible and profitable. To determine the significance of a format, it therefore makes sense to carve out its relationships to its direct and indirect environment, whether a physical medium, a physical location (for instance, a museum), a technological infrastructure, or a larger media ecology. In conjunction with which storage media and transmission channels can certain formats be found, and where are they not found? What intended and unintended kinds of circulation have emerged? How and why are some obsolete formats repurposed and in what contexts?

As many of the abovementioned examples make apparent, the majority of formats involve considerable degrees of standardization (see also Schueler, Fickers, and Hommels 2008). Although the terms standard and format can overlap their meanings and practical uses, the main difference between the two lies in the simple fact that formats most commonly standardize objects and processes that deal with and display symbolic or aesthetic content. As Sterne writes, "Without standards, content could not travel as well as it does and could not be as well controlled as it is" (Sterne 2012, 6).

Many formats can thus be thought of as media standards to the extent that they designate specific configurations of media artifacts and determine the processes and practices connected to them, enabling greater consistency, predictability, and accountability by way of regulating costs, promoting usability, and providing for legal protections such as copyrights and licenses.

Because formats specify media, they also differentiate them, for instance, by dividing the vast continuum of possible manifestations of media into a few set fixations. In this regard, it is worth noting that formats often come in predefined sets or families, such as the ISO A, B, and C series of paper sizes. In the case of paper, the fixed dimensions channel the sheer infinite possibilities of potential sizes and aspect ratios to a number of fixed choices or grids. Formats render media into concrete forms and can thus considerably reduce complexity. Ideally, this reduction of complexity facilitates compatibility and interoperability between media devices from different manufacturers or software applications on different operating systems, which, in turn, can render complex processes and workflows more flexible and predictable. In reality, as we likely experience all too often, a counterforce to this straightforward strategy is that rivalling formats or a general plurality of formats tend to cause friction, glitches, errors, and incompatibilities in everyday media use (see, for instance, Marek Jancovic's chapter on archival practices and cultural memory in this volume). Or to put it differently, wherever formats aim to provide compatibility, they also create the potential for exclusions and incompatibility.

Three Entry Points into Format Studies

Format matters are important for media studies because they determine not only the aesthetic conditions but also the practical affordances of media. Not coincidentally, Sterne (2012, 7) has argued: "If there is such a thing as media theory, there should also be format theory." In this section, I will take up some of Sterne's thoughts on format theory and add some of my own suggestions for how format studies could be conceptualized in more theoretical terms. Certainly not all formats are of equal importance and not all formats matter in the same way. Therefore, I would like to offer three basic entry points into the study of formats that might help us determine the significance of formats—both in contemporary media culture and the broader course of media history—by suggesting that format studies should acknowledge the relations of formats to practices, pay attention to how formats organize and govern forms of cooperation, and consider formats within broader media-historical transformations by assessing strategies and dynamics of specialization and universalization.

Formats Reflect Practices

Many of the fundamental properties of technical media, such as the photosensitivity of chemical substances that became the foundation of photography, were not so much invented as discovered. On account of this, media scholars have repeatedly suggested that each medium possesses its own inherent specificity or intrinsic tendency that influences its general aesthetics and "affordances" (Gibson 1979). Formats are, quite to the contrary, of a radically decisionistic nature. Although some formats have grown historically and unintentionally, they are usually the materializations of contingent historical conditions and thus reflect economic and political strategies as well as decision and negotiation processes. As Sterne writes,

> Format denotes a whole range of decisions that affect the look, feel, experience, and workings of a medium. It also names a set of rules according to which a technology can operate. . . . Most crucial dimensions of format are codified in some way—sometimes through policy, sometimes through the technology's construction, and sometimes through sedimented habit. They have a contractual and conventional nature. (Sterne 2012, 7–8)

Due to their "contractual and conventional nature," formats inform not only our understanding of the aesthetic and experiential dimensions of media technologies but also how—and on what terms—media are turned into commodities and how people create, work with, and consume them. In other words, since formats are usually designed with specific applications, workflows, and communities of practice in mind, format studies must pay close attention to how particular format specifications are linked to or originate from practices. Recently, Nick Couldry (2012) has prominently advocated for an approach to media and communication studies that he calls *media practice theory*. Couldry's approach encourages media and audience research scholars not to limit themselves to the philology of media texts or the political economy of media institutions but to direct their focus toward "what people . . . are doing with media" (ix) and specifically toward how they integrate media, and especially digital media, into the routines of their everyday lives.

The growing experiences with digitally networked media have indeed revealed the diverse ways people consume, alter, and redistribute media objects in active and participative ways. Format studies can profit from such a practice-focused perspective because formats shape and are shaped by practices. However, upon taking such a perspective, it seems wise to zoom out from the objects of audience research, such as end-user practices, to acknowledge the wide range of professional and amateur cultures that revolve around formats in not only the reception but also the conception, production, and distribution of media. Moreover, infrastructure studies has drawn attention to the quotidian practices of "infrastructuring" (Star and Bowker 2002) that comprise media practices in people's daily work and personal lives. Practice-centered studies of *format cultures* can thus supplement traditional media approaches by accounting for diverse actors groups, their politics, and their sanctioned as well as clandestine use practices situated along the operational chains that run through the—often separated—domains of media production, distribution, and reception. Formats live in the realms of practice and media use, in the fields of economics, law, and other profane domains and thus point to arguably less obvious but nevertheless equally ubiquitous practices that involve media, such as bureaucratic, juridical, and infrastructural practices.

Formats as Media of Cooperation

According to Sterne, "format is what specifies the protocols by which a medium will operate" (2012, 8). Formats, however, determine the protocols of not only technologies but also people. This can be seen, for instance, when an academic journal allows for only a limited range of file formats to be uploaded or when a new media format prevents users from doing the things they used to do with a prior format. Another frequent example would be the limitation of characters in online forms, not least for complaints. In this way, formats function as means to regulate the relations between and, to a certain extent, the behaviors of different stakeholders or actors groups and can thus be understood as what German media scholar Erhard Schüttpelz (2017, 24) has recently termed "media of cooperation." Conceiving of media in terms of cooperation, rather than merely in terms of communication or mass entertainment, shifts attention from the storage, transmission, and processing of information or the production, distribution, and reception of content toward the relations between different users or user groups, their goals, and their practices. Guided by a praxeological understanding of media that prioritizes practices over artifacts or technologies, Schüttpelz argues that "all media are cooperatively developed conditions of cooperation and have evolved as such" (14). Formats enable, shape, and sustain diverse forms of cooperation, both on and beyond the local scale. Many formats originated historically from temporary and non-public "work media" or "media of work" (Schüttpelz 2017, 25), such as paper documents, scientific instruments, dictaphone recordings, or production prints in film production, that were conceived to support labor practices in contexts of media production and distribution rather than exhibition and reception. Book formats, for instance, emerged in the 16th century as practical means to facilitate the manufacturing of books in the printing industry (Gaskell 1972; see also the chapter by Marek Jancovic in this volume). Formats thus invite us to rethink media not just as technologies and systems that provide informational and aesthetic content but as "logistical media" (Peters 2015, 37) conceived to create and organize conditions of cooperation.

As media of cooperation, formats can both facilitate or impose cooperative behaviors and transactions. For instance, to ensure the smooth operation of a bureaucratic procedure or a hand-over, say between departments in the process of film postproduction, formats represent landmarks in the muddle of practice by prompting the corresponding parties to prepare or rather format an object or a piece of information in a specific way. Media work is formatting work. At the same time, formats serve as means also to nudge or force people to comply with certain procedures or prevent them from doing things (see, for example, Florian Hoof's chapter on media piracy in this volume). Failure to comply with the requirements of format, in turn, might cause a standstill or termination of an ongoing process and may even entail penalties, as, for instance, when the approval of a wrongly formatted media artifact is denied.

In exercising this sort of appeal function, which routinely prompts media users to compare between actual states and target states, formats ensure the creation of stable media objects and artefacts that are able to travel within technical infrastructures as well as along the lines of complex production and value chains. Moreover, preassigned formats facilitate the manifestation of collective and collaborative work practices and thus play a vital role in establishing and sustaining finely grained divisions of labor. Formats, which in such a way forge people together in specific "conditions of cooperation," as Schüttpelz (2017, 14) calls them, are importantly also an expression of uneven power relations, as can be observed in the commodification of early portrait photography (see Roland Meyer's chapter in this volume) or in microwork platforms such as Amazon Mechanical Turk or CrowdFlower (see Ekbia and Nardi 2017). Therefore, formats can act as important interfaces or "boundary objects" for encounters between "heterogeneous social worlds" (Star and Griesemer 1989), involving both humans and nonhuman actors, and should be considered and approached as such.

Formats represent affordances that are less intrinsic to the medium in question than the result of conscious design meant to show people how to use technologies and how not to use them. In other words, formats crystallize the often-cooperative efforts that went into shaping a medium to yield specific affordances. The study of formats can thus reveal these efforts and their underlying intentions. Because the features of formats are always set by someone and often mutually made or, as Schüttpelz (2017, 14) frames it, "cooperatively developed," studies of format direct our attention to the politics of format making and the people who are involved in such processes (see also Sterne 2012, 128–47). Formats render media in tamed or domesticated form. At the same time, however, excavating the intended uses of a medium by studying the biography of a format, possibly also in relation to other competitive formats, may serve as a reference to contextualize unintended, critical, or even illicit forms of media use and appropriation.

Formats Embody Dynamics Between Specialization and Generalization

Sterne (2012, 16) argues that one of the main characteristics of formats is their ability to "cut across" different media. Notably, however, not all formats are fully amenable to translating to other media. They can do so only if they share a certain universality or openness. Paper formats, for instance, generally specify the geometric dimensions of paper sheets but not their material qualities, hence they can be applied to different media, such as office paper, books, photographic prints, or digital pages, as on word processors. Likewise, to use Sterne's own example, the MP3 digital audio format can serve to encode the soundtrack of a movie on a digital storage device like a DVD or in digital broadcasting but it can be used equally well to store music on personal computers and to share it over the internet, not least after the code of the original MP3 codec was hacked and rereleased for free in 1995 (see Sterne 2012, 201–202). The implications of special and general purpose along with strategies of opening up or limiting the presumed scope of formats (by facilitating or preventing compatibility and interoperability, for instance) can be considered constitutive of the evolution of media. If formats equipped with more universal properties and designed to facilitate connectivity thus bear a higher potential of migrating into new contexts and application areas, format studies may benefit from

tracing dynamics of specialization and generalization to rethink and recon-
ceptualize media-historical change.

The history of video telephony is a fitting example in this context. As a
technology, visual telephony is basically as old as television itself, and yet,
almost nobody was using it on a regular basis before the era of Skype.
When television emerged in the 1920s, it remained unclear whether the
new medium would become a visual extension of the telephone service
or a new form of radio broadcasting with an image component. The latter
won out for the obvious reason that it is easier to distribute a low number
of high-bandwidth signals to many receivers than to route a multitude
of signals from end-user to end-user individually. Nonetheless, the 20th
century saw many attempts to establish video telephony (after all, the
name television was modeled after the term telephone). As early as 1936,
the German postal service introduced the *Fernsehsprechdienst* (literally
"televisionphone service") between the central post offices of some of the
major German cities. However, the service was discontinued in 1940 in
response to the outbreak of the Second World War.

In 1970, AT&T marketed a similar service called Picturephone, this time
packaged in the form of sleek desktop devices for home and office use.
Due to high equipment and calling costs, as well as a considerable lack of
consumer demand, however, it reputedly became AT&T's biggest economic
failure (see Noll 1992). Kenneth Lipartito (2003) has sought to rehabilitate
AT&T's investment in Picturephone by arguing that although the service
failed as a product, its vision of video telephony nevertheless represented
a trailblazing innovation in the second half of the 20th century, ensuing
from and fueling the widespread cultural narrative of a technological
future based on information and communication technology. In a prescient
conclusion, unaware of how near the future really was, Lipartito writes
that "perhaps in the end we shall have videophones after all" (80–81).
And indeed, in August of the same year, the tech start-up company Skype
Technologies was founded. Initially conceived and installed as an IP-
telephony service that enabled computer users to place voice calls, Skype
added video chat functionality to its software client only two years later
(see LeClaire 2005). Today, users place billions of video calls and video conference calls per month.

What transformed failure into an everyday media experience was not a
special-purpose device but a new format on a general-purpose medium.
Skype was able to innovate on the grounds of readily available personal
computers, publicly available research on data compression, and new

broadband access to the internet. The developers benefitted intensely from the multimedia transmission standards developed by the Moving Picture Experts Group, best known for its MPEG family of standards, including the MPEG video and MP3 audio formats. Originally conceived for applications such as digital television, digital video storage, and video conferencing, the audio and video coding schemes opened up possibilities for the creation of new specialized applications and services as well. Skype, for its part, applied these already-available compression techniques to the already-established digital information infrastructure of the internet, with its TCP/IP and HTTP protocols, and was thus able to set up IP-telephony with comparatively low investments in hardware, software, and infrastructure. So what finally led videophones to catch on was not the invention of yet another expensive special-purpose device but the simple coupling of digital general-purpose hardware, network infrastructure, and compression formats for digital video.

The same is true for the still-picture standard JPEG. The main reason why JPEG is by far the most ubiquitous file format for digital photographic images is that JPEG was conceived, according to one of its key engineers, as a publicly available "general-purpose compression standard" meant to

> meet the needs of almost all continuous-tone still-image applications. If this goal proves attainable, not only will individual applications flourish, but exchange of images across application boundaries will be facilitated. This latter feature will become increasingly important as more image applications are implemented on general-purpose computing systems, which are themselves becoming increasingly inter-operable and internetworked. (Wallace 1991, 2)

To be fair, the original JPEG standard from 1988 was kept even so general that no particular algorithmic implementation of the compression method was recommended, which meant that, technically, different and ultimately incompatible individual formats could have accrued from the standard. Only after libjpeg, a free software library built to handle the JPEG image standard, had been developed and distributed by the co-called Independent JPEG Group (IJG), did the JPEG standard actually come into use as a concrete format (for instance, in internet browsers). Nevertheless, it is the degree of designed universality as an affordance that enables general-purpose formats such as the JPEG to "cut across" media and communication technologies. If we want to estimate the impact of formats, then, it makes sense to analyze them over longer historical trajectories, with an eye to their tendencies toward specialization (special purpose) and generalization (general purpose).

Conclusion

In this paper, I have presented some elements that might serve as a foundation for a theoretical and methodological framework for format studies. I started out by identifying basic types of formats and distilled from those a number of common features that indicate the relevance of formats as research objects for media studies. Formats frame, limit, and confine both physical media and their content and thereby produce both standards and artifacts that can be handled in and applied to different contexts of media use. They also structure data spatially and temporally and thereby affect how these data will be stored on inscription surfaces or transmitted over transmission channels. Formats thus represent reflections of the relation between a medium's content and its material conditions, infrastructural surroundings, and economic constraints. More-over, formats assume fundamental logistic and economic functions within media systems, as they render use and labor practices more consistent, predictable, and accountable. While material media such as photographic paper, shellac, celluloid, magnetic tape, or digital representation gained considerable traction and diffusion, it was their respective formats that determined their range of use, mainly by governing compatibility and inter-operability between devices.

More specifically, I have argued that formats invite us to study or recon-struct the practices that both evolved around formats and led to their formation. Therefore, format studies seems particularly suitable for praxe-ological approaches to media studies (see Schüttpelz 2017; Bergermann et al. 2020). Due to the specific possibilities and affordances of formats to facilitate connections, relations, and labor chains, formats not only determine the aesthetic and individual experience of media content but also provide the terms and conditions for both desired and enforced forms of cooperation and collaboration. Formats therefore need to be considered as fundamental elements of governmental technologies and as important expressions or materializations of the microphysics of power within media. Formats can also serve as means to amplify or hamper the affordances of a medium or to extend or limit the reach or scope of a media system, business model, or value chain. Instead of speaking of the affordances of certain media in general, such as the digital binary code (analog vs. digital), one should therefore look at or consider more closely the formations and formatting of media, such as tendencies toward specialization and universalization.

To define the role of format studies, I would claim that the medium is still the message of media studies but that this message needs to be acknowledged as being fundamentally determined by its format. Digital photography on the basis of JPEG image files, for instance, still generates pictorial representations by projecting light through a system of lenses on a light-sensitive recording medium in a camera. However, the infrastructures and publics of photography, which affect both the practices of circulation and exhibition as well as the media industries and economies involved, have radically changed—and this transformation cannot be accounted for by the replacement of an analog film by a digital sensor inside a camera but rather occurs according to the cooperative reformatting of digital images in a general-purpose and publicly available digital network infrastructure. The more media scholars shift their attention from the general formations we have habitually called "media" to the concrete practices, forms of cooperation, and materialized politics of specialization and universalization, the more format will emerge as a relevant object of study. In the end, format studies will surely not—and is not supposed to—substitute for media studies, but in prompting us to ask different questions, follow different routes, and write different histories, it definitely has the potential to reformat contemporary media studies.

Acknowledgements
This research has been funded by the German Research Foundation (DFG) as part of the A01 project of the Collaborative Research Center "Media of Cooperation" (SFB 1187 Medien der Kooperation) at the University of Siegen. I would like to thank Erhard Schüttpelz and Marek Jancovic for valuable remarks and express my gratitude to Kyle Stine for copy editing this paper and for providing critical insights and suggestions.

References

Anders, Günther. 1956. *Die Antiquiertheit des Menschen: Über die Seele im Zeitalter der zweiten industriellen Revolution*. Munich: C. H. Beck.

Bergermann, Ulrike, Monika Dommann, Erhard Schüttpelz, Jeremy Stolow, and Nadine Taha. 2020. *Connect and Divide: The Practice Turn in Media Studies*. Berlin and Zürich: Diaphanes.

Couldry, Nick. 2012. *Media, Society, World: Social Theory and Digital Media Practice*. Cambridge and Malden, MA: Polity.

Derrida, Jacques. 1997. *Of Grammatology*. Baltimore, MD: Johns Hopkins University Press.

Edwards, Paul N., Geoffrey C. Bowker, Steven J. Jackson, and Robin Williams. 2009. "Introduction: An Agenda for Infrastructure Studies." *Journal of the Association for Information Systems* 10 (5): 6.

Ekbia, Hamid R., and Bonnie A. Nardi. 2017. *Heteromation, and Other Stories of Computing and Capitalism*. Cambridge, MA: MIT Press.

Engemann, Christoph, Till Heilmann, and Florian Sprenger. 2019. "Wege und Ziele. Die unstete Methodik der Medienwissenschaft." *Zeitschrift für Medienwissenschaft* 15 (1): 151–61.

Gaskell, Philip. 1972. *A New Introduction to Bibliography*. Oxford: Clarendon Press.

Gibson, James J. 1979. *The Ecological Approach to Visual Perception*. Boston: Houghton Mifflin.

Gitelman, Lisa. 2014. *Paper Knowledge: Toward a Media History of Documents*. Durham, NC: Duke University Press.

Harris, Roy. 1995. *Signs of Writing*. London and New York: Routledge.

Hickethier, Knut. 2010. *Einführung in die Medienwissenschaft*. 2., aktualisierte und überarb. Aufl. Stuttgart and Weimar: Metzler.

Hoffmann, Stefan. 2002. *Geschichte des Medienbegriffs*. Hamburg: Felix Meiner Verlag.

Krämer, Sybille. 1998. "Das Medium als Spur und als Apparat." In *Medien, Computer, Realität: Wirklichkeitsvorstellungen und Neue Medien*, edited by Sybille Krämer, 73–94. Frankfurt am Main: Suhrkamp.

LeClaire, Jennifer. 2005. "Skype Makes New Video, Blogging Friends." December 2, 2005. https://www.technewsworld.com/story/47650.html.

Lipartito, Kenneth. 2003. "Picturephone and the Information Age: The Social Meaning of Failure." *Technology and Culture* 44 (1): 50–81. https://doi.org/10.1353/tech.2003.0033.

Müller, Susanne. 2014. "Formatieren." In *Historisches Wörterbuch des Mediengebrauchs*, edited by Heiko Christians, Matthias Bickenbach, and Nikolaus Wegmann, 253–67. Cologne u.a.: Böhlau Verlag.

Niehaus, Michael. 2018. *Was ist ein Format?* Kleine Formate 1. Hannover: Wehrhahn Verlag.

Noll, A. Michael. 1992. "Anatomy of a Failure: Picturephone Revisited." *Telecommunications Policy* 16 (4): 307–16. https://doi.org/10.1016/0308-5961(92)90039-R.

Parks, Lisa, and Nicole Starosielski, eds. 2015. *Signal Traffic: Critical Studies of Media Infrastructures*. Urbana: University of Illinois Press.

Peters, John Durham. 2015. *The Marvelous Clouds: Toward a Philosophy of Elemental Media*. Chicago: University Of Chicago Press.

Schmidt, Kjeld, and Ina Wagner. 2018. "Writ Large: On the Logics of the Spatial Ordering of Coordinative Artefacts in Cooperative Work." *Working Paper Series/SFB 1187 Medien der Kooperation* 5.

Schröter, Jens, and Alexander Böhnke, eds. 2004. *Analog/Digital – Opposition oder Kontinuum? Zur Theorie und Geschichte einer Unterscheidung*. Bielefeld: transcript.

Schueler, Judith, Andreas Fickers, and Anique Hommels, eds. 2008. *Bargaining Norms, Arguing Standards: Negotiating Technical Standards*. Vol. 74, Stichting toekomstbeeld der techniek. The Hague: STT Netherlands Study Centre for Technology Trends.

Schüttpelz, Erhard. 2017. "Infrastructural Media and Public Media." *Media in Action* 1 (1): 13–61.

Star, Susan Leigh, and Geoffrey C. Bowker. 2002. "How to Infrastructure." In *Handbook of New Media: Social Shaping and Social Consequences of ICTs*, edited by Leah A. Lievrouw and Sonia Livingstone, 151–62. London: Sage.

Star, Susan Leigh, and James R. Griesemer. 1989. "Institutional Ecology, 'Translations' and Boundary Objects: Amateurs and Professionals in Berkeley's Museum of Vertebrate Zoology, 1907–39." *Social Studies of Science* 19 (3): 387–420. https://doi.org/10.1177/030631289019003001.

Star, Susan Leigh, and Karen Ruhleder. 1996. "Steps toward an Ecology of Infrastructure: Design and Access for Large Information Spaces." *Information Systems Research* 7 (1): 111–34.

Sterne, Jonathan. 2012. *MP3: The Meaning of a Format*. Durham, NC: Duke University Press.

Turkle, Sherry. 1995. *Life on the Screen: Identity in the Age of the Internet*. New York: Simon & Schuster.

Volmar, Axel. 2017. "Formats as Media of Cooperation." *Media in Action* 1 (2): 9–28. https://www001.zimt.uni-siegen.de/ojs/index.php/mia/article/view/19/23.

Wallace, Gregory K. 1991. "The JPEG Still Picture Compression Standard." *Communications of the ACM* 34 (4): 30–44.

Young, Liam Cole. 2017. *List Cultures: Knowledge and Poetics from Mesopotamia to Buzzfeed.* Amsterdam: Amsterdam University Press.

2

Let's Dance: GIF 1.0 versus GIF 2.0

Wanda Strauven

Flash-forward

Anno 2024, the Graphics Interchange Format (GIF) has come to be commonly used for the recording of living cells. By repurposing a compression format into a scientific tool, the human species has now at its disposal "black boxes" of human bodies, including their brains. They no longer need memory implants, as envisioned 20 years earlier by Omar Naim's sci-fi movie *The Final Cut* (2004); instead, bacteria are currently programmed "to snuggle up to cells in the human body and to record what they are doing, in essence making a 'movie' of each cell's life" (Kolata 2017). In less than a decade, scientists have managed to improve their DNA experiments with moving images from in-cell storage to in-cell recording.

In the summer of 2017, the first results of storing moving images in the DNA of living cells had indeed seemed very promising. The research team at Harvard Medical School and Harvard University had also expressed quite optimistic views on the system's recording capacity (Shipman et al. 2017). The use of *biological* DNA and the perspective to deploy it not only for archiving but also for recording had marked a clear difference from previous efforts to store visual data in DNA. In the spring of 2016, celebrating its centenary year, Technicolor had showcased the successful encoding of Georges Méliès's *A Trip to the Moon* (1902) into *synthetic* DNA, storing a million copies of the digitized version of this early cinema classic into a few droplets of water (Taggart 2016). Technicolor had thus set the trend for film archives and image banks worldwide: digitization was no longer the final stop but the first necessary step for encoding into (nonbiological) DNA.[1]

The biological DNA applied as (visual) information storage system in the 2017 experiments had belonged to a population of gut bacteria. The online version of *The New York Times* had published the breaking news at the time, captivating the attention of the reader with two (almost!) identical looping animated GIFs of a racing horse, placed directly under the headline. Thanks to its wide circulation on social media, the newspaper article had of course intrigued many film scholars. They had immediately recognized the double GIF animation, despite its strong pixilation, as the pioneering photographic experiment carried out 139 years earlier, in 1878, by Eadweard Muybridge, commissioned by Leland Stanford to prove that all four feet of a horse were off the ground at the same time while trotting. The scholarly audience had been baffled by this Muybridge strip being encoded as a sequence of DNA molecules and had paid little attention to the fact that *The New York Times* totally neglected the visual difference between the two GIFs, that is, the "original image" or encoded GIF, stored in the DNA of the living gut bacteria, and the "reconstructed image" or recall GIF, retrieved from those very same bacteria (Kolata 2017).

From the perspective of format theory, it would have been relevant to look more closely at the dancing dots that had made their appearance in the recall GIF, all around the horse; moreover, a white dot had provided the animal with an eye and a black dot at the bottom had seemed like a signature. In other words, instead of losing information, new data had been added from one phase to the other, from storage to retrieval. Clearly, in the 2017 DNA storage experiments, the GIF was no longer functioning as a lossless compression format, but it had become the content of a new format, the living cell, and as such was subject to alteration.[2] Like the audio file format MP3, the GIF had been a "container technology" par excellence. Borrowed from Lewis Mumford, the notion of "container technology" entered format studies by way of Jonathan Sterne (2006). Often overlooked by technology scholars because of their (seeming) passivity, containers are

1   Technicolor's laboratories developed their revolutionary storage technology in collaboration with Harvard University. Already in 2012, Harvard scientists had "successfully stored 5.5 petabits of data—around 700 terabytes—in a single gram of DNA, smashing the previous DNA data density record by a factor of one thousand" (Taggart 2016). For a more detailed research report, see Goela and Bolot (2017).

2   This altered outcome had to do with the coverage (or depth) in DNA sequencing, which is counted in numbers of reads. The higher the number of reads, the less "noise" we get. See Shipman et al. (2017).

not experienced as such; they are not experienced for what they are (e.g., file formats) but for what they contain (e.g., music, animation). About MP3s, Sterne writes: "they are important precisely because they are useful but do not call attention to themselves in practice" (Sterne 2006, 826). Just as the MP3 had become synonymous with the song it contained, being ascribed the "status of a thing" (Sterne 2006, 830), so the GIF had been objectified: it had become the animated loop to be added to your GIF collection.

In 2017, however, the GIF had become not only the "contained" of a new "container" but also an essential part of medical research. In fact, the main goal of the Harvard scientists had not been to solve archiving issues of moving images but rather to understand "both the basic biology of bacterial adaptation and its technological applications" (Shipman et al. 2017, 345). Thus, the GIF had been turned into a tool, that is, the active counterpart of Mumford's container technology. The aim of this chapter is precisely to reconstruct the GIF's function as tool, to study—retro-spectively—how the GIF became a format to be actively used, for multiple purposes, from time-lapse weather maps to grassroots net design, from communicative strategies on social media to genetics and DNA storage "with an eye towards future biological recordings" (Shipman et al. 2017, 345). The method used at the time by the Harvard scientists was CRISPR-Cas, a powerful editing system that allowed for modifying DNA. CRISPR stands for clustered regularly interspaced short palindromic repeats. CRISPRs are short DNA segments that are repeated, like looping animated GIFs, over and over again. One might also hypothesize that the trans-parency of the used GIF, rendering a black racing horse against a white or neutral background, played in favor of the successful completion of the experiment. As will be further discussed below, both loop and trans-parency are two defining characteristics of the GIF. As for the dancing dots that appeared around the racing horse in the recall GIF of the 2017 exper-iment, it will be compelling to find an (unrelated) progenitor in the early history of the World Wide Web.

Flashback

In 1983, David Bowie released his album *Let's Dance*. The same year, on June 20, Terry Welch filed the patent for a new lossless data compression algorithm, LZW, called after its three inventors: Lempel–Ziv–Welch.[3] It was an improved version of a previous compression algorithm, LZ78 (1978). The

---

3   The LZW inventors' full names are Abraham Lempel, Jacob Ziv, and Terry Welch.

LZW patent was granted on December 10, 1985.[4] In the meantime, Welch had published an article in the *IEEE Computer* magazine in which he gave a very detailed and, for computer programmers, readily understandable and usable description of the algorithm, without however mentioning that its patent was still pending. Welch referred to the lossless-ness of the new compression technique in terms of both transparency, in that "the computer programmer is not aware of the existence of compression except in system performance," and "noiseless"-ness, in that "the decompressed data is an exact replica of the input data" (Welch 1984, 8).

In June 1987, four years after the filing of the LZW patent, the graphics development team at CompuServe Information Service (also known as CIS) released the Graphics Interchange Format. As one of America's major information network systems, CompuServe offered, before the existence of the web, "hourly subscription services that provided access to email, forums, file transfers, and chat" (Eppink 2014, 299). The company had already introduced a black-and-white image format, RLE,[5] which the GIF supplanted as a color alternative. From its origin, the GIF could handle anything from two to 256 colors,[6] with its graphics data compressed using LZW. CompuServe was not the first but also not the last company to implement this algorithm, acting in good faith convinced it was freeware.

One year earlier, in September 1986, the Sperry Corporation, for which Welch was working when he filed the infamous patent, had merged with the Burroughs Corporation to form the Unisys Corporation. Unisys retained all of Sperry's patents, including LZW, of which they apparently were not well informed. It took more than seven years, till December 1994, before Unisys took action. By then the GIF was used widely by not only software developers but also commercial sites; moreover, it had become extremely popular among end users. Unisys's tactics to capitalize on the GIF led to a lot of controversy. Subsequently, the LZW patent became known as the "GIF tax" (Battilana 2004), and the League for Programming Freedom launched "a 'Burn All GIFs' campaign" (Eppink 2014, 300). Yet this did not stop GIF's

---

4   The US patent number of the LZW algorithm is 4,558,302.
5   RLE stands for run-length encoding.
6   Nowadays the GIF still has a 256 color palette, but there are tricks to circumvent this restriction. As specified on the *Tech Terms Computer Dictionary*, "A GIF image can actually store more than 256 colors. This is accomplished by separating the image into multiple blocks, which each continue unique 256 color palettes. The blocks can be combined into a single rectangular image, which can theoretically produce a 'true color' or 24-bit image. However, this method is rarely used because the resulting file size is much larger than a comparable .JPEG file."

popularity from rising even more, and the controversy continued until Welch's patent finally expired, 20 years after filing, on June 20, 2003.[7]

Important to stress in terms of format is that the LZW algorithm has remained the leading technique for general-purpose data compression due to its simplicity and versatility. It remains the basis of many PC utilities that claim to double the capacity of hard drives. In the mid-1980s, it was a matter not only of space but also and especially of speed because back then modems used costly telephone lines to dial into Internet service providers. Not surprisingly, one of the main reasons why the graphics development team at CompuServe developed the GIF was to facilitate and accelerate the process of downloading. But the GIF was also designed, as already mentioned, as a color alternative to its monochrome predecessor because "the company wanted to display things like color weather maps," which is how Steve Wilhite, who had "an interest in compression technologies," invented the GIF (O'Leary 2013). As the official father of the format, Wilhite insists, even today, that the correct pronunciation of the acronym is with a soft *g* (as in jif).[8]

GIF87a vs. GIF89a

The alleged first GIF created by Wilhite was a picture of an airplane, now coming back to life online with an animated and looped background and passing as the very first GIF ever.[9] Yet Wilhite claims that he never made an animated GIF himself. In fact, the airplane GIF with animated background is not an original GIF from 1987, because, very simply, its format is not GIF87a. As one can verify by opening the file in a text editor, it is instead GIF89a, which is the enhanced version of the format, released two years later.

Besides combining indexed color with lossless data compression (that is, on the one hand, giving in on image quality and, on the other, preventing image degradation),[10] the real asset of the GIF, its key to success, lies of course in its capacity to store multiple images in a single file. While this spec was already defined in GIF87a, it was not originally meant to make animations possible, but "to save memory by eliminating redundant data"

---

7   This is a simplified version of the legal issues and litigations, regarding GIF using LZW. For a more detailed version, see Battilana (2004).
8   For the heated debate about the acronym's correct pronunciation, see "The GIF Pronunciation Page" (Olsen, n.d.).
9   See "The First GIF Ever," *Know Your Meme*: https://knowyourmeme.com/photos/1267516-gif.
10 This makes the GIF still today an attractive alternative to, for instance, JPEG.

(Eppink 2014, 299). GIF89a added background transparency and some other specs, such as delay times and image replacement parameters, to make the multiple-image-storage feature more useful for animation.[11] This could be identified as the first pivotal moment in GIF's history, marking its shift from format to tool. As documented in CompuServe Monthly Status Reports, the first implementation of GIF animation was a non-repetitive "time-lapse weather map" (Eppink 2014, 299).

Up to 1995, an animated GIF would play only once. It was not until the release of Netscape Navigator 2.0 that GIFs could be displayed in looped sequences, thanks to the Netscape Looping Application Extension, which became the most popular Application Extension Block of GIF89a.[12] This meant another turning point, whereby the browser was given a leading role. In fact, one could say that it is the browser that loops (or even makes) the GIF, turning the data storage file into a continuously moving image. But, technically speaking, it is the Application Extension Block within the GIF's syntax that tells the browser to loop the file. So, the command is embedded in the GIF itself, which means a reinforcement of its function as tool.

All this happened in 1995 when Unisys started claiming royalties for its LZW patent. CompuServe and other developers began working on a freely usable successor to GIF, which led to the creation of PNG (officially, "Portable Network Graphics"; unofficially, "Png is Not Gif"). While PNG was endorsed by the World Wide Web Consortium (W3C) as a "W3C Rec-ommendation," most Internet browsers could not directly handle this new format and continued to support GIFs, in particular animated GIFs (Battilana 2004). Software developer Mike Battilana adds: "As a result, GIF became more difficult to replace with PNG, since PNG was not designed to support animation" (Battilana 2004). Then there were efforts to create a meta-PNG, which led to the development of MNG ("Multiple-image Network Graphics"), Version 1.0 of which was released in 2001. But it did not really kick off before the expiration date of the LZW patent, two years later.

11   Animation delay is an animation property that configures the delay between the time when the element is loaded and the beginning of the animation sequence. In the late 1980s computers were "slow enough that even a 0 delay was good enough for animation; as they got faster browsers added extra delays to make old animations work correctly" (shachaf 2013).
12   As explained on the cover sheet of the GIF89a Specification report, CompuServe had decided to host an unofficial directory for voluntary participation: "There will be a Courtesy Directory file located on CompuServe in the PICS forum. This directory will contain Application Identifiers for Application Extension Blocks that have been used by developers of GIF applications" (CompuServe 1990).

In terms of animation, there is another interesting side story. In 1996, a video with a 3D-rendered dancing baby went viral, in the sense that it became globally popular via email chains. Later that same year, web developer John Woodell created a highly compressed animated GIF from the source movie, as part of a demo of the movie-to-GIF process, which further enabled the spread of the Dancing Baby across the Internet (Romano 2017). This early GIF animation remains one of Wilhite's favorites (O'Leary 2013). It is also a good demonstration of the functionality of GIF's transparency, the black background of the video being removed by the conversion into GIF and therefore usable (or shareable) on any type of background. This shareability due to GIF's transparency was crucial to its success in the early days of the web and its application as Internet art. In those very same years, 1995–1996, a group of artists, among them the Russian GIF artist Olia Lialina, formed the Internet art movement, "net.art."[13] Within this framework, the GIF became an artistic practice. On a more conceptual level, as discussed below, this meant a shift from format to medium, from container to context.

WWW

According to Olia Lialina (2016b), the history of the GIF animation has nothing to do with CompuServe; it is instead a "real grassroots Net story."[14] For her, the World Wide Web (Web 1.0) was the best thing that happened to the Internet because it gave people the opportunity to program without having advanced programming skills. Net.art is a form of art that uses the World Wide Web as its medium and cannot be experienced in any other way. Hence, the importance of the browser. In Lialina's view, the GIF only exists online.

In those years, the GIF was becoming something more than just a file format; it was becoming a part of a page (a personal web page or home page, as it was called back then). As Lialina points out, "*Technically there are two features that are specific to GIFs: loop and transparency*. [One] only talks about the loop, the endless animation, a moment that exists *forever*. Transparency is about the possibility to exist *everywhere* (on any page and any background), which is historically much more important for the development of the file format into the medium." She adds: "GIF89a is a format

13   The other main members are Vuk Ćosić, Jodi.org, Alexei Shulgin, and Health Bunting.
14   In the grassroots spirit, the GIF is "a community-originated format, unlike the top-down development of emoji" (Miltner and Highfield 2017, 4). Becoming extremely popular in the 2010s, emoji originated on Japanese mobile phones in 1997.

to be distributed. The ability for one image to appear in countless contexts made it the success that it is" (Lialina 2012). Thus, for Lialina, distribution means not simply free circulation; instead, it refers more specifically to GIF's appearance (or recycling) on other home pages.[15]

This is when GIF banners became increasing popular: banner ads, "under construction" signs, flames, etc. And let's not forget the Dancing Banana! In 1996, Lialina made her first animated GIF, a black-and-white window, consisting of four frames (size: 6 KB). This GIF was a part of a page, a browser-based Internet artwork, entitled *My Boyfriend Came Back from the War* (MBCBFTW). Conceived as a "netfilm," the work is an example of interactive hypertext storytelling about two lovers who are trying to reconnect after the war. Today it is considered as "one of the most influential net art pieces of the mid nineties" (Bosma 2016).

Yet Lialina became probably more famous because of her creative use of the Dancing Girl, a little animated figure dressed in red, swinging her hips and her black ponytail. It is a found GIF (hulagirl.gif) that Lialina appropriated and integrated into new net.art works, such as the *Rhizome.org* splash-page from 1998.[16] A splash-page is an introduction page, enticing the user to explore the rest of the website, in this case inviting them to dance along with the GIF, which is flanked by two lines of copyright symbols. In Lialina's (2011b) words, it is a "free girl from a free collection dancing among copyright decoration" telling us that "information wants to be free."

When looking carefully at the Dancing Girl, one notices a black spot at the bottom right. It is a "forgotten pixel" that has been blinking incessantly ever since the original hulagirl.gif was uploaded on the World Wide Web. Why is it still there? Why did no one remove it? One could say it has become the "signature" of the Dancing Girl GIF, similar to the dancing dots in the recall GIF of Muybridge's horse-in-motion of the 2017 DNA storage experiments. But the former is not a DNA sequencing. So, where does its black dot come from? Where does the Dancing Girl come from?

Only recently, Lialina discovered that the Dancing Girl GIF was made by a retired pilot from the US Air Force, Chuck Poynter, who passed away in 2001 (Lialina 2011b). Poynter was the owner and developer of the website *Original Animation for Download*, in which he stored his GIF collection. The Dancing Girl appeared on the top of all the pages on the site, so it clearly was one of

---

15   For a more general discussion of GIF's free, unrestricted circulation, see for instance Uhlin (2014).
16   See http://archive.rhizome.org:8080/splash/olia/.

Poynter's personal favorites. As we can read further on Lialina's blog, she also found out that the Dancing Girl GIF was a demo animation made from VideoWorks, a black-and-white animation program for the early Macintosh of the mid-1980s. Among its sample animations, there were three dancing figures, forming the so-called Dance Fever Cast (Lialina 2011a). All three figures have been colored in and adapted to the GIF format by Poynter in the mid-1990s. Without going into too much detail, a comparison between the VideoWorks Dancing Girl and the GIF version shows that Poynter not only removed two frames but also got rid of the shadow. One might guess that the "forgotten pixel" is an un-removed piece of the girl's shadow—in fact, it shows up only in frames 3 and 7, which are those with the most extended shadow area in the VideoWorks file. But this hypothesis does not hold: a close-up frame-by-frame analysis reveals that the "blinking dot" is outside the shadow area.[17]

To date, it is still a mystery where the pixel comes from. But it has become the authenticity marker of GIF 1.0, a trace of its original "error-laden" style, its "DIY aesthetics" (Kane 2016, 59). The dot belongs to the format's history, to its dancing appearance in the good old days of the WWW, for which it is cherished, if not fetishized, by net artists and archivists. But there is more at stake than pure nostalgia; it is a form of resistance against the "progres-sive rationalization of aesthetics" in contemporary media culture (Kane 2016, 52). The dot is a critique of digital cleanness. Do not dare to remove it!

GIF 2.0 and Its Multiple Uses

By 2005, two years after the LZW patent had expired, GIFs became out-dated. No serious web designer would use animated GIFs any longer. But it is precisely during that period that social networking sites were gaining in popularity. MySpace was founded in 2003, with Facebook following in 2004, Twitter in 2006, and, most importantly, Tumblr in 2007. Supporting the format since its foundation, Tumblr played an important role in GIF's revival, its combination of microblogging and built-in virality through reblogging leading to an increase in the circulation of GIFs. Twitter and Facebook have supported animated GIFs only since June 2014 and May 2015, respectively.

So, GIF 2.0 is a relatively recent phenomenon. Compared to GIF 1.0, it is more diversified in terms of style, form, and function. On social media

---

17   Such an analysis has been carried out by Lialina's husband and collaborator Dragan Espenschied (Lialina 2011a) as well as by the person behind the Real_Dancing_Girl (2013) creation.

sites, it has mainly become a communication tool, characterized by polysemy, decontextualization, flexibility, and repetition (Miltner and Highfield 2017). There are also many new forms of GIF art, ranging from Scorpion Dagger's humorous, sacrilegious work to Lorna Mills's low-res GIF collages and Bill Domonkos's sophisticated black-and-white cinemagraphs (Tanni and Verini 2016). Another noteworthy case is the Valencia-based collective Sal Viral, consisting of two young women, Alicia Adarve and Regina Rivas, who are net archivists/activists and meme researchers. In 2016, they made an installation with the multiple appearances of the so-called Confused Travolta GIF, combining a barcode-like sliding door, a video compilation of 220 GIFs and printouts of GIF encoded files.[18] Ripped from Quentin Tarantino's cult film *Pulp Fiction* (1994), the GIF, hashtagged with #travoltaconfused, is transparent, meaning that the living room setting from the movie scene has been removed and the cutout figure of the gangster Vincent Vega (played by John Travolta) can be stuck against all kinds of backgrounds, appearing "lost" in the most diverse situations and contexts.

The Confused Travolta GIF is a good example of a reaction GIF: "By putting a single gesture on loop [in this case of a man turning to the side with his hand out], the reaction GIF acts as a proxy for, or expression of, emotion and/or effect" (Miltner and Highfield 2017, 5). Posted on social media sites, in "reaction" to other posts, it is an effective tool of communication. Another famous example is the slowly clapping Orson Welles, extracted from the classic movie *Citizen Kane* (1941) and GIF-ized into a loop. Decontexualized, its original meaning of sincere support may be altered, ranging from an ironic to a ridiculing or begrudging clap. It becomes indeed "applicable to any situation, by anybody, regardless of their familiarity with, or awareness of, its original context" (Miltner and Highfield 2017, 5). In the early days of net culture, one could express dislike, disgust or disagreement by using the Peeman.gif (also known as peeguy.gif, peepee.gif or piss.gif). A reaction GIF avant la lettre, Peeman needed to be contextualized, instead of decontextualized. Or as Lialina (2017) put it, "Peeman can only fulfill his purpose when combined with a second image which he can pee upon."

Most of today's GIFs are video-to-GIF clips, or GIF-ized clips, which Lialina (2016b) labels "Animated JPEGs." They are made "to be posted or shared and not to become a part of a web page" (Lialina 2016a). As already pointed out, for Lialina, GIF's most important and original feature was its transparency. And that is what "Animated JPEGs" lack. In Lialina's (2016a) words, "They

---

18   The collective posted a short video on Vimeo, documenting the Confused Travolta installation (Sal Viral 2016).

are always a 'content', not a part of the page." This seems to imply that the GIF is making an evolution from container to context to content. But as demonstrated by the Confused Travolta GIF, things are not that simple: thanks to its transparency, Travolta's confused gesture can be placed in many different contexts (even web pages!), becoming the content of new (reaction) GIFs and as such the container of an expression.

Nevertheless, one might wonder if GIF 2.0 is not altogether a new format. Because if a format "denotes a whole range of decisions that affect the look, feel, experience, and workings of a medium" (Sterne 2012, 7), there seems to be quite a gap between GIF 1.0 and GIF 2.0.[19] Hence the nostalgia for the original format (as a web design tool) and the wave of "retro-GIF-makers" (Kane 2016, 50). For instance, the Real_Dancing_Girl is a true ode to the hulagirl.gif of 1996. With accounts on Tumblr and Twitter since April 2013, she is claiming to be an old symbol in a new look:

> I've been dancing ever since I was created back in the days.
>
> With the arise of the internet I became a vernacular symbol of freedom among the net, and a source of inspiration for countless users in the pre-history of the web.
>
> The advent of social networks brought a severe, consequently change in the aesthetic of the internet; that's why I felt the need to renew my look, giving myself a more "topical" appearance.
>
> But don't be fooled by this: my "hula" remains the same ;-)
>
> Feel free—as you've always been—to make me dance among your web universe! (Real_Dancing_Girl 2013)

The Real_Dancing_Girl is not an animated figure, but a live-action GIF of a young dancing woman, dressed in red (or blue), who swings her hips and ponytail, like the hulagirl.gif. As might be expected, the Real_Dancing_Girl GIF is transparent and below her left foot appears a blinking dot. This residue of GIF 1.0 has been deliberately added; it is an obsolete piece of technology that is nurtured for its symbolism, for its sense of freedom, for its shareability on different web pages (and backgrounds). The blinking dot disguises GIF 2.0 as GIF 1.0. A similar mechanism has been noted by Sterne (2012) in the case of the 128k standard for sound files: "A characteristic

---

19   This gap reflects the changing net culture, in particular the effects of Web 2.0, which meant "the culmination of approximately seven years of neglecting and denying the experience of web users—where experience is Erfahrung, rather than Erlebnis" (Lialina 2018, 178).

that might first appear as the result of numb technological imperatives is actually revealed as something that had an aesthetic and cultural function, even if it is subsequently transformed" (15).

More generally, one could say that GIF's transparency feature has been overruled by its looped animation, which was originally a browser's extension. So, is the browser still making the GIF? Lialina argues that the looped GIF is never identical, that each repetition is unique, precisely because it depends on the speed and performance of the browser (and computer) used. To illustrate this point, she made a web-based animation of herself on a swing, moving up and down, while in the location bar the URL constantly changes, switching from one address (or context) to the next.[20] Besides this technical/navigational aspect, it is also true that the loop is never the same because our viewing experience changes over the course of the loop's repetition, a point to which I will return in the final section.

To conclude the discussion of the format's loss of transparency, it seems apt to (mis)quote here Anna McCarthy's remark about GIF's to-be-looked-at-ness. She writes: "GIFs are things to look *at*, not through" (McCarthy 2017, 116). Instead of dealing with the technical spec of GIFs' transparency, she analyzes their "visual pleasure" (turning Laura Mulvey's feminist reading of classical narrative cinema into a witty critique of today's capitalist, corporate online culture), which she connects to the to-be-looked-at-ness of our smartphones. GIFs' raison d'être is to catch our attention; they impose themselves, unsolicited and unannounced, "in the indeterminate *durée* that is the flow of social media" (McCarthy 2017, 114).

Sleepless Images

GIFs are sleepless images because of their nonstop operation, their continual looping and animated presence on the Internet. According to Jonathan Crary (2013), today's human life is inscribed into duration without breaks. In his condensed study about our new 24/7 temporality, he writes: "Sleeplessness is the state in which producing, consuming, and discarding occur without pause, hastening the exhaustion of life and the depletion of resources" (17). We are living in a "time without time," or a "non-stop time," where the borders between private and professional time are dissolved, where we are supposed to be always available, day and night. While not dealing explicitly with GIFs as "24/7 feeds" (Kane 2016, 58), Crary's book

---

20   See http://www.todayandtomorrow.net/olia/summer.

discloses how "our productivity as workers relies on our consumption of commodities from smartphones to streaming movies to (mostly useless) information itself" (Heuer 2013). *Rhizome.org* nicely illustrates this point with an animated GIF by Zoe Burnett, entitled *Life*, which shows the repetitive action of a thumb scrolling over the screen of a smartphone.

Burnett's GIF also captures well McCarthy's point about the to-be-look-at-ness of the smartphone and the hypnotic effect of certain GIFs. McCarthy (2017) draws attention to the reproductive capacity of GIFs, in the way they accumulate layers and traces of their online circulation, that is, of their "GIFfing" (113). While circulating, GIFs acquire new meanings and literally transform (or change form). According to McCarthy, GIFs are like zombies:

> They may come back, but they're never the same. Something has changed: resolution, aspect ratio, size. Or the image material has become encrusted with memes. [. . .] Part of the enjoyment of GIFs in the context of social media involves observing their constant transformations. (114)

A case in point is, once more, the Confused Travolta reaction GIF. McCarthy, however, is attracted by different GIFs that are hashtagged with #satisfying and extracted from industrial films, showing the perfection (or precision) of machinery. These GIFs are particularly mesmerizing because of the never-ending repetition of a short flawless fragment.

This dialectics of endless shortness (or eternal ephemerality) typifies today's online loops. In this respect, Maria Poulaki (2015) distinguishes between "background loops" and "foreground loops" (92–93). The former "prolong the duration of non-action" (92), and the latter "contain a distinctive action" (93), which is however weakened by the repetitive operation of the loop. A typical example of a background loop is, for instance, the static video of fire burning in a fireplace. Most GIFs are instead, according to Poulaki, foreground loops. Yet they lose the strength of their eventfulness precisely because of the repetition of the looping:

> After multiple watching, the even superficial narrative of the event-based foreground loops is dismantled and the event itself (e.g. the visual gag) now becomes the incentive for the repetitive operation of the loop to take place. The event acquires its dynamics not from a narrative goal to be executed but from the loop's movement and self-generated dynamics. (93)

Above we have seen that, technically speaking, each repetition of an animated GIF is unique. Here we can add that the loop is never the same because the viewer's experience also alters. That is, the sameness changes through repetitive viewing. Such a shift in viewing experience happened, for instance, to Arild Fetveit (2018), who narrates how the incessant looping of the black-and-white Sexy Prince GIF turned the flirtatious pop star into an automaton. Circulating widely after Prince's death in April 2016, this particular GIF proved itself "effective in providing a passage, not merely from the dead towards the living, but as much, from the living towards the dead" (Fetveit 2018). The split between life and death is somehow reinforced by the zooming in from medium shot to close-up, which interrupts, at each repetition, the perfect loop.[21]

In her analysis of online loop cultures, Poulaki calls attention to the looping point, or "short-cut," as she calls it, which makes the endless loop intermittent. She writes: "This looping point is a moment of reflexivity, where the present reflects the past and becomes again a new starting point, in a continuous feedback between the present and the eternal" (2015, 94). It is this continuous feedback, this repetition of the looping point, that constitutes the essence of the GIF as gesture, or—to say it with Walter Benjamin—as "creative innervation" (2005, 204). In the original version of his famous Artwork essay (1936), Benjamin observed that the decay of aura in art is matched by a huge increase of room-for-play (*Spiel-Raum*), especially in and thanks to film.[22] He also suggested to explore "the great law that presides over the rules and rhythms of the entire world of play: the law of repetition" (2005, 120). The GIF as repetitive sequence of images fits Benjamin's definition of play rather well. For Poulaki, the loop is indeed a form of play; it is a "play with self-reference, as its duration is created through self-multiplication" (2015, 94).

From sleepless to playful image, the GIF allows, lastly, for a connection with 19th-century optical toys, which were also based on the looping principle: in particular, the thaumatrope, the phenakistiscope, and the zoetrope were rotating *dispositifs* that produced repetitive "pre-GIF" visual patterns. The loop was inscribed in the circular form of their *dispositif*: the thaumatrope's circular cardboard, the phenakistiscope's disk, and the zoetrope's drum. It therefore comes as no surprise that these 19th-century visual patterns are nowadays turned into GIFs. They are literally awakened to become sleepless images among their 21st-century companions, eternally put into rotation without the need of manual operation. What is more, the content

---

21   The "Sexy Prince GIF" can be found on *Giphy*: https://giphy.com/gifs/
       justin-prince-26AHrsRVKw5lDjRba.
22   For an in-depth discussion of Benjamin's notion of *Spiel-Raum*, see Hansen (2004).

of the optical device is now its format (GIF), which runs without its original *dispositif*.

Conclusion

It is fascinating to see how a bitmap image format with a limited color palette, introduced more than 30 years ago, is surviving and thriving in the 21st century and how it challenges our notions of format (or container), medium (or context), and image (or content). As I have suggested throughout this chapter, the GIF can best be considered as a tool. It used to be a tool for programming, for creating your own animations as web designer or net artist, while nowadays it has become a tool for animating JPEGs, for looping short video clips ripped from existing movies or TV shows and for conceptualizing, theorizing, and historicizing online phenomena. As such, the GIF clearly crosses disciplinary boundaries: from information technology to art and activism, from social media and communication studies to genetics and brain science.

Moreover, the GIF epitomizes changes in our screen culture, from the desktop computer screen and Web 1.0 browsers to the cellular touch-screens through which we access—nonstop—online platforms. It is difficult to predict the future, but since reality often catches up with science fiction, it is quite possible that the human species will soon have GIFs in its brains.

References

Battilana, Mike. 2004. "The GIF Controversy: A Software Developer's Perspective." *Mike.pub.* Accessed July 22, 2018. https://mike.pub/19950127-gif-lzw.

Benjamin, Walter. 2005. *Selected Writings*, vol. 2, pt. 1, *1927–1930*, edited by Michael W. Jennings, Howard Eiland, and Gary Smith. Cambridge and London: The Belknap Press of Harvard University Press.

Bosma, Josephine. 2016. "Olia Lialina—20 Years of My Boyfriend Came Back from the War." *Josephine Bosma*. Accessed July 22, 2018. http://www.josephinebosma.com/web/node/112.

CompuServe. 1990. "GIF89a Specification." *W3.org*. Accessed February 2, 2019. https://www.w3.org/Graphics/GIF/spec-gif89a.txt.

Crary, Jonathan. 2013. *24/7: Late Capitalism and the Ends of Sleep*. London and New York: Verso.

Eppink, Jason. 2014. "A Brief History of the GIF (so far)." *Journal of Visual Culture* 13 (3): 298–306.

Fetveit, Arild. 2018. "The Uncanny Mediality of the Photographic GIF." *NECSUS* (Spring). https://necsus-ejms.org/the-uncanny-mediality-of-the-photographic-gif/#_ednref1.

Goela, Naveen, and Jean Bolot. 2017. "Advances in DNA Storage." *2017 Information Theory and Applications Workshop (ITA)*, San Diego, CA. doi: 10.1109/ITA.2017.8023453.

Hansen, Miriam. 2004. "Room-For-Play: Benjamin's Gamble with Cinema." *Canadian Journal of Film Studies / Revue Canadienne d'Etudes Cinématographiques* 13 (1): 1–27.

Heuer, Megan. 2013. "Who Sleeps? Jonathan Crary's '24/7.'" *Rhizome.org*, September 17. Accessed July 22, 2018. http://rhizome.org/editorial/2013/sep/17/who-sleeps-jonathan-crarys-247/.

Kane, Carolyn L. 2016. "GIFs That Glitch: Eyeball Aesthetics for the Attention Economy." *Communication Design* 4 (1–2): 41–62.

Kolata, Gina. 2017. "Who Needs Hard Drives? Scientists Store Film Clip in DNA." *New York Times*, July 12. Accessed July 22, 2018. https://www.nytimes.com/2017/07/12/science/film-clip-stored-in-dna.html.

Lialina, Olia. 2011a. "Dancing Girl File Not Closed Yet." *One Terabyte of Kilobyte Age*. Accessed July 22, 2018. http://blog.geocities.institute/archives/2559.

———. 2011b. "In Memory of Chuck Poynter, User and GIF Maker." *One Terabyte of Kilobyte Age*. Accessed July 22, 2018. http://blog.geocities.institute/archives/2466#footnote_0_2466.

———. 2012. "Animated GIF as a Medium." *Art.teleportacia.org*. Accessed July 22, 2018. http://art.teleportacia.org/observation/GIF-as-medium/.

———. 2016a. "Animated JPEGs." Email correspondence with author. December 4.

———. 2016b. "Telling GIFs and Animated JPEGs Apart." Keynote lecture at Viral Art: The New Imageries of GIF Culture, International Conference, University of Bologna, November 24–25.

———. 2017. "Peeman." *Art.teleportacia.org*. Accessed February 2, 2019. http://art.teleportacia.org/exhibition/peeman/.

———. 2018. "Rich User Experience, UX and the Desktopiation of War." *Interface Critique Journal* 1: 176–93.

McCarthy, Anna. 2017. "Visual Pleasure and GIFs." In *Compact Cinematics: The Moving Image in the Age of Bit-Sized Media*, edited by Pepita Hesselberth and Maria Poulaki, 113–22. New York and London: Bloomsbury.

Miltner, Kate M., and Tim Highfield. 2017. "Never Gonna GIF You Up: Analyzing the Cultural Significance of the Animated GIF." *Social Media and Society* 3 (3): 1–11.

O'Leary, Amy. 2013. "An Honor for the Creator of the GIF." *Bits* (blog), *New York Times*, May 21. Accessed July 22, 2018. https://bits.blogs.nytimes.com/2013/05/21/an-honor-for-the-creator-of-the-gif/.

Olsen, Steve. n.d. "GIF Pronunciation Page." *Olsenhome.com*. Accessed May 24, 2019. http://www.olsenhome.com/gif/.

Poulaki, Maria. 2015. "Featuring Shortness in Online Loop Cultures." *Empedocles: European Journal for the Philosophy of Communication* 5 (1–2): 91–96.

Real_Dancing_Girl. 2013. "Who_Am_I." *Real_Dancing_Girl*. Accessed August 3, 2018. http://realdancingirl.tumblr.com/WHOAMI.

Romano, Aja. 2017. "The GIF Is 30 Years Old. It Didn't Just Shape the Internet—It Grew Up with the Internet." *Vox*, June 15. Accessed August 3, 2018. https://www.vox.com/culture/2017/6/15/15802136/gif-turns-30-evolution-internet-history.

Sal Viral. 2016. "Obra Confused Travolta por Sal Viral en el Pam!16." *Vimeo*. Uploaded May 7. https://vimeo.com/165702273.

shachaf. 2013. "The Mystery of the Spotty Animated GIF." *Hacker News*, May 11. Accessed August 3, 2018. https://news.ycombinator.com/item?id=5689941.

Shipman, Seth L., Jeff Nivala, Jeffrey D. Macklis, and George M. Church. 2017. "CRISPR-Cas Encoding of a Digital Movie Into the Genomes of a Population of Living Bacteria." *Nature* 547: 345–49. doi: 10.1038/nature23017.

Sterne, Jonathan. 2006. "The MP3 as Cultural Artifact." *New Media and Society* 8 (5): 825–42. doi: 10.1177/1461444806067737.

———. 2012. *MP3: The Meaning of a Format*. Durham, NC: Duke University Press.

Taggart, Frankie. 2016. "Technicolor Stores Hollywood History in a Bottle." *Phys.org*, April 5. Accessed February 1, 2019. https://phys.org/news/2016-04-technicolor-hollywood-history-bottle.html.

Tanni, Valentina, and Saverio Verini. 2016. *Stop and Go. L'arte delle GIF animate*. Roma: Litografia Bruni.

Tech Terms Computer Dictionary, s.v., "GIF." Accessed May 23, 2019. https://techterms.com/definition/gif.

Uhlin, Graig. 2014. "Playing in the Gif(t) Economy." *Games and Culture* 9 (6): 517–27. doi: 10.1177/1555412014549805.

Welch, Terry. 1984. "A Technique for High-Performance Data Compression." *IEEE Computer* (June): 8–19.

[3]

Formats and Formalization in Internet Advertising

Ramon Lobato and Julian Thomas

Leaderboards, pushdowns, skyscrapers, expandables, interstitials, carousel ads, sponsored search results, promoted tweets, full-page takeovers, recommendation widgets—these are a few of the advertising formats that consumers are likely to encounter in their everyday internet use. Since the invention of graphical web browsers in the early 1990s, hundreds of ad formats have appeared and disappeared from the web, from familiar banners and billboards to bespoke video, audio, and mobile formats for specific platforms like Snapchat and Spotify. With the rapid development of mobile media, ad formats designed for smartphones have further proliferated and cross-pollinated with desktop-specific formats.

These formats are of interest to media scholars for several reasons. They have introduced new and diverse aesthetic forms into everyday digital culture; generated distinctive economic practices, including real-time bidding and complex "ad-tech" value chains; and, in the case of pop-ups and video ads, attracted criticism for degrading users' online experience, spreading malware, wasting bandwidth, and spawning a new ad-blocking industry. Notwithstanding the important work of internet advertising scholars (Turow 2011; Gehl 2014; Crain 2013), and the parallel professional literature on the effectiveness of particular ad formats (Rejón-Guardia and Martínez-López 2017), research in this area remains somewhat scarce. Consequently, the histories of these ad formats, and the complex distribution and governance systems behind them, remain poorly understood.

This chapter tells one part of the larger story. Our focus here is on how internet ad formats came to be standardized (to some degree at least) and what this means for wider debates about the institutional and technical governance of media formats. For almost twenty years the industry's key lobby and standards group, the Interactive Advertising Bureau (IAB), has been trying to "formalize" (Lobato and Thomas 2015) the unruly advertising markets of the internet, to establish interoperable technical standards, and to weed out aberrant formats and practices—with only limited success. In this chapter we explore the reasons for this partial failure of formalization. We argue that internet advertising, compared to older advertising formats in print and broadcast media, is characterized by a *proliferation* of formats as well as their *instability*. Beyond the legitimate concerns about internet advertising, automation, and surveillance, we suggest there is also another story to be told here about the limits of standardization—its success and failure—in a highly fragmented, increasingly automated, and internally con-flicted sector of the media industries.

Internet Advertising Formats

The term *format* has a specific meaning within internet advertising. Beyond referring to the many different kinds of advertising that appear online (video, mobile, text, in-app, and so on), format also designates the technical attributes that determine how an ad appears and behaves to the user. These attributes include basic properties such as dimensions and ratio, as well as more technical attributes such as file type, file size, definition, CPU load, autoplay features, file requests, expandability, and the presence or absence of close buttons. We may also see a distinction between the formats of ad *inventory*, the spaces publishers provide on websites or in apps for ad content, and the formats of *creative*, the term used to denote actual ad content. The two are not always the same. In some cases, format is also used to refer to the trading and distribution systems underlying specific ad types, such as real-time bidding and retargeting. There is, in other words, a looseness in how the term is used both within and beyond advertising industry practice.

When studying internet ads, it is helpful to begin with a distinction between standard formats and custom formats. Standard formats, such as the bill-board and the leaderboard, are the basic display units of web advertising. Most of these have evolved in an ad-hoc way over many years of trial and experimentation among publishers. Witnessing the enormous expansion of web and later mobile advertising since the 1990s and the simultaneous proliferation of screen sizes and device types, advertising industry stake-holders have long recognized the need for standardization.

One of the industry bodies charged with responsibility for stand-ardizing formats is the Interactive Advertising Bureau, which has been issuing standards and protocols to encourage interoperability in internet advertising since its founding in 1996. Based in New York, with 43 offices around the world, the IAB is the private standard-setting body for inter-net advertising. Its funding comes from annual member contributions paid by major brands, ad agencies, technology providers, and other companies seeking a seat at the table for regulatory and technical discus-sions affecting the industry. The IAB also performs a dispute-settlement function by mediating conflicts as they arise in the industry and proposing technical solutions to address industry problems (though IAB policies, which are private in nature and have no legal standing, are frequently ignored by advertisers). Over the last two decades, as internet advertising has migrated from the web to platforms, the IAB has been increasingly torn between its core membership base—most of whom are publishers, agencies, and ad-tech providers—and the new "duopoly" of Google and Facebook whose business models pose a direct threat to many of its other members. As such, the IAB is an inherently fragmented and conflict-ridden organization.

The IAB's key standards document is the IAB Ad Portfolio, which is pub-lished annually and contains a list of approved formats and their technical specifications. The aim of the portfolio is to minimize production costs for advertisers and enable automated placement of their artwork across millions of different websites, platforms, and apps. Because the ever-increasing number of mobile devices and screen sizes poses a challenge for any standardized portfolio, the IAB has in recent years moved away from fixed-size ads toward flexible size ad formats (22 in total) that can be scaled up and down as needed. These flexible size formats are shown in table 1. Also included is a selection of other current and some historic "delisted" ad formats, which have disappeared from mainstream use but still appear at the margins of the web (on casino and torrent sites, for example).

Current IAB flexible display formats	Other common formats in use	Older display formats delisted by IAB
2x1 horizontal (Half page)	Paid search	Pop-ups
4x1 horizontal (Billboard)	Recommendation widgets	Floating ads
6x1 horizontal (Smartphone banner)	Promoted listing	Auto-expansion
8x1 horizontal (Leaderboard)	In-game ads	Hover or rollover expansion
10x1 horizontal (Super leaderboard/pushdown)	In-banner video	Forced countdown
1x2 vertical	Video 360	Scroll over / scrolling overlay
1x3 vertical (Portrait)	Push notifications	Flashing animation
1x4 vertical (Skyscraper)	Lockscreen ads	Adhesion / sticky ads
1x1 tiles (Medium Rectangle)	Audio in-stream ads	Expand while scrolling
2x1 tiles (Financial)	Chatbots	Underlay ads
Full page portrait (various dimensions)	VR and AR ads	
Full page landscape (various dimensions)	Branded emojis	
Feature phone sizes (small, medium, large banner)		

[Table 1] Interactive advertising formats. Sources: IAB (2017) and Reina (2017).

Custom formats are the second family of internet advertising formats. Unlike standard formats, which require a high degree of technical uniformity, custom formats are owned and controlled by specific platforms. For example, Twitter's signature ad format is the Promoted Tweet; Snapchat is known for its Lenses and Filters that overlay brand information onto users' photos; and Spotify offers Sponsored Playlists and Sponsored Sessions. Custom formats, in other words, are all about differentiation and novelty, rather than standardization.

One of the most famous custom formats is Adwords, Google's signature ad product, which was launched in beta in 2000. The Adwords format is deceptively simple. Advertisers provide a few lines of text, a target URL, and the search terms they want their ads to appear alongside (for example, "toothache" is an attractive term for local dentists). Every time a user searches on Google, a real-time auction occurs between potential advertisers bidding on the designated keyword(s) to determine whose ad appears in the results. Where the ad appears then depends also on its relevance to the search, calculated by Google's algorithms. The humble Adwords format, with its unfashionable plain-text aesthetic and its self-serve, cost-per-click model, has been extraordinarily successful; it is the core of Google's vast advertising and artificial intelligence enterprise.

While Google phased out the Adwords brand in 2018, replacing it with the moniker Google Ads, this was a purely cosmetic change; the underlying technology and business processes of Adwords continue to generate most of Google's revenues.

Understood in these terms, the success of Adwords can be seen as a reaction to the inefficiencies or perceived failures of its rival formats, and the banner format in particular. In the context of the tech crash of the early 2000s, the banner was an expensive, intrusive format. It was the creation of print media publishers (the first banner ads appeared in *Wired*'s online publication *Hotwired* circa 1994), and it emulated the display ads of print media. As the trade paper *Digiday* put it, "For years, the banner ad was the workhorse of digital advertising, and what a miserable nag it was: Banners had diminished click-through rates, stymied publishers' web designers and infuriated a generation of readers who saw sites get more and more crowded with ads" (Willens 2016). In contrast, the Adwords format was new, inexpensive, lower-bandwidth, and automated. And unlike the banner, its price reflected a market operating in real time and its relevance to users rather than a price set by publishers. We return to the Adwords format below in the context of automation.

Other titans of the tech economy have their own custom formats. Amazon, an e-commerce platform with a lucrative advertising and infrastructure business on the side, sells a range of custom formats, including landing pages for brands, sponsored search results, and daily deal "site stripes." At the same time, Amazon also sells display ads in standard IAB formats, such as banners and rectangles, which appear in various places as the user searches for products on the Amazon website or app. The end result is an unusually dense commercial environment offering a wide array of touch points. A user shopping for jeans, for example, might see a Levi's video ad, a Levi's landing page, or Levi's-sponsored search results at various points in their search. Each of these formats is the result of a long process of research and development, as well as careful calculation weighing the revenue potential against the risk of user experience degradation.

As these examples suggest, novel, custom ad formats are a key foundation of the internet economy. More than simply technical specifications to ensure interoperability, formats are nexus points where the media buying side of advertising interacts with the creative side; where commercial, aesthetic and technical logics intertwine; and where the dueling forces of standardization and differentiation enter into productive tension.

The Political Economy of Ad Formats

Internet advertising relies on a constant churn of formats. Compared to other areas of the media industries—such as broadcast and radio—interactive formats are highly unstable. While the 30-second ad has been the mainstay of television advertising since the 1970s, many formats used in web, mobile, and online video advertising are barely a few years old. In other words, there is enormous innovation, and instability, in this sector of the media industries.

The long reign of the 30-second television commercial relied on the extended postwar hegemony of the commercial TV broadcasting system. Hardware and technical standards evolved slowly and incrementally, and standard analog screen resolutions persisted over an extended period, with a gradual transition to digital equivalents from the turn of the century. Periodic user-driven disruptions—remote controls, video recorders— challenged ad formats and shaped industry responses, just as ad blockers are now disrupting internet advertising. But screen sizes and program formats remained relatively stable.

The contemporary situation is different. Convergence has destabilized the format system, as advertisers, publishers, and platforms experiment with new ways to command user attention. It could be argued that formats themselves are the basic "products" of the internet advertising industry, even though they cannot be bought by a consumer. For platforms especially, formats are a point of competitive difference: the business of running a platform involves inventing, refining, and marketing new ad formats that can reach audiences in effective ways. These formats can then be priced as premium ad products delivering effective, targeted messaging that cannot be replicated by other platforms.

Consider the case of Facebook, which has developed dozens of custom formats since its early years as an online college directory. Facebook's first ad format was the Flyer, a vertical text-and-image display box that appeared on the side of the home screen. The Flyer was akin to a classified advertisement and was used mostly by US college students and local businesses catering to those students. Later Facebook ad formats included Pages, Sponsored Groups, and Sponsored Stories (fig. 1). Facebook has full control over these formats and can therefore specify what constitutes appropriate conduct, context, and disclosure. This gives Facebook a clear competitive advantage over other publishers and platforms that rely on standard ad formats.

[Figure 1] Example of a Facebook Sponsored Story ad (2011). Image credit: Chris Messina. Available from Flickr (CC license).

The vital context here was the shift to mobile media. From around 2010 onwards, the smartphone changed advertising, and therefore advertising formats, in ways that amounted to a bifurcation of the "interactive" advertising world into mobile and desktop domains, each with specific characteristics, constraints, and dynamics—and distinct political economies. Mobile meant many things: smaller screens and touch-based interfaces, dramatically refined locational services, and an app economy that began to displace the central role of the browser in desktop media (Burgess 2012; Snickars and Vonderau 2012). Mobile platforms were more controlled than desktop environments, especially in the case of Apple's iOS ecosystem. Users spent more time connected. The smartphone was a personal device, designed with single users in mind, in contrast to the multi-user affordances of desktop systems.

All this created, very rapidly, whole new realms of advertising opportunity and, at the same time, an urgent need to reconsider and reinvent formats from the ground up. The display ad formats that worked on the desktop web failed on the phone. "Mobile [banner] ads are easily ignored," recalled one industry observer, "and when they aren't, they're accidentally clicked" (Bilton 2014). Formats tailor-made for smartphones, however, were very successful. Pop unders became pointless; notifications emerged.

Facebook's response was to evolve its signature ad formats to align with the smartphone user experience. "In-feed" mobile ads became the new gold standard because they were integrated into the flow of the news feed and therefore difficult to avoid. The Sponsored Stories format, which effectively broadcast a user's Likes to all their friends, was particularly important: it revealed the extraordinary potential of in-feed formats, and the problems they raised. The format was phased out in 2014, partly as a result of privacy concerns and a related US$20 million class action lawsuit.

Facebook has also trialed a number of video ad formats over the years, including short GIFs, cinemagraphs, and video takeover ads, all designed for in-feed viewing. Clearly, Facebook's success has been premised on the continual invention of new advertising formats that integrate paid ads into the stream of user-to-user communications as discreetly (some would say deceptively) as possible. A further advantage of Facebook's custom formats is that they are somewhat more difficult for adblockers to detect. Since 2016, Facebook has been claiming it can outsmart desktop adblockers because of the way it embeds its ads in the platform, although Adblock Plus developers have also invented new workarounds in response (Bosworth 2016; Tan 2017). The end result is the familiar "whack-a-mole game of constantly creating ad formats to block the blockers, only to have them figure out a work-around" (Innovation Media 2017). So, while no format is totally impervious to adblocking, custom formats may be harder to block because of their deep integration into the platform.

As these examples suggest, the political economy of formats helps us to understand why and how the internet advertising economy has evolved in recent years into a "duopoly" of Facebook and Google, the two companies that now command the vast majority of new advertising expenditure and whose domination of advertising and media is so bitterly contested. Control over formats was a precondition for this massive concentration of industry power.

Format Governance

The story of Google and Facebook, and their mastery of custom ad formats, reminds us of what is at stake here commercially. Both companies have invested enormous resources in standardizing, scaling, and automating their advertising infrastructure. They now offer end-to-end advertising solutions in which all elements of the transaction are controlled and monitored in-platform. However, the situation is different in advertising supply chains that rely on standard display ad formats, such as those shown on most websites and in apps. These supply chains remain highly complex, volatile, and conflicted. In the display advertising ecology, the process of standardization has been only partially successful.

These tensions can be seen plainly in the history of the IAB, the industry's reluctant and ineffectual watchdog. As explained earlier, the IAB was founded in 1996 to lend some order to an increasingly disorganized industry. Many readers will recall that the mid 1990s were the rough-and-ready years of banner advertising, when banners were proliferating across the web in a wide range of sizes, shapes, and color schemes. By 1996, there were an estimated 250 different banner sizes in use (Collins 1996). As Robert Gehl (2014) notes,

> Websites varied wildly; even with the standards-setting body the W3C, the "browser wars" between Microsoft's Internet Explorer and Netscape's Navigator, coupled with the inevitable growing pains of any new medium, meant that users confronted a sometimes bizarre mediascape of sites "under construction," dead links, and pop-up ads. A common metaphor of the 1990s was that the World Wide Web was the "Wild Wild West." In this space, interaction was as open-ended as many other human activities; uncertainty, surprise, and anxiety were the order of the day. (99)

The IAB's first mission was to dramatically reduce the number of banner ad sizes from 250 down to eight. The organization issued a "Proposal for Voluntary Model Banner Sizes" (IAB 1996) in December 1996 which defined specs for the eight most common web advertising banners. These became the standard IAB units, which publishers and advertisers were encouraged to adopt. In later years, the IAB would extend its standardization agenda to include video ads, mobile ads, and other issues like privacy and tracking (table 2). It would also change its name to the Interactive Advertising Bureau to indicate its newly enlarged focus.

1996:	Founded as Internet Advertising Bureau; sets banner size standards
1997:	Establishes first international chapters
1998:	Issues Online Audience Measurement Guidelines; defines the ad "impression"
2000:	Issues IAB Privacy Guidelines
2002:	Issues Universal Ad Package Guidelines
2004:	Issues Pop-Up/Under Guidelines
2007:	Opens IAB Public Policy Office
2008:	Issues video ad guidelines and standards
2011:	Releases Mobile Rich Media Ad Interface Definitions (MRAID) and Guiding Principles of Digital Measurement
2012:	Develops video ad protocols
2013:	Develops video standards
2016:	Develops LEAN (lightweight, encrypted, AdChoice-supported, noninvasive) principles; phases out set ad sizes in favor of ratios; delists the pop-up

[Table 2] Interactive Advertising Bureau key milestones

The IAB standards process formed the basis for a wider rationalization of internet advertising (Gehl 2014, 100). The clean-up operation enabled the growth of ad networks, which emerged around 1997 and whose primary function was to sell banner advertising across multiple sites (which was only feasible at scale for websites that adopted IAB standard sizes). IAB standards were thus integral to the automation of adverting generally and the advertising architectures that would emerge in the social media platforms of the 2000s. In effect, as Gehl (2014) suggests, the IAB "produced the standards necessary for effective social media surveillance" (94). This process of size standardization was relatively uncontroversial and therefore relatively effective in its stated objective. A diverse and unruly set of formats and commercial practices was rationalized into something more uniform. However, other IAB campaigns have been notably less effective, especially those related to usability and privacy.

As an example, consider the IAB's largely ineffectual campaign against pop-up ads. The pop-up—an ad that suddenly appears as a new window either in front of the user's browser, or even behind it (the pop-under)—began to rival the banner as the internet's default ad format during the late 1990s. Initially appearing on sites like Tripod.com, pop-ups were awful for the user experience. Over time, key stakeholders in the industry began to wonder whether pop-ups might be damaging the reputation and integrity of internet advertising as a whole. The IAB—whose members were often reliant on revenue from pop-ups—took a long time to come around to this way of thinking. While it issued a 2004 pop-up guidelines document requiring advertisers to include close buttons and frequency caps, it wasn't until 2016 that the IAB finally "delisted" the pop-up, removing it from its Portfolio of approved ad formats. By this time, users had taken matters into their own hands by installing adblockers. The major browsers—Firefox, Chrome, Internet Explorer, Opera, Safari—had also introduced pop-up blocker functions.

[Figure 2] The dreaded pop-up ad. Image by Random Literature Council. Available from Flickr (CC license).

The IAB is now starting to govern bad formats more proactively. In recent years, it has issued guidelines restricting the use of forced countdown ads, non-closable interstitials, and the older-style flashing ads. It is also developing guidelines and standards of practice on other contentious issues, such as autoplay video, data allowance, battery use, and tracking script within ad code and cookies. Through these processes, the format is called upon to perform a kind of technical governance: IAB standards aspire to formalize a chaotic and opaque industry by specifying acceptable and unacceptable practices; to smooth out the industry's rough edges; and, in general, to professionalize what is still a fragmented and conflicted sector of the media industries that has had relatively little regard for usability, transparency, or privacy.

Formats in the Age of Automation

Advertising has long been at the forefront of automation in the media industries, and ad formats have played a central role in the automation process. We have already seen how Google combined an automated auction with a relevance algorithm to determine the purchase and placement of Adwords in the early 2000s. Clearly, the simple, text-based Adwords format facilitated the development of Google's system, and its commercial success. Adwords was framed as advertising "for the rest of us," to borrow the rhetoric of an earlier era of personal computing. It was designed for a burgeoning and diverse web, with the promise of expanding markets and latent commercial opportunity. In its early phase, the service was marketed with a question and invitation that underlined the system's speed and ease of use: "Have a credit card and 5 minutes? Get your ad on Google today" (Levy 2011, 86).

The Adwords format took on the stripped-back, minimal aesthetic of Google's overall search design, setting ads alongside "organic" search results in a way that offered some differentiation from them—in order to meet Google's legal and consumer obligations—while giving them consistency with the "house style" of Google's website. The question of whether the format enabled consumers to distinguish clearly between the ads and actual search results remains contentious (Daly and Scardamaglia 2017). Like Facebook Stories or Twitter's promoted tweets, the potential value of the custom ad format lies at least in part in the implication that this particular content has been produced under the auspices of a trusted service (a search engine, social network, or micro-blog). In any case, the stability and simplicity of the Adwords format seems to have provided a form of assurance for both would-be advertisers and consumers while at the same time simplifying the integration of ads into Google's websites. A simple, standardized format, made possible by complex, large-scale automation, served aesthetic, technical, and commercial purposes.

Real-time bidding and automated placement did not emerge in the wider advertising market for display ads until around 2010, heralding the era of "programmatic advertising," a general term for the large-scale automation of buying and selling advertising. A diverse array of new intermediaries appeared to manage the complex interactions between the suppliers of advertising inventory and the market of media buyers: some in competition with each other, some playing complementary roles, and some controlled by large tech platforms or advertising conglomerates. Ad exchanges, supply-side and demand-side platforms (SSPs, DSPs), and data management platforms (DMPs) emerged to coordinate and control transactions in what was a rapidly growing market, with the spectacular growth of mobile media, the appearance of in-app advertising, and a strong trend toward video. A precondition of this new ecosystem, as noted above, was the standardization and modernization of formats, a process heavily promoted by the IAB, without which automated buying and selling would not be possible. In this system, ad formats comprise one of a range of "ad slot parameters" involved in automated market calculations, alongside geographic, demographic, system, and user information.

If the automation of advertising has driven the standardization of formats, the currency of algorithmically valued impressions has also enabled new forms of malpractice. Many forms of ad fraud become possible in a system involving an array of different parties, and the format and placement of ads is also subject to misrepresentation. Two techniques are notable: "pixel stuffing" involves resizing paid ads to 1x1 pixel size, rendering them effectively invisible on the page, while "ad stacking," another technique, involves the vertical stacking of large numbers of ads of the same format, so that only the top few may be visible. There are now so many inter-mediaries involved in programmatic ad placements that it is often difficult to pinpoint the source of the fraud. These deceptive practices, and the wider problem of opacity and revenue leakage within ad-tech, are major challenges for publishers. For example, *The Guardian*'s Chief Digital Officer Hamish Nicklin has stated that up to 70 percent of the revenue generated from ad placements on *The Guardian*'s websites is siphoned off to ad-tech intermediaries.

The problems of ad fraud and revenue leakage underline the degree to which questions of ad formats are also questions of control, governance, and power across the industry. Students of media history are familiar with debates about "format wars," such as Beta vs. VHS, which emphasize the heady and contingent mix of technological change, capital investment, first-mover advantage, and intellectual property control that tend to decide such wars. There is also a rich literature in the history of science and technology that emphasizes the social as well as technical factors that have determined the outcome of many other standard and format wars, from railway gauges to electrification (Hughes 1983). Invariably, these are stories of power, politics, and money. There is no virtuous victory for the best idea, the best invention. Out of this process, new formats and standards and codes emerge as phenomena that "take on a sheen of ontology when they are more precisely the product of contingency" (Sterne 2012, 298).

These histories reveal the difficulty of building and maintaining con-sensus around formats in any large industry. Consensus is especially challenging in internet advertising because the supply chain has so many participants with wildly divergent incentives. Publishers want to increase their ad revenue, platforms want to build and monetize a user base, ad exchanges and middle-men want to optimize auction bids and take a cut along the way, third-party ad-tech suppliers offer proprietary tweaks to the auction formula, data management platforms sell user data overlays (often unethically obtained) to improve ad targeting, ad networks aim to build the largest possible inventory base, and so on. Together with that systemic complexity, there is also ongoing change in the composition and interests of the key actors. Publishers, for example, range from legacy media businesses with print or broadcast markets to entirely web-based media firms and app creators for smartphones or tablets, all with different problems and competitive pressures.

This gives some sense of how difficult it is to govern such a complex system. While the size and shape of ads can, and has been, standardized, it is much harder to police other transgressions like the use of invasive tracking scripts in ad code that slow down page load times. Advertisers get away with this because most users do not realize that the ads are causing the delay, or latency; nor do users understand that the ad script may be draining their phone batteries and causing sluggish phone performance. This provides an alibi for poorly designed ad creative because the advertiser's incentives to reduce ad file size are not in place. In this context, the "end-to-end" offering of the platforms starts to look appealing to advertisers as well as to consumers, who despair of the inefficiency, opacity, and poor user experience inherent in web advertising. In other words, the chaos of web-based display advertising and its apparent impossibility of formalization is contributing to what many in the industry—publishers especially—see as a greater threat: the further empowerment of Google and Facebook at the expense of the open web business model (Hern 2018; Orlowski 2018).

The main effect of the technical and formal transformations described here—both industrial and cultural—has been to open huge new advertising markets over a short historical period. These new markets have stimulated the growth of extraordinarily powerful advertising platforms, resulting in a degree of consolidation with few precedents in the pre-internet media environment. In the case of advertising, however, standardization of ad sizes has created chaos as well as concentration. Standardized and automated ads feed not only are the titans of the internet but also create spaces for its demimonde: the bots, spammers, scammers, and skimmers who evolve and adapt fastest in a huge and complex ecosystem. When it comes to formats, their expertise continues to match that of the largest media companies on the planet.

Acknowledgements
Many thanks to Sam Kininmonth for research assistance, and to Nic Carah for expert advice.

References

Bilton, Ricardo. 2014. "Publishers Invest in Home-Grown Mobile Ad Innovations." *Digiday*, May 13, https://digiday.com/media/publishers-invest-mobile-ad-innovations/.

Bosworth, Andrew. 2016. "A New Way to Control the Ads You See on Facebook, and an Update on Ad Blocking." Facebook press release, August 9, https://newsroom.fb.com/news/2016/08/a-new-way-to-control-the-ads-you-see-on-facebook-and-an-update-on-ad-blocking/.

Burgess, Jean. 2012. "The iPhone Moment, the Apple Brand, and the Creative Consumer: From 'Hackability and Usability' to Cultural Generativity." In *Studying Mobile Media: Cultural Technologies, Mobile Communication, and the iPhone*, edited by Larissa Hjorth, Jean Burgess, and Ingrid Richardson, 24–42. London: Routledge.

Collins, Glenn. 2006. "Trade Groups Propose Web Banner Guidelines." *New York Times*, December 12, https://www.nytimes.com/1996/12/12/business/trade-groups-propose-web-banner-guidelines.html.

Crain, Matthew. 2013. "The Revolution Will Be Commercialized: Finance, Public Policy, and the Construction of Internet Advertising." PhD thesis, University of Illinois, Urbana-Champaign.

Daly, Angela, and Amanda Scardamaglia. 2017. "Profiling the Australian Google Consumer: Implications of Search Engine Practices for Consumer Law and Policy." *Journal of Consumer Policy* 40 (3): 299–320.

Gehl, Robert. 2014. *Reverse Engineering Social Media: Software, Culture, and Political Economy in New Media Capitalism*. Temple, PA: Temple University Press.

Hern, Alex. 2018. "Can We Really Trust Google as Judge, Jury and Executioner of Online Ads?" *The Guardian*, February 15, https://www.theguardian.com/technology/2018/feb/15/google-chrome-adblocking-online-ads.

Hughes, Thomas P. 1983. *Networks of Power: Electrification in Western Society, 1880–1930*. Baltimore, MD: Johns Hopkins University Press.

IAB. 1996. "Internet Advertising Bureau and CASIE Identify Most Commonly Used Banners on the Web." Internet Advertising Bureau, press release, December 10, https://www.iab.com/news/voluntary-guidelines-banner-advertising-process-exploring-future-internet-advertising-forms-announced-industry-groups/.

———. 2017. "IAB New Standard Ad Unit Portfolio, July 2017: Version 1.1." New York: Interactive Advertising Bureau.

Innovation Media. 2017. Magazines Report 2017–2018. https://innovation.media/magazines/monetisation-how-the-heck-do-you-make-in-magazine-media-these-days.

Levy, Steven. 2011. *In The Plex: How Google Thinks, Works, and Shapes Our Lives*. New York: Simon and Schuster.

Lobato, Ramon, and Julian Thomas. 2015. *The Informal Media Economy*. Cambridge: Polity Press.

Lyon, Vicki. 2016. "Back to the Basics: Ad Creative Formats Holding Back the Future of OTT Monetization." Ooyala whitepaper, July 21, http://www.ooyala.com/resources/videomind-blog/back-basics-ad-creative-formats-holding-back-future-ott-monetization.

Orlowski, Andrew. 2018. "Chrome Adblockalypse Will 'Accelerate Google–Facebook Duopoly.'" *The Register*, February 16, https://www.theregister.co.uk/2018/02/16/chrome_adblockalypse_ads_and_media_analysis/.

Pidgeon, David. 2016. "Where Did the Money Go? Guardian Buys Its Own Ad Inventory." *Mediatel Newsline*, October 4, https://mediatel.co.uk/newsline/2016/10/04/where-did-the-money-go-guardian-buys-its-own-ad-inventory.

Reina, Edoardo. 2017. "Mobile Advertising: An Exploration of Innovative Formats and the Adoption in the Italian Market." MSc thesis. Politecnico di Milano.

Rejón-Guardia, Francisco, and Francisco J. Martínez-López. 2017. "A Review of Internet and Social Network Advertising Formats." In *Digital Advertising: Theory and Practice*, edited by Shelly Rodgers and Esther Thorson, 362–81. New York: Routledge.

Sinclair, John. 2012. *Advertising, the Media and Globalisation: A World in Motion*. London: Routledge.

Snickars, Pelle, and Patrick Vonderau, eds. 2012. *Moving Data: The iPhone and the Future of Media*. New York: Columbia University Press.

Spotify. 2018. "Spotify for Brands." Accessed on March 21, 2019. https://spotifyforbrands.com/en-AU/ad-experiences/.

Sterne, Jonathan. 2012. *MP3: The Meaning of a Format*. Durham, NC: Duke University Press.

Tan, Emily. 2017. "Adblock Plus Cracks how to Block Facebook Ads." *Campaign*, September 27, https://www.campaignlive.co.uk/article/adblock-plus-cracks-block-facebook-ads/1445772.

Turow, Joseph. 2011. *The Daily You: How the New Advertising Industry Is Defining Your Identity and Your Worth*. New Haven, CT: Yale University Press.

Willens, Max. 2016. "The Promise and Peril of the Custom Banner Ad." *Digiday*, October 28, https://digiday.com/media/promise-peril-custom-banner-ad/.

4

Liveness Formats: A Historical Perspective on Live Sports Broadcasting

Florian Hoof

No Radio, No Home TV

In 2015, the English Premiere League sold its television broadcasting rights for the next three seasons to the pay-TV company Sky and the telecommunications company BT Group for $8 billion. This record-breaking deal is only a recent reminder that sports, as an intrinsic part of Western modernity, have always been deeply intertwined with film and media history on a global scale. In particular, live sports have been a driving force in developing, standardizing, and stabilizing pay TV practices and technology for delivering and securing live broadcasting events (Sies, 2008). An early advertising slogan for pay-per-view boxing fights, "No Radio, No Home TV," sums up the vital purpose—to restrict access to live sports broadcasts—of such attempts: It includes transmission and projection technologies that have the capacity to grant access to the live broadcasting signal for people who have paid for the event and at the same time deny access to anyone else. My case study investigates the media history of strategies of fortification and control in the context of pay TV for live sports. A business model that depends on controlling the circulation of moving images by either restricting access to the broadcasting signal or controlling the infrastructure needed to circulate the broadcasting signal.

In recent decades, there have been decisive shifts in critical understandings of circulation in the emerging global cultural economy. Such cultural flows and transactions have been explained more broadly by an interplay between ideologies, cultures, technologies, and economies

(Appadurai 1990). The boundary-expanding dynamics unleashed by media convergence and digital-network markets have been described as the dissemination of moving images and information goods beyond existing media *dispositifs* (e.g., Jenkins 2006). How this affects media circulation was researched by focusing on media infrastructures that would enable and restrict the circulation of moving images (Parks and Starosielski 2015; Starosielski 2015; Schabacher 2013). Those perspectives have recently been accompanied by approaches that are more cautious about associating such boundary-expanding capacities with digital media. Instead, they focus on technologies and politics of control to understand decentralized media networks (Galloway 2006; O'Neil 2016).

These are different lenses for looking at media culture, but they also hint at a methodological challenge for film and media studies. Media convergence, the digitization of film and media culture, and the advent of media ecosystems make it increasingly difficult to distinguish between single media *dispositifs* and media networks. Even entities such as "film" and "television" seem no longer to be stable (Wasson 2015; Sterne 2012). Streaming container formats, such as MPEG and QuickTime, show that the boundaries between media that store moving images (celluloid film, DVD), the infrastructures that distribute them (postal system, video store), and the media *dispositifs* that exhibit them (cinema, television) have become almost irrelevant. As Jonathan Sterne explains, streaming container formats that encapsulate media technologies and aesthetics "carry the traces of other infrastructures" (2012, 2). What then comes to the center of attention are "architectures of control" (Lessig 2006) embedded in media standards, containers, and data formats that structure the circulation of moving images. I specifically look at strategies of control that emerge out of economic necessities to standardize and control the distribution and logistics of goods (Rossiter 2016), and how these concepts and architectures become "sources of order in underorganized systems" (Weick 1985, 106). From this angle, I look at the history of sports broadcasting as "a series of small crises of cultural control" (Hilmes 1997, xiii) that arise when economic interests temporarily fail to control the circulation of their product. Looking at the materiality of historically emerging forms of cultural control offers a more precise perspective "than the concept of an ahistorical, unchanging, and thus rather expansive, concept of a medium" (Wasson 2015, 58). To account for the changing politics of cultural control (Winner 1980; Gillespie 2010; Warnke 2013; Vonderau 2014), I define and lay out two concepts of control. The first, "fortifying," tries to control live broadcasts by protecting the medium that stores the signal; the second, "infrastructuring," tries to dominate the distribution network used to circulate or distribute live broadcasts.

Bifurcated Concept of Format Control: Fortifying–Infrastructuring

Live sports broadcasting is a specifically suitable example to look at shifting concepts of control. Sports events are extremely valuable resources for content providers. But because a program's economic value diminishes greatly after the event has taken place, it is essential for rights holders to protect and secure such broadcasts. By definition, the practice of pay-TV live broadcasting is a compromise between easy and fast circulation of live sports events and the protection of those signals from illegal duplication and bootlegging. The priority is to precisely manage and control access to the live signal, while storing the event for later distribution or providing for the "best" possible image quality are subordinate aspects. Live broadcasting is optimized toward immediate circulation and is thus closely linked to distribution. Therefore, broadcasting signals rely on physical infrastructure that is embedded into social arrangements and technologies, such as standardized practices, norms, and protocols. This is not unique to media infrastructure but the basis of any logistical system. As Susan Leigh Star and Karen Ruhleder explain, such "infrastructure is transparent to use, in the sense that it does not have to be reinvented each time or assembled for each task, but invisibly supports those tasks" (1996, 113). In the case of media infrastructures this specifically concerns the interoperability between media event, storage or broadcasting medium, and projection device. Interoperability is guaranteed by standardized norms that cover these requirements. Media formats such as 35mm film, Betamax, or MPEG incorporate certain standards that make them compatible with certain film projectors or software decoders. This facilitates circulation and distribution of audiovisual signals because of the standardized and modularized infrastructure arrangements. While such technological standards fulfill basic technological specifications, they seem to be an insufficient explanation to account for the sociomaterial aspects of media culture. Furthermore, such an explanation downplays the role of culture and social practices that stabilize such norms and standards. To open a broader perspective on media distribution, Sterne suggests the need for a more comprehensive definition of the term "format" to account for the question of interoperability. He argues that formats are "attempt[s] to solve the problem of exchangeable formats across segments of the media industry" but also "artifact[s] shaped by several practices" (Sterne 2006, 826). Using this basic definition of formats, I look at live broadcasting as an arrangement of formats that guarantees the interoperability of technological specifications, such as norms and standards, with the cultural and economic sphere. Here, inter-operability is particularly important because live broadcasting formats depend on immediate distribution and circulation, making them loosely coupled and only weakly determined structures. As piracy has always been a driving force for media history (Johns 2009; Dommann 2019) this openness has resulted in continuous negotiations between the industry, the consumers, and the state about format control.

To better understand these negotiations, I devise a bifurcated concept of control that includes two ideal typical strategies of format control. The first branch focuses on "fortifying" and securing the broadcasting signal. The second branch focuses on controlling the infrastructure that facilitates the circulation of live broadcasts. I understand these two ideal types of control as a "unified analytical construct" that "is formed by the one-sided *accentuation* of one or more points of view" (Weber 1949, 90, emphasis in original). Thus, while the two ideal types, "fortifying" and "infrastructuring," are analytically separate, concepts of control cut across these ideal-typical branches and thus do not fall neatly into only one particular branch.

Firstly, "control through fortification" can be executed by securing and controlling the boundaries of a storage medium, such as celluloid film, videotape, or a digital data format. The architecture of such a "fortified" storage medium clearly distinguishes between two spaces, the space within the storage medium and the space that surrounds the medium. To be able to maintain this boundary, measures have to be taken to stabilize and fortify a format either by restricting access to the storage medium or by making it inaccessible. An exemplary case is contemporary digital rights management (DRM) systems. DRM systems, a compound of hardware and encrypted software code, try to control how digital media formats can be used, duplicated, and circulated. Examples are Apple's so-called "FairPlay Streaming DRM" and Microsoft's "Windows Media Digital Rights Management System" (see Diehl 2012, 120–32). The data container itself is a useless black box unless one is provided with the encryption key necessary to decode the data container.

Secondly, "control through infrastructuring" can be executed by dominating the "material forms that allow for the possibility of exchange over space" (Larkin 2013, 327). Here, the infrastructure where those formats can be circulated and the devices on which those formats can be viewed are used to control market and user behavior. Exemplary cases are media ecosystems established by companies such as Apple and Amazon. Infrastructuring relies on dominating architectures, norms, and standards to make it more difficult to circulate any given storage medium inside such a proprietary system. Infrastructure control is executed by an interplay between media formats and digital infrastructures. Examples are the ever-changing standards and protocols in media ecosystems to prevent workarounds implemented by third party providers.

I argue that these two ideal typical forms of control are not unique to digital network markets but can be traced back throughout the twentieth century. Together they form "multiple, overlapping and perhaps contradictory infrastructural arrangements" (Bowker and Star 2010, 230). I trace the history of liveness format control starting at the end of the 19th century from early "sports bulletin boards" and "fighting films" to "theatre television," to pay TV and pay-per-view, and finally to contemporary forms of over-the-top (OTT) streaming services. Hereby, I rely partly on existing accounts on the media history of live broadcasting (Gomery 1985; Schubin 2018; Sies 2008; Streible 2008), complement them with new archival material, and rearrange and discuss them under my overall perspective on a history of strategies of media fortification.

A Media History of Live Broadcasting

Live broadcasting encompasses not only a technological and economical dimension it is also a media cultural phenomenon with strong ties to media history. Starting with early radio and television stations, where live broadcasting was the only technological option available the possibilities of media to synchronize time and space resulted in certain cultural conceptions of live broadcasting. Jane Feuer describes these established conventions to perceive a broadcast as a constructed form of participating at an event from a distance as "liveness" (1983). Conventions that address and stabilize the idea of immediacy and direct access are not restricted to broadcasting but can also be found in context of documentary film. Here it echoes in concepts such as "direct cinema" and "cinema vérité" (Comolli 1969) when filmmakers argue to use the film camera as a technology of "mechanical objectivity" (Daston and Galison 2007) that would guarantee an unaltered direct mode of observation or perception of the world. But because technology and culture are always intertwined practices, the mediated "feeling of being here" (Leacock 2011) is always a constructed format that relies on practices such as montage and narration.

Consequently, diverse media networks, including radio, television, and film, can provide for liveness experiences even if such media are not capable of delivering live and direct access to a given event. Thus, it is possible to trace the history of liveness not so much as the history of a technological paradigm but as a media cultural history of certain media cultural formats to connect and synchronize different spaces. If we take this perspective as a point of departure, we see that quite a wide array of different concepts were capable of delivering or creating the experience of liveness, even before the advent of the mass-media broadcasting systems of radio and live TV.

Moving Picture Sports Boards, 1889–1930

In the last quarter of the 19th century, newspapers started to report on sports events on a regular basis. By 1900 urban newspapers included daily sports sections that were vital to boost the sales figures of the papers and made spectator sports a popular pastime within society (Oriard, 2004, 25). Not only did this draw huge crowds to sports venues to watch events; it also opened up all sorts of considerations on how to make available the experience of an event at a distance. To be broadcast or reported on, sports events first had to be turned into serialized and standardized formats (see Stauff in this volume). Spectator sports formats then could be disseminated by relying on the media technology available at that time. Among the early concepts for providing a live experience of sports were scoreboards and bulletin boards that would display the results of baseball games to distant audiences. Mostly, they were used by newspaper companies to attract large crowds in front of their buildings (Schubin 2018) and to promote their own newspaper sports sections. In 1889 Edward Sims van Zile was granted a patent for his "Bulletin-Board and Base-Ball Indicator" (fig. 1). According to the patent description, the "invention relates to display or bulletin boards or tables, and is intended to show the progress of a base-ball game at some place distant from the playground. The invention consists in the construction of the board and the arrangements of its parts whereby the exact conditions of the game may be indicated at any time" (Van Zile 1889, 1). Furthermore, the patent specifies where to use the invention: "The board is to be posted in some conspicuous place, as in a pool-room or, as it has been used, in front of a newspaper-office, com-munication being had by telephone or telegraph with the base-ball ground" (Van Zile 1889, 1). One person would operate the scoreboard according to the information given to him by an announcer who would track the game by phone or over the wire. As the operators publicly displayed such bulletin boards to promote newspaper sales, access was not restricted. But the "quality" of the liveness experience was poor due to the tiny score board, which displayed only the game statistics with little information about the event. Thus, the scoreboard captured the dynamics of the game only partially.

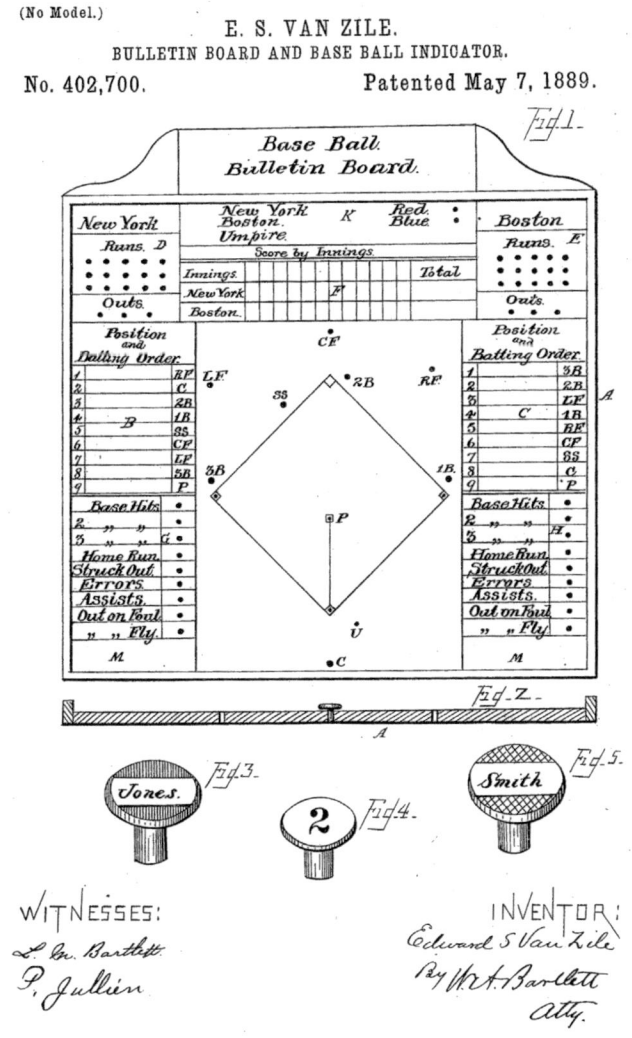

[Figure 1] Bulletin Board and Base Ball Indicator. Source: Van Zile 1889.

Alongside public bulletin boards, more advanced systems existed as well. The so-called Coleman Lifelike Scoreboard (fig. 2, fig. 3) was used in 1914 for the first time and connected the concept of live broadcasting or live displaying to the cinematic space. It was a technically complex system that would be placed in front of a cinema screen or on a theater stage. The system consisted of "nineteen thousand feet of wire and 400 electric bulbs" (Popular Science Monthly 1924, 78) and was operated by a group of up to five people. One person was in charge of the teletype machine that would communicate the changes on the baseball ground. The other people would then operate the electric system to indicate the game play by switching on and off light bulbs. The system not only promised to show statistics but also the dynamics of the game. Consequently, the patent that was filed in 1924 was entitled "Moving Picture Baseball Board" (Coleman 1924). It should provide "a novel form of multiple projection apparatus whereby pictures representing the players executing the plays, or executing any acts incidental to the playing of the game, or the actions of others such as umpires or coaches, may be shown on a board, screen, or other surface marked off to represent a baseball field" (Coleman 1927, 1). To be able to project the dynamics of the game, the system depended on a semi-dark environment, such as a theater or movie venue. This made it into "virtually a motion picture machine without film or projector" (Popular Mechanics 1924, 966). The bulletin board, albeit a sturdy structure made of wood, metal, and fabric, turned into a transparent medium for live broadcasting as a baseball game unfolded in the distance (Heider 1926).

While the newspaper scoreboards were part of the already existing news gathering infrastructure of the newspaper company, the "moving picture" baseball boards depended on a more complex infrastructure and a different business model. As with the cinema or theater, Coleman Lifelike broadcasts were financed through entrance fees, making it an early pay-per-view broadcast concept. The elaborate, sturdy technological construction and infrastructure that was needed to set up and deliver this kind of liveness experience—the actual transmission of the event to the cinema space via the teletype machine—was controlled by the operators of the system. The encapsulated cinematic space set a clear and stable boundary that surrounded the media device, in this case the bulletin board allowing for restricted access through the box office. One might infringe the patent and plagiarize the technology, but there would be no option to simply duplicate the live broadcast by interfering with the system installed in the cinema venues. The liveness experience was deeply inter-twined with the infrastructure that provided for the transmission of this temporal experience. Consequently, the Coleman system was at the same time a system of fortification and of infrastructure control. The setup was a unique system, as it did not rely on standardized devices that could be easily repurposed.

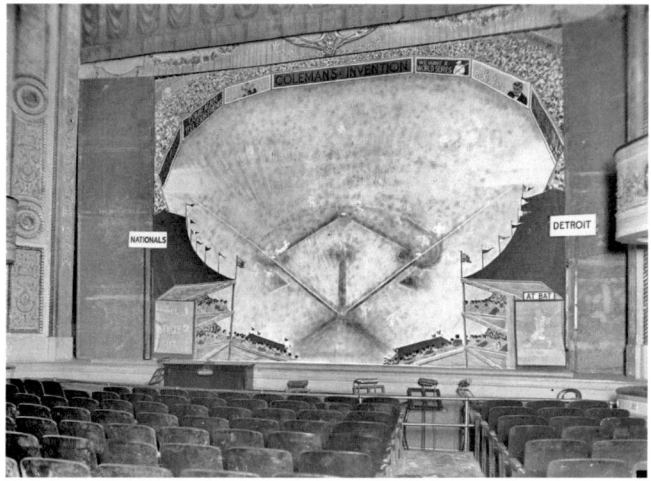

[Figure 2] Coleman Lifelike Scoreboard installation in the National Theatre, Washington, D.C., August 2, 1924. Source: Shorpy.com, https://www.shorpy.com/node/8283.

[Figure 3] Behind the screen of the Coleman Lifelike Scoreboard. Source: Shorpy.com, https://www.shorpy.com/node/8285.

Celluloid Film, 1894–1947

A different situation could be found in the context of boxing, another popular sport at this time. Besides boxing reports in newspaper sports sections, and until the advent of radio in the 1920s, celluloid film was the preferred medium for providing quasi-live experiences of boxing. Moreover, as Streible (2008) has shown in his study of early "fight pictures," the popularity of boxing sports in the 1890s is closely connected with the moving image. Film companies started to produce boxing films, especially films that were shot on location and showed a non-staged boxing match turned out to be successful (Streible 2008, 43). While baseball depended on game play that strongly relied on statistics to make sense of a baseball event, boxing drew its fascination from the unexpected moments that characterized a fight between two boxers. Only film was capable of capturing the knockout, the decisive moment of a boxing match. Even an official ban on boxing films between 1915 and 1927 issued by state authorities did not stop the production of boxing films. The circulation of boxing films and, by the late 1920s, boxing broadcasts via radio turned boxing matches into major public events.

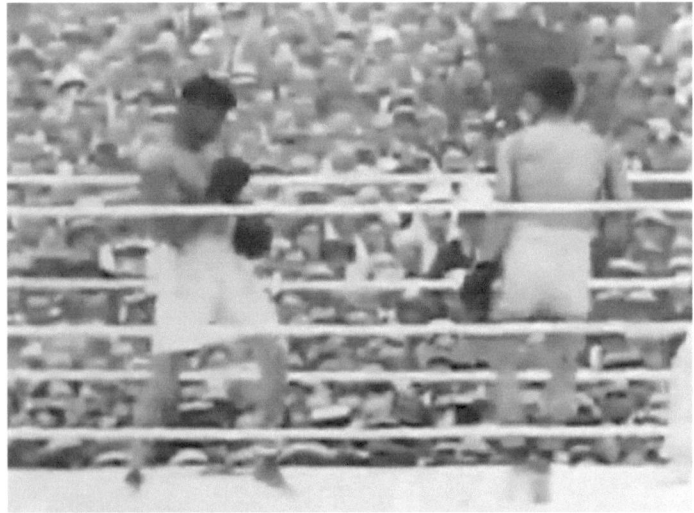

[Figure 4] Still from the boxing film *Jack Dempsey vs. Georges Carpentier.* July 2, 1921. Author unknown. Source: Archive.org, https://archive.org/details/JackDempseyVsGeorgesCarpentier.

In the 1920s, boxing promoters organized boxing matches such as the 1921 fight between Jack Dempsey and Georges Carpentier in Jersey City

in front of 90,000 people (fig. 4) and the 1927 fight between Dempsey and
Gene Tunney where an audience of 105,000 gathered at Soldier Field in
Chicago. Besides being popular events, boxing matches became significant
testing grounds for new media broadcasting technologies. For Dempsey
versus Carpentier, the Radio Corporation of America (RCA), the US Navy,
and the National Wireless Amateur Association cooperated for the first
large-scale experiment in radio boxing broadcasting. Using a telephone
line, a "blow-by-blow" description from the arena was sent to the Hoboken
terminal of the Lackawanna Railroad company where the RCA set up a
temporary radio station. Here, a technician listened to the comments and
spoke his own version of the description into a microphone that would
then be broadcast (Barnouw 1966, 80–81). Across a 200-mile radius, the
signal was picked up by radio amateurs and transmitted to theaters and
other venues. Approximately 300,000 people listened to the broadcast,
paying an admission fee as part of a fundraising campaign for the benefit of the American Committee for Devastated France (White 1921, 2). But
besides early experimental forms of radio broadcasting, film remained the
key medium of the boxing sports business. Not least because early radio
relied on a different business strategy. Radio stations were either owned
by radio manufacturers or by newspapers. In this context, sportscasts
were used to sell radio devices, so-called "Radio Music Boxes" (Hagen 2005,
185–86), or to boost newspaper sales in a way similar to the purpose of
baseball bulletin boards. Radio became a medium that used sportscasts to
maximize potential audiences. But at this time, there was no need to control the circulation of live broadcasts, for example, by developing methods
of encryption for commercial radio.

In the context of film, the situation was different as the economic model
was based on selling access to fight pictures. For the 1921 fight between
Dempsey and Carpentier, the film company Pathé bought the international
film rights and produced a boxing film to be distributed throughout the
world. The company sent among others a salesman to London to market
the film in the United Kingdom. But on his arrival, he realized that the
boxing film produced for this occasion had already been screened in the
London cinemas. One of the Pathé cameramen had stolen an incomplete,
raw version of the film from the film laboratory in Chicago, shipped it to
London immediately, and sold copies to the local cinema operators (Streible
2008, 273). This incident was no exception. The producers of boxing
films were heavily affected by piracy, against which they were unable to
take legal action because the production and circulation of boxing films
was—depending on the state jurisdiction—partly illegal. Distributing

on-location recordings of boxing matches on film, and in this way providing a kind of delayed liveness experience, turned out to be a rather weak and unprotected means of delivery. It was quite easy to duplicate and distribute such films, not least because of the standardized celluloid formats, which could be projected by any standardized projection device. In this respect, the contradiction between two strategies of control—fortifying and infrastructuring—becomes visible. In July 1916, right after the US Supreme Court ruled against the patent trust of the Motion Picture Patents Company (MPPC), which had controlled film infrastructure through monopoly for nearly a decade, the standardization group within the Society of Motion Picture Engineers (SMPE) declared that "of prime importance, and of immediate necessity for the welfare of the industry, was the standardization of materials, mechanisms, and practices" (Jones 1933, 280). To be able to improve the capability of the film industry to circulate celluloid film, four committees were founded that would focus on the standardization of "'Cameras and Perforations,' 'Motion Picture Electrical Devices,' 'Picture Theater Equipment,' and 'Optics'" (Jones 1933, 281). The aim of the committees that were dissolved only in 1932 was to create a cinema infrastructure that would allow for interchangeability of the devices needed to produce, circulate, and screen moving images. Or as the SMPE put it, "The way to standardize is to standardize" (Jones 1933, 282). This included the 35mm film standard for theaters and from 1918 on a "new size of narrow width, slow burning film as the standard for all portable projectors" (Jones 1933, 285). The standardized infrastructure for the moving images industry as envisioned by the SMPE consisted of 35mm, 28mm, and 16mm film gauges, interoperable cameras, and projector devices. The standardization efforts of the SMPE aimed toward securing the growth of the film industry. But after the end of the MPPC trust, the cinema infrastructure could no longer be controlled by legal measures. Without legal protection, it became obvious that the different parts of the infrastructure were only loosely coupled and could be easily repurposed, for example, to establish informal ways of duplicating, distributing, and screening moving images. In contrast to the baseball scoreboards mentioned above, where the liveness experience provided to the audience was deeply intertwined with the transmission infrastructure and thus bound to a specific place, boxing film was prone to piracy. While the scoreboards were unique constructions that could not be easily duplicated, the standardized film infrastructure made it easy to repurpose the medium for an informal film economy.

As a result, the producers of boxing films adopted other strategies to make it more difficult to produce and circulate pirated copies. Or to put it differently, they tried to regain control of the infrastructure that would facilitate the circulation of their weakly protected celluloid films. One of these measures was to exploit the "live" aspect of fight pictures and avoid long distribution channels in order to reduce the risk of police detection and piracy of film copies. Speeding up distribution meant that in 1923 a boxing match staged in New York was shown in theaters and cinemas on Broadway only 48 hours later (Streible 2008, 275). This not only contributed to an almost-live effect but also made piracy more difficult. Just a few copies were in circulation, and the films were not shipped throughout the United States but distributed only in New York. New film formats for 16mm home projection further increased the speed of film distribution. In 1927, the producers of boxing films were able to start to sell their films to cinemas but also for home projection only 18 hours after the fight (Streible 2008, 277). After the ban on boxing films was lifted later that year, the popularity of the films rose, as did the illegal duplication and bootlegging of boxing films.

It was impossible to fortify boxing films because they were standardized and thus interchangeable parts of a larger film infrastructure. Celluloid film could easily be stolen, duplicated, and illegally distributed by reusing the standardized devices of the film infrastructure. Consequently, film producers tried to protect their films by speeding up circulation and concentrating it locally, taking measures to control the film infrastructure.

Theater Television and Closed-Circuit Television, 1948–1977

This situation changed with the advent of "real-time" live broadcasting systems for moving images. In the 1920s and 1930s, film ceased to be the only audiovisual medium capable of showing boxing fights due to the first experiments of live television broadcasting. The CBS television networks relied on live sports events and boxing matches in particular. In 1928, J. Andrew White, the president of the company at that time argued that "the first and most logical application of television apparatus would be for events such as championship boxing matches" (quoted in Streible 2008, 287). In England, the first television broadcast of a boxing match took place in 1938, followed by a broadcast in the United States one year later. In 1941, the Radio Corporation of America (RCA) organized a live broadcast of a boxing match from Madison Square Garden to the New Yorker Theatre in New York on a 15-by-20-foot screen promising the 1,200 attendees "a better-than-ringside view of the battle" (Radio News 1941). In this case, a mobile television unit transmitted the signals of television cameras and parabolic microphones via a stabilized telephone wire to the NBC studios in Radio City where they were relayed to the New Yorker Theatre. Here, the signal was split and the light impulses were fed into a second projection device that had to be installed inside the cinemas to screen theater television. The second signal distributed the sound to 16 loudspeakers that were set up inside the auditorium (Popular Mechanics 1941, 6).

[Figure 5] Screenshot, live broadcast of the boxing match Jersey Joe Walcott vs. Rocky Marciano, September 23, 1952. Source: YouTube.com, https://www.youtube.com/watch?v=ZaKPg7gXtW4.

This system became known as Theatre Television and made it possible to directly broadcast sports events, such as boxing, horse racing, wrestling, or the baseball World Series, on a screen in a film theater. Cinemas were sold out, for example, during the 1948 broadcast of the heavyweight fight between Joe Louis and Jersey Joe Walcott. Warner Bros. film studio, at that time still possessing its cinema chain, used this sports event to showcase the advantages of the RCA broadcasting system (Gomery 1985, 57). The diverse systems of Theatre Television developed by the media industry were originally intended to transmit different TV shows and events to the cinemas. In no small part, these systems were introduced by the film industry to compete with the new medium television. But only live sports events, especially American football, baseball and boxing, turned out to be successful content for Theatre Television (Gomery 1985, 58).

In 1952, Theatre Television reached its first peak when 50 cinemas in 30 different cities across the United States were interconnected using AT&T's cable network to broadcast the heavyweight boxing match between Jersey Joe Walcott and Rocky Marciano (fig. 5). However, Theatre Television turned out to be an economic failure, except for boxing (Gomery 1985, 59). The only profitable events that attracted a large number of viewers to the cinemas were live broadcasts of Rocky Marciano's heavyweight boxing matches and, from the 1960s onward, those of Muhammad Ali. Events such as the 1974 "Rumble in the Jungle" heavyweight fight between George Foreman and Muhammad Ali in Kinshasa, were broadcasted by Theatre Television. This system, later also described as closed-circuit television, was the basis for pay-per-view live broadcasts of boxing events until the 1970s. While the signal itself was not protected, the infrastructure to distribute, convert, and screen these signals remained under centralized control. This included the spatial concept of the movie theater, a protected room only accessible through the box office. Like the Coleman Lifelike baseball board, this gave the operators a robust position against piracy.

Satellite Networks, 1975–2006

This situation only changed in the 1970s. New providers with a modified transmission technology established themselves after the US Federal Communications Commission (FCC) changed the broadcasting regulatory policy toward satellite signal transmission in 1972. In this very year, the pay-TV company HBO (Home Box Office) was founded and used satellite-supported signal transmission for the first time. Now, a program signal could be synchronously fed into previously unconnected local cable networks. The concept of theater television that was previously restricted to venues such as cinemas, hotels, and opera houses could be extended to a large number of private households, creating a completely new market for live sports broadcasts. The first live sporting event to be broadcast via satellite technology was a boxing match, the Thrilla in Manila between Muhammad Ali and Joe Frazier in 1975 (fig. 6).

Ted Turner's WTCG, the second broadcasting company that used satellite transmission, also focused on live sports broadcasts, including baseball and basketball. After a further deregulatory decision, the Cable Act of 1984, live sports, in particular boxing, became an integral part of the now-common pay-TV and pay-per-view packages (Miller and Kim 2013). HBO, for example, concluded exclusive contracts with organizers and individual athletes for the pay-per-view rights (Roberts and Smith 2014).

With the expansion of the customer base to potentially all private households, the broadcast signal became non-excludable, and piracy was back.
The architecture of the venues and the enclosed distribution channels
of Theatre Television provided for some protection against piracy. This
situation changed when pay-TV and pay-per-view providers started
to introduce smart-card systems to decode satellite signals at home.
Encryption systems had to be introduced to retain control of the now-
decentralized infrastructure necessary to broadcast live events (Diehl
2012, 98–102). Every single household with a pay-TV subscription had to be
secured by an encryption system that consisted of hardware and software
components and relied on concepts such as the analog scrambling principle
(Diehl 2012, 99). The early scrambling algorithms were rather simplistic,
and the 11-bit encryption keys could easily be reengineered, so that hackers
managed to decipher and disable the security technology on a regular basis
and within minutes (Diehl 2012, 100). This gave rise to an informal market
in which plagiarism tools and valid monthly access codes were traded. For
the pay-TV industry, this became an unresolvable, permanent issue of their
decentralized distribution systems.

[Figure 6] Screenshot, HBO live broadcast of the boxing match *Thrilla in Manila*, Muhammad
Ali vs. Joe Frazier, October 1, 1975. Source: YouTube.com, https://www.youtube.com/
watch?v=oNEfN2R4oRc.

An exemplary case is the hacking of the widely used Nagravision encryption
system in 2008. Pay-TV companies that relied on this system, such as
the German-based Premiere, were now easily accessible without a valid

subscription. The problem became so severe that Premiere decided to switch to the then-secure NDS Videoguard system (Premiere 2008). To this day, Premiere's successor, Sky, is still struggling with an informal market that offers solutions to circumvent encryption technologies. In response, Sky and the suppliers of encryption solutions are constantly changing their encryption algorithms, most recently in May 2016, when Sky totally blocked access via unlicensed hardware (Digitalfernsehen 2016). After the concept of theater television based on centralized infrastructure was replaced by satellite networks, pay-TV companies were no longer able to control the infrastructure. The logical step of the content providers was to turn their signals into highly protected and encrypted formats that would serve as fortresses to try to regain control in a decentralized digital network market (Galloway 2004).

Over-the-Top Live Streaming Services, 2006–Present

The situation of a decentralized infrastructure prevailed through the transition from satellite to internet-based streaming infrastructure. The technological process of streaming, the segmentation and then continuous transmission of electric signals, had already been described in a patent from 1927 (Squier et al.). Initially, streaming was used to transmit audio signals for internet radio services through internet-based network structures. Improved compression and network expansion allowed for the transmission of larger amounts of data and made it possible for streaming to become the new standard of moving image distribution as early as 2006 when Google acquired YouTube. The pay-TV companies were gradually forced to abandon their card-based systems, which required a lengthy process of shipping and installing technological equipment on the consumer side, and turn their service into streaming platforms, not least due to economic considerations to extend the range of potential customers.

As with the standardization of celluloid film in the 1910s and 1920s, streaming widened the options for pay-TV companies to reach out to new customers but at the same time further weakened their options for protecting live broadcasts. Significantly, streaming is not confined to a specific technology but can run on standard computer equipment. To circumvent the encryption technologies used in hardware-based decoder smart-card systems, one at least needed some technological knowledge to hack the system. Today, streaming platforms offer illegal live streams that are easily available. Streaming software solutions such as Periscope allow illegal streams to be set up without any specialist knowledge. To find and access such streams one needs only to be able to operate a common search engine. OTT streaming no longer relies on exclusive distribution infrastructure but utilizes the same openly available digital infrastructure that is used to circulate illegal live streams (Hoof 2015).

[Figure 7] Screenshot, HBO/Showtime live broadcast of the boxing match Floyd Mayweather Jr. vs. Manny Pacquiao, May 2, 2015. Source: YouTube.com, https://www.youtube.com/watch?v=6lJkUcPJvzMe.

How this changed the situation of live sports broadcasting shows up in the Mayweather versus Pacquiao fight from 2015 (fig. 7). It was promoted by HBO and Showtime as the fight of the century. Prices for this pay-per-view event ranged from $89.95 for standard resolution to $99.95 for the high-definition stream. Before the fight took place, the streaming platforms Sportship.org and Boxinghd.net already advertised their illegal services as follows: "[I]f you can't afford to buy tickets then simply watch Mayweather vs Pacquiao here. We will provide with nothing but the freshest and the most reliable high quality live links" (United States District Court 2015, 5). *The New Yorker* even ran an article with the title "Pirates Crash the Mayweather–Pacquiao Fight" (Thompson 2015). HBO, the owner of the broadcasting rights, handed in a copyright infringement lawsuit against the operators of these streaming portals, even before the actual boxing match took place. Furthermore, they issued a takedown notice against the company Periscope to prevent the allocation of illegal live streams on their platform. This "pre-crime" scheme is not restricted to this case but seems to characterize the new approach to how pay-TV and pay-per-view companies attempt to prevent the illegal circulation of live sports streams. By using legal measures, they try to reduce the options available to the consumer to use streaming technology and thereby regain control of the distribution infrastructure. The key players are tech companies that provide encryption systems, such as the Kudelski Group that offers the Nagravision smart-card system for pay-TV operators. The company no longer focuses on encryption technology alone but has turned into a full-service anti-piracy provider. According to its service description, in digital network markets,

> the entire media value chain is at stake and content piracy is more than ever a moving target fueled by ubiquitous broadband networks. This calls for a much more holistic approach to content protection than technology alone can deliver. . . . Our end-to-end solution combats all forms of piracy, such as key sharing, web streaming and IPTV piracy, among others, and leverages a full range of intelligence building, monitoring, technical, forensic and legal capabilities. (Kudelski 2017)

As even encrypted, fortified formats are no longer capable of preventing piracy, Kudelski adopted an approach to "defeat piracy through active security" (Kudelski 2018). Players such as Kudelski and its customers, the pay-TV providers, are trying to extend the strategy of fortifying content by encrypting formats to a bifurcated strategy with an infrastructuring surveillance approach to society. Their approach is comparable to the contemporary concept of proprietary media ecosystems, such as the Apple and Amazon device families, but with the small but decisive difference that they are targeting, surveilling, and policing potentially every user in digital culture. This makes the ongoing conflict between liveness formats, piracy, and infrastructure a highly political issue. While HBO uses legal action as a kind of pre-crime procedure to try to prevent copyright infringements before they actually happen, providers for cybersecurity no longer simply provide technical solutions, such as encrypted "fortress formats," but also offer so-called forensic and intelligence services to hunt down piracy and secure the value chain. This includes measures like infiltrating private internet forums and other "intelligence services." Instead of controlling the devices that enable the circulation of media formats, "active security" aims at policing culture and social processes as they are suspected to harbor potential criminal energy.

Conclusion: The Politics of Format Control

I have shown how perspectives change when film and media history is approached from an angle that looks at concepts of control that emerge on the level of standards, norms, and formats that facilitate and administrate the circulation of media culture. This enables us to distinguish more precisely between different phases in film and media history with regard to the circulation and dissemination of media culture. Thus, it allows us to establish a broader perspective on how different concepts of control relate to and have an impact on culture and society. I have suggested thinking about cultural control not in an essential way but as a relational, ever-shifting concept that revolves around (a) the fortification of storage media and (b) attempts to control the infrastructure and distribution logistics necessary for media industries to thrive. These two ideal typical forms of control relate to the materiality and practices of media.

Harold Innis, who understood media as anything that enables communication or the logistics of goods, introduced a helpful concept to better understand the politics and administrative power of this bifurcated system of control. Innis argued that the capability of a medium to control time and space is determined by its form and materiality (Innis 1950). On a basic level he distinguishes between different media such as stone and paper, and how these media affect the abilities to exert administrative power over time and space. He argues that the materiality of each medium structures the process of circulation and the stability of the meaning engraved in that medium. This effects the way administrative power can be exerted over time and space. Here, he distinguishes between "time-biased" and "space-biased" media. The character of "time-biased" media, such as stone tables, is linked to a sturdy materiality that remains stable over time (Innis 1951). While the meaning engraved into a stone tablet endures over time, its materiality hinders its circulation over distances. In contrast, "space-biased" media, such as paper or papyrus, are easy to circulate but lack the sturdy inner structure necessary to function as a storage medium that can transcend time.

In line with this distinction between "time-biased" and "space-biased" media, strategies of "fortification" can be understood as "time-biased" for their strong and durable character. These are centralized and proprietary media networks, such as early sports bulletin boards, theater television, and closed-circuit television, whose rigidly defined structures can be easily controlled. On the other hand, there are decentralized and weakly protected liveness formats, such as boxing films, encrypted pay-TV systems, and streaming services. Here, control focuses on the distribution infrastructure. This latter strategy tends to dominate space, reaching beyond distinct formats and thus deeper into society and culture.

The contemporary situation seems to fall into the latter category. Durable, sturdy, and stable storage media are not the dominant structures of the digital network society; instead, approaches to contain and control uncertainty, which derive from an increasingly elusive digital infrastructure, are on the rise. The consequences for culture and society are severe, as such approaches are no longer bound to identifiable formats but abet strategies of control and legal frameworks that pathologize digital culture beyond commercial interests.

References

Appadurai, Arjun. 1990. "Disjuncture and Difference in the Global Cultural Economy." *Theory, Culture, and Society* 7: 295–310.

Barnouw, Erik. A. 1966. *Tower in Babel: A History of Broadcasting in the United States Volume 1 – to 1933.* New York: Oxford University Press.

Coleman, G. S. 1927. Moving Picture Baseball Scoreboard. US Patent 1,616,304, filed December 1, 1924, and issued February 1, 1927.

———. 1924. Moving Picture Baseball Scoreboard. US Patent 1,507,583, filed October 27, 1922, and issued September 9, 1924.

Comolli, Jean-Louis. 1969. "Le Détour par le Directe." *Cahiers du Cinéma* 209: 48–53; 211: 40–45.

Daston, Lorraine J., and Peter Galison. 2007. *Objectivity*. New York: Zone Books.

Diehl, Eric. 2012. *Securing Digital Video: Techniques for DRM and Content Protection*. Dotrecht: Springer.

Digitalfernsehen. 2016. "Sky optimiert Verschlüsselungssystem." *Digitalfernsehen*. Accessed October 20, 2016. http://www.digitalfernsehen.de/Sky-optimiert-Verschluesselungssystem.139829.0.html.

Dommann, Monika. 2019. *Authors and Apparatus: A Media History of Copyright*. Ithaca, NY: Cornell University Press.

Feuer, Jane. 1983. "The Concept of Live Television: Ontology as Ideology." In *Regarding Television: Critical Approaches—An Anthology,* edited by Anne E. Kaplan, 12–21. Los Angeles: University Publications of America.

Galloway, Alexander R. 2004. *Protocol: How Control Exists after Decentralization*. Cambridge, MA: MIT Press.

Gillespie, Tarleton. 2010. "The Politics of 'Platforms.'" *New Media and Society* 3 (12): 347–64.

Gomery, Douglas. 1985. "Theatre Television: The Missing Link of Technological Change in the US Motion Picture Industry." *The Velvet Light Trap* 21: 54–61.

Hagen, Wolfgang. 2005. *Das Radio: Zur Theorie und Geschichte des Hörfunks Deutschland/USA*. Munich: Fink 2005.

Heider, Fritz. 1926. "Ding und Medium." *Symposion, Philosophische Zeitschrift für Forschung und Aussprache* 1: 109–57.

Hilmes, Michele. 1997. *Radio Voices: American Broadcasting, 1922-1952*. Minneapolis: University of Minnesota Press.

Hoof, Florian. 2015. "Live Sports, Piracy, and Uncertainty: Understanding Illegal Streaming Aggregation Platforms." In *Geoblocking and Global Video Culture*, edited by Ramon Lobato and Jonathan Meese, 86–93, Amsterdam: Institute of Network Cultures.

Innis, Harold A. 1951. *The Bias of Communication.* Toronto: University of Toronto Press.

———. 1950. *Empire and Communications.* Oxford: Oxford University Press.

Jenkins, Henry. 2006. *Convergence Culture: Where Old and New Media Collide.* New York: New York University Press.

Johns, Adrian. 2009. *Piracy: The Intellectual Property Wars from Gutenberg to Gates.* Chicago: University of Chicago Press.

Jones, Loyd A. 1933. "A Historical Summary of Standardization in the Society of Motion Picture Engineers." *Journal of the Society of Motion Picture Engineers* 21 (4): 280–93.

Kudelski Group. 2018. "Anti-Piracy Services." *Nagra Kudelski*, accessed October 12, 2018. https://dtv.nagra.com/anti-piracy-services/.

———. 2017. *Nagra Kudelski*, accessed December 4, 2017. https://www.nagra.com.

Larkin, Brian. 2013. "The Politics and Poetics of Infrastructure." *Annual Review of Anthropology* 42: 327–43.

Leacock, Richard. 2011. *The Feeling of Being There: A Filmmaker's Memoir.* Égreville: Semeïon Éditions.

Lessig, Lawrence. 2006. *Code: And other Laws of Cyberspace.* New York: Basic Books.

Messner, Holger. 2013. *Pay-TV in Deutschland: Ein schwieriges Geschäftsmodell.* Wiesbaden: Springer VS.

Miller, Toby, and Linda J. Kim. 2013. "It Isn't TV, It's the 'Real King of the Ring.'" In *The Essential HBO Reader,* edited by Jeffrey P. Johns and Gary R. Edgerton, 217–36. Lexington: The University Press of Kentucky.

Oriard, Michael. 2004. *King Football: Sport and Spectacle in the Golden Age of Radio and Newsreels, Movies and Magazines, the Weekly and the Daily Press.* Chapel Hill: The University of North Carolina Press.

O'Neil, Cathy. 2018. *Weapons of Math Destruction: How Big Data Increases Inequality and Threatens Democracy.* New York: Random House.

Parks, Lisa, and Nicole Starosielski, eds. 2015. *Signal Traffic: Critical Studies of Media Infrastructures.* Urbana: University of Illinois Press.

Premiere. 2008. "Neue Premiere Verschlüsselung: Kriminelle Hacker sehen schwarz." *Info. sky.de*, accessed October 20, 2016. https://info.sky.de/inhalt/de/medienzentrum_news_uk_15042008.jsp.

Popular Mechanics. 1941. "Theatre Audience Attends Fight by Television." *Popular Mechanics* 76 (3): 6.

———. 1924. "Every Move in Ball Game Is Shown on Screen." *Popular Mechanics* 59 (12): 966.

Popular Science Monthly. 1924. "Lifelike Ball Games on the Screen." *Popular Science Monthly* 5 (105): 78.

Radio News. 1941. "Big Image Television Demonstrated." *Radio News*, July.

Roberts, Randy, and Andrew R. M. Smith. 2014. "Boxing: The Manly Art." In *Companion to American Sport History,* edited by Steven A. Riess, 271–91. Hoboken, NJ: John Wiley & Sons.

Rossiter, Ned. 2016. *Software, Infrastructure, Labor: A Media Theory of Logistical Nightmares.* New York: Routledge.

Schabacher, Gabriele. 2013. "Medium Infrastruktur: Trajektorien soziotechnischer Netzwerke in der ANT." *Zeitschrift für Medien- und Kulturforschung* 2: 129–48.

Schubin, Mark. 2018. "Watching Remote Baseball Games before Television." *Proceedings of the IEEE* 106 (10): 1854–60.

Sies, Luther F. 2008. "Sports." In *Encyclopedia of American Radio, 1920–1960,* 2nd ed., edited by Luther F. Sies, 633–36. Jefferson, NC: McFarland & Company.

Squier, Georg O., Joseph O. Mauborgne, and Cohen Louis. 1927. Electric Signaling. US Patent 1,641,608, filed June 12, 1922, and issued September 6, 1927.

Star, Susan L., and Karen Ruhleder. 1996. "Steps Toward an Ecology of Infrastructure: Design and Access for Large Information Spaces." *Information Systems Research* 7: 111–34.

Starosielski, N. (2015). *The Undersea Network*. Durham, NC: Duke University Press.

Sterne, Jonathan. 2006. "The MP3 as Cultural Artifact." *New Media and Society* 8 (5): 825–42. doi: 10.1177/1461444806067737.

———. 2012. *MP3: The Meaning of a Format*. Durham, NC: Duke University Press.

Streible, Dan. 2008. *Fight Pictures: A History of Boxing and Early Cinema.* Berkeley: University of California Press.

Thompson, Nicolas. 2015. "Pirates Crash the Mayweather–Pacquiao Fight." *The New Yorker*, May 4. Accessed October 20, 2016. http://www.newyorker.com/business/currency/pirates-crash-the-mayweather-pacquiao-fight.

United States District Court for the Central District of California, Case No. 2:15-cv-03147.

Van Zile, Edward Sims. 1889. Bulletin Board and Base Ball Indicator. US Patent 402,700, filed December 14, 1888, and issued May 7, 1889.

Vonderau, Patrick. 2014. "The Politics of Content Aggregation." *Television and New Media* 16 (8): 717–33.

Warnke, Martin. 2013. "Databases as Citadels in the Web 2.0." In *Unlike Us Reader: Social Media Monopolies and their Alternatives*, edited by Geert Lovink and Miriam Rasch, 76–88. Amsterdam: Institute of Network Cultures.

Wasson, Haidee. 2015. "Formatting Film Studies." *Film Studies* 12: 57–61

Weber, Max. 1949. *The Methodology of the Social Sciences*. Glencoe, IL: Free Press.

Weick, Karl. 1985. "Sources of Order in Underorganized Systems: Themes in Recent Organizational Theory." In *Organizational Theory and Inquiry*, edited by Yvonna. S. Lincoln, 106–36. Beverly Hills, CA: Sage.

White, J. Andrew. 1921. "Report: First Broadcast, Dempsey–Carpentier Fight," July 2, 1921, Box 1, David Sarnoff Papers (Accession 2464.55), Hagley Museum and Library, Wilmington, DE 19807.

Winner, Langdon. 1980. "Do Artifacts Have Politics?" *Daedalus* 1 (109): 121–36.

ARCHAEOLOGIES OF SUCCESS AND FAILURE

5

Formatting Cross-Media Circulation: On the Epistemology and Economy of Sports Highlights

Markus Stauff

In 1999 Elihu Katz argued for a more systematic development of a theory of diffusion: an interdisciplinary theory that could help to compare the spread of viruses, the circulation of goods and materials, the innovation of technologies and the adaptation and transformation of cultural values and meanings. The difficulty for such a theory, he argued then, results from the "ostensible incommensurability of diffusing items [and] their refusal to hold still in transit" (Katz 1999, 144). Media studies' recently surging interest in the concept of "format" (e.g., Moran 1998; Sterne 2012) can be considered a contribution to such a theory of diffusion; at least, the format's potential to enable diffusion by ordering content (or information) according to a material, technical, or legal framework is a shared concern of otherwise pretty heterogeneous approaches.

In the following, I take the omnipresence of sports highlights in media culture as a starting point to analyze the interrelation between formatting practices and cross-media circulation: Condensed representations of sports events featuring a number of selected moments and the result of a competition, arguably, belong to the most consistently and most dynamically circulating items in media culture for the last 100 years. Crossing all media (from film to television to online video and games), a number of different genres (news and entertainment), and often also the borders created by languages or nation states, sports highlights guarantee the "spreadability" (Jenkins, Ford, and Green 2013) of the results, narratives and mythologies of modern competitive sports.

Sports highlights don't show the same material rigidity or institutional consistency as more paradigmatic examples of formats—say a painting's physical frame or a sound file's technical and legal standards. But in offering selections and condensations of sports' special moments, they not only format—that is, standardize—observations on and knowledge about sport events, whether on film, television, or social media platforms, but also structure the very reality of sports. Simultaneously, these highlights, as with the formats of the TV industry (Magder 2004), allow for the constant modulation and local adaptation of content and form. This volatility gets harnessed and constrained through conflicting strategies of fans, rights holders, media platforms, and national governments, which all have a share in highlights' formatting potential. Thus, I want to argue that sports highlights' combination of standardization and flexibility makes it an especially rich example for a conceptual and empirical discussion of formats—or rather of formatting practices.

Taking my lead from television studies, I will argue that the sports highlight is a *cultural technology of diffusion*. Its cross-media circulation clearly results from a highly flexible but still regulated manner of transformation. This chapter, thus, aims to analyze how sports highlights travel because of a combination of epistemological, legal, and aesthetic strategies that result less in one particular format (with standardized characteristics) but rather in constantly adapting formatting practices. Sports becomes formatted into both an object of knowledge and a toolset for media industry; at the same time, the sports highlight provokes new industrial and legal strategies.

The first two sections of this chapter will sketch the historical and conceptual framework. First, I will describe how in the 19th century modern sports was made possible through representational forms that gave a reliable and condensed account of the competitions. Second, I will use the established notion of the TV format to specify some key characteristics of sports highlights as a format.

Thereafter, in the analytical part of this chapter, I will take a closer look at some of the dynamics that contribute to the recognizability and transformability of sports highlights. Each of the four sections of this second part focuses on one aspect of the actual work that highlights do, not only for sports but also for the media industries and media policy: (a) the sports-highlights compilation is a derivative format that achieves its identity from the task of condensing and circulating selected aspects of a competition; (b) its formal scalability and modularity allows the sports highlight to adapt this task to the requirements of different media and different cultural circumstances; (c) such flexibility extends its task, so that beyond the role of summarizing sports, the sports highlight becomes a tool to promote sport organizations and media industries; (d) because of its ambivalent status as both a derivative format *and* a valuable commodity, the sports highlight is harnessed for economic and political strategies.

Historical Framing: Formatting Sports

In the 19th century, the emergence of competitive spectator sports was made possible through condensed representations of its various events in the mass press. The reports on competitions from different places (and from different sports) created a public that got interested in a more comprehensive and more expansive comparison of performances. This interest contributed to the serialization and standardization of sporting events (Werron 2014; 2010; 2009), a process that can itself be described as formatting: for example, instead of informal and spontaneous contests adapted to the given space and available time, horse races and running competitions became differentiated according to standardized lengths and ball games got framed by lines of fixed dimensions separating playing fields from spectators (Bale 1996).

This formatting of the sporting practices happens in close interrelation-ship with the formatting of the modes of observation and reporting. Most drastically, the result of a competition is condensed in a quantitative manner, as in the score of a football game (e.g., 3–1) and the places and finishing times of a horse race. Results of different events are aggregated in tables and rankings. Leagues, with their weekly changing tables, and World Records are two different, but nevertheless characteristic phenomena of the later 19th century. Both imply that performances that take place at different times and at different places can be compared, thanks to the standardization of the actual competition and of the way it is recorded and communicated (Heintz and Werron 2011, 276).

Next to results, rankings, and statistics, the condensed communication of sports events in newspapers and special-interest magazines harnessed narrative, allegorical, and pictorial modes of observation, too, which embellished and contextualized the sober quantitative formatting of individual events. This implies the selection of distinctive moments from a competition that are considered either to have led to the result or to be remarkable independent of that result. In both cases, the mere result is supplemented with representations of what are considered the *highlights* of the event (Gamache 2010). A goal scored in a team sport and crossing the finish line in a race are both clear examples of the results-oriented aspect of highlights; yet especially artful or skilled movements can become part of highlights compilations too, as can controversial referee decisions or eventually any athlete's (or even audience member's) remarkable, especially fair or unfair, spectacular or dumb behavior. While there are clear cornerstones for sports highlights, they always leave room for more subjective impression and therefore open a discussion about the most appropriate way of condensing an event.

While sports highlights mainly are conceived of as representations in hindsight of the event, they were quickly also contributing to the expectations for upcoming competitions. Characteristically, reporting on the 1908 Olympic Games in London announced the marathon race two days in advance, singling out stretches of the course expected to create especially exciting moments or considered to be advantageous or disadvantageous for particular types of athletes (Stauff 2018a).

To wrap up this short historical introduction, highlights have an epistemological function. They serve as formats to observe, select, define, and organize, but also to question or debate, the moments of an event considered to be relevant, memorable, and spreadable. As with most formats, highlights compilations often aggregate sub-formats; they include results, statistics, tables, and highly formatted narratives. Sports highlights result from the intersection of two interrelated formatting processes. They are defined partly by the format of each sport, its dramaturgy and rules, and partly by the formatted modes of observation. A decisive move or particular turn of events becomes a highlight when it can be condensed into a recognizable and repeatable representation, which is as much dependent on the rules of the sport as on the forms and technologies harnessed to give an account of a competition. Modern competitive sports only exist because of formats that shape their observation and provoke a selection of key moments that can easily be circulated. The diffusion is stimulated by effective condensations that harness different media forms (numbers, narratives, images) and therefore allow for easy adaptation to different media systems (press, film, television). The ongoing debate about whether the most important moments are selected and if the mode of representation is appropriate further spurs the diffusion process.

Before I go into detail about the dynamics that contribute to the formatting function of highlights, I will first offer some more conceptual remarks concerning the notion of format. Taking my lead from television studies, I argue that the concept of format is intriguing because it allows one to describe a highly flexible but still regulated manner of transformation.

Conceptual Framing: Form/Format/TV Format

The sports highlight, I argued in the first section, fosters the diffusion of sports' remarkable events and results. Thus, it has close affinities to the concept of format, given that formats can be defined as *modes of presentation* that are made to enable and facilitate certain modes of circulation.[1] As Gerard Genette explains in *Paratexts*, the format of a book (originally resulting from folding the paper in different manners) is one of the earliest uses of the term; the format materially shapes mobility and moreover connotes a certain position on the ladder of cultural respectability—as we know especially from paperbacks or "pocket editions" (Genette 1997, 18).

Since the sports highlight misses the clear material delineation characterizing the different book formats (or technical formats like MP3), it might seem likely to describe it as a genre or even more general as a form. Caroline Levine (2016), at least, has convincingly argued that forms order signs, materialities, and meanings in a restraining and recognizable manner. The most basic result hereof is that forms differ: it is often easy to distinguish one form from another. Additionally, this allows forms to travel. They move across different materials and media, across different cultures and regions, and not least between media representations (or art, if you like) on the one hand and social reality on the other (Levine 2016, 4–7).

The concept of format, however, highlights how some forms are more closely bound to a set of practices and an institutional context than others. Understanding highlights as format (and not merely as form or genre), thus allows one to underline their specific function for the institutional system of sports media and the implicit and explicit regulations of highlight compilations that come with that (and which will be outlined in the following sections).

A format is connected to a series of decisions and a set of explicit rules that have to be followed to make it work for a particular medium and to intentionally foster the circulation process. Liam Young (2017, 38), for

1   According to Lothar Mikos, formats are modes of presentation ("Präsentationsformen") that adapt to media's capabilities to show and tell; thereby, he contrasts formats with genres' function of ordering content according to patterns of cultural meaning (Mikos 1995, 170). For a similar distinction between format and genre, though focusing more on the trade aspect, see Keane and Moran (2008, 158).

example, argues that the list is a *form* in the context of art practices (the famous lists of Homer) but a *format* in the context of administration because it is used to fulfil explicit tasks and gains a particular epis- temological function. The making of the list and its circulation is shaped by patterned practices and institutional concerns. While Young bases his reflections on the format mainly on Jonathan Sterne's (2012) analysis of the MP3, I will refer here to the notion of format in the television industry and television studies. Sterne's work on the MP3 approaches the format as a "crystallized set of social and material relations" (2006, 826) that inscribes certain assumptions about human listening into a technical standard (2012, 2). The TV format, with its focus on adaptability to different contexts, rather multiplies than crystallizes and thus seems the more fitting model for sports highlights' cross-media mutations—not least because sports- highlights compilations, even if emphatically cross-media, developed most explosively in the context of television.

For a long time, TV formats were mostly agents of standardization and crystallization, too. The program schedule establishes a grid of predefined segments of 30 or 60 minutes and additionally establishes an intricate entanglement of specific positions in the grid with allegedly appropriate content and values. The differences between daytime and prime-time programming and between weekday and weekend programming are the most conspicuous formatting dynamics here. Additionally, the enormous technical and organizational investment necessitated by broadcasting led to the establishment of basic routines of content production that shaped the standardized setup of cameras and lighting, editing, and modes of address. Live studio production and live-on-tape production, but also outdoor live events with huge trucks and kilometers of cable, can all be considered patterned production practices that become applied to varying content.

A somewhat different concept of format developed in the context of global program exchange which is much facilitated by the licensing of content, or rather ideas and concepts that can be multiplied and adapted to different contexts. Such TV formats had been around since the 1950s, but only emerged as a dominant tool for the distribution of TV content with the globalization and nonlinearization of the TV industry in the 1990s (Moran 2009). Until then, international program exchange was dominated by so- called "canned programs" (e.g., Waisbord 2004) in which programs were sold and distributed on celluloid or video tape and adapted slightly at times to the local context through the addition of subtitles, dubbing, or some re- editing. As an answer to the growing demand for new, cheap, and low-risk content, however, companies in the 1990s started to sell programming *templates,* which enabled the production of local and seasonal variants of already successful programs. While first mainly applied to quiz and game shows and reality programs, it by now has become a tool for the circulation of scripted content as well (Chalaby 2016).

The format, here, is first of all a manual for producing not only multiple episodes of a program but also different national variations based on a formula that has proven its success and allows for flexible scaling to available budgets (Moran 1998; 2009). Instead of a "canned program," customers receive a so-called "paper format," which outlines key aesthetic elements and provides guidelines for the production and marketing "that can be tailored to each locale" (Magder 2004, 147). According to Silvio Waisbord (2004), the format thus "bridges transnational economic interests and national sentiments of belonging" (368). *Big Brother* might be the most famous example. As of November 2018, Wikipedia announces, "there have been 445 seasons of *Big Brother* in over 54 franchise countries and regions" ("Big Brother (Franchise)" 2018). Additionally, when formats travel, it sometimes is less the textual form that is exchanged than knowledge about the organizational and technological ways of running a show, thus fostering particular forms of craftsmanship as well as industrialized, factory-like productions and their local adaptations (Keinonen 2017).

Canned programs and paper formats imply a different way of organizing production, different systems of distribution, and specific concepts of the audience (Moran 2009). In the case of canned programs, the formatting takes places in the production process and circulates as stable text and as material technology (a tape, a file, etc.). In the case of paper formats, it is rather contractual regulations, format information, and know-how "in the shape of a set of services designed to help in the production of the program elsewhere" (Moran 2009, 17). Characteristically, TV formats, while allowing for the flexible adaptation of content to local contexts, emerged together with a new global system of trade comprising, among other things, interdependent economic agents, global institutions, and copyright rules (Chalaby 2015). In this sense, TV formats clearly shaped the infrastructure they circulate on.

The TV format presents an interesting example for diffusion theory because what travels is not a thing or a recognizable form that is placed in different contexts. What circulates are composites of forms, practices, materials, and regulations that enable the generation and reconstruction of a number of versions. Much more flexible than the canned program, the TV format can be considered a "cultural technology" that "governs the flow of program ideas across time and space" (Moran 1998, 23). It functions as a generative matrix, regulating formal innovation and the cross-cultural travel of ideas, narratives, technologies, and economic strategies. In the following sections, I will build on that to analyze how sports highlight compilations work as a generative matrix that organizes diffusion across different media through practices of formatting.

Selection/Condensation: Highlights as Operational Forms

To a certain extent, sports-highlights compilations are a forerunner of the TV format. Since the 1950s, mega events like the Olympics or World Cup have sold media access to sports competitions and provided rules (a proto paper format) outlining how broadcasters are allowed to adapt the content to their national interests. Unlike TV formats, though, most sports highlights are not defined by a template or a program bible. In contrast to a paper format that is sold, adapted, and modulated for different seasons and countries, sports highlights are a much more elusive entity. Yet Albert Moran (1998) helpfully clarifies: "The term [format] has meaning not so much because of what it is, but rather because of what it permits or facilitates" (18). And as composites of forms, practices, materials, and regulations, sports highlights, I argue, can be considered formats because of the work that they do. Similarly to the TV format, they allow for flexible but patterned adaptation to different contexts and especially to different media and related social practices. I want to use the remainder of this paper to discuss how sports highlights govern the flow of images and ideas across time and space due to a particular overlap of formal conventions, technological innovations, economic strategies, and legal dynamics.

As I outlined in the historical framing at the start of this paper, a first aspect of the formatting work that sports-highlights compilations perform is the "creation of a visual shorthand" for decisive, telling, and thrilling moments of a competition "through the use of condensation and remediation" (Gamache 2010, 10). A certain formal stability results from this operational aspect of the highlights: they have to give an account of why and how one side won the contest while the other lost. The formal conventions at least partly depend on the rules, the temporal and spatial characteristics of specific sports.

During the 19th century, narrative reports in the press, maybe augmented by numbers, drawings, or photographs, contributed to the development of what one might call a highlight sensibility. Rudimentary forms of sports-highlights compilations also existed from the start of cinema in the 1890s. Dan Streible's (2008) history of the early boxing film shows that for quite a while, the distinction between highlights and full-event coverage was less systematic than dependent on technical capabilities, spontaneous practices, and legal disputes. Early cinema often displayed boxing as an attraction without aiming to present an actual competition; if actual competitions (or re-enactments of them) were staged to be filmed, they became adapted to the medium, such as by having rounds of only one minute to fit the length of a film reel (Streible 2008, 6). When kinetoscope parlors presented the individual rounds of a fight in separate kinetoscopes, often the audience turned out to watch the knockout round only (Gamache 2010, 20).

With consolidation of the institutional and technological settings of cinema, highlights compilations eventually achieved a conventionalized form, as Raymond Gamache (2010) details in his comprehensive *A History of Sports Highlights*. Not least because of sports' regular schedule throughout the year, highlights quickly became a staple of newsreels in the early 1910s and thereby emerged as the dominant framework for presenting sports as a separate segment of news. The newsreel highlights contributed to the familiarization of a broad audience with American football and other sports (Gamache 2010, 4). Just like magazine formats on television in the 1950s (like BBC's *Match of the Day* and *Grandstand*), they made sports accessible to a broader, nonexpert audience (Whannel 1991) and thereby also diffused sports' racial and gender hierarchies into common culture (Gamache 2010, 67).

The conventionalized form typically presented a "composite story of a sporting event comprised of multiple parts" (Gamache 2010, 39); it started with the venue and the presentation of teams, included a selection of high-light moments and shots of the audience reacting, and ended with images of the winners' celebration. When film sound was available in the late 1920s, the commentators fostered a more individualizing perspective, adding per-sonal stories (Gamache 2010, 51).

In the 1940s, when television started, sports-highlights compilations soon became part of the schedule too. "While the delivery systems of sportscast highlights have changed, what has not undergone significant change is the highlight form itself" (Gamache 2010, 10). With new technology, close ups, slow-motion replays, and data visualizations were successively integrated into an overall pretty stable form as specific but complimentary means to do the work of selection and condensation, evaluation and admiration.

It speaks to the stability of the format and its function that most sports computer games present a selection of highlights after each game played, which follow pretty much the formal pattern established in film and television throughout the past 100 years. Not surprisingly, experiments in computer-based video analytics have come up with several models for the automated detection of highlights in television footage (e.g., Radhakrishnan et al. 2005; Hao Tang et al. 2011; Assfalg et al. 2003).

Nevertheless, as I will argue in the following section, the formatting work of highlights results first of all from the scalability and adaptability of this otherwise recognizable form. On the one hand, sports highlights easily integrate heterogeneous media; the formatting work thus results less from the form or materiality of a particular medium than from a more general endeavor to diffuse sports through efficient (if controversial) selection and condensation of key moments. On the other hand, the work sports-highlights compilations do also comprises the flexible formatting of selection and condensation according to different media infrastructures and cultural contexts.

Scalability/Modularity: Adapting to Media and Cultural Contexts

Interestingly, Gamache (2010, 49–66) describes the patterns in the history of sports highlights as resulting from habits, just as Magder (2004) in his discussion of format states that the day-to-day business of television "runs on habit" (143). Recent discussion of the concept has underlined the generative potential of habits: instead of blindly and automatedly executing the same actions, habits, this research argues, function as modes of embodied thinking that allow behaviors to adapt to changing environments (Bennett 2016; Grosz 2013). Taking my lead from such a perspective, I want to argue that the ostensive formal simplicity of sports highlights, resulting from the half-automated operation of selecting and condensing the decisive and remarkable moments, allows for its adaption to different temporal and infrastructural circumstances.

First of all, the formatting work of highlights-compilations becomes visible in their intense scalability.[2] They allow for a very flexible transition between the full event and the highly condensed representation of the mere result. This transition is possible because of the highlights' flexible combination of different media forms like numbers, lists, spectacular images, and over-arching narratives. In games that consist of a series of distinct moves, such as baseball and billiards, every single action could be documented even before the invention of moving image technology. In 1881, Vienna's *Allgemeine Sport-Zeitung*, for instance, noted down every single strike of a game of pool in a table full of numbers, providing a very condensed rep-resentation of the full event without actually determining its highlights (*Allgemeine Sport-Zeitung* 1881).

The more common practice in today's media landscape is a live trans-mission of events in which commentators and the use of replays already clearly signal relevant or remarkable highlights. Directly after the game, these highlights become part of a post-game show in which athletes and experts comment on isolated moments to further evaluate their significance. A more strictly and coherently narrativized compilation of highlights occurs in shows that summarize entire game days in retrospect (like the British *Grandstand*, or the German *Sportschau*). Shorter versions of these are often presented at the end of news programs or increasingly on the apps of broadcasters and sports organizations, such as the National Football League (NFL) and National Basketball Association (NBA) in the United States, and their media partners, such as Facebook and YouTube.

In Germany, for example, the evening news program of public service broadcaster ARD, *Tagesschau*, presents condensed highlights of some games just 15 minutes after the longer versions of these compilations have been presented in the *Sportschau* on the same channel. About two hours later, the competing public service broadcaster ZDF also summarizes the game day, but unlike the rather sober and linear highlight reels of the *Sportschau*, these focus on more idiosyncratic aspects of the matches (the development of a young talent, the fate of a coach, the relationship of a club with its fans, and so on).

The number of remarkable moments, their formal treatment, and their re-contextualization can easily be modified. Sports highlights can thus be molded to fit timing from the original event, audience prior knowledge,

2   On the epistemological and methodological implications of scaling, see McCarthy (2006).

cultural and national context, and strategic industrial and institutional function.

This can be illustrated by means of a very well-known example. The 1966 men's World Cup final between England and Germany was represented in condensed form by newspapers and magazines, on television, and in movie theaters. Already the number of cameras at the event allowed for varying presentations of the same highlight moments (next to the TV cameras were film cameras recording in black and white and in color). Additionally, the game included one especially controversial moment: a shot by the English team that bounced from the crossbar down to the goal line and from there back into the field, which was called a goal by the referee. This moment became a point of focus in later highlight reels of the game and provoked a proliferation of re-contextualization and forensic scrutiny (Stauff 2018b), with, of course, opposing national narratives. The contemporary newsreel in German cinemas—the *Fox Tönende Wochenschau*—announced the scene as "the most controversial goal of the tournament" and showed it from two different camera angles. The second was presented in slow motion with the commentary stating, "these images prove that it was not a goal."[3]

Forty years later this moment was included in a DVD with highlights from BBC's Match of the Day (*BBC Match of the Day* 2004) and in a DVD celebrating 100 years of FIFA (*FIFA Fever* 2002). On the FIFA DVD, the controversial goal is actually presented twice, first in the chapter on controversial World Cup decisions, where it becomes part of a series of similar situations that all are isolated from their original context, and then a second time in a special chapter on Germany's World Cup successes. There, the goal is supplemented by an interview with one of the German players from 1966, claiming that it was a bad call by the referee but that the sportsmanlike manner in which his team accepted the decision advanced Germany's global reputation. This is only included in the German version of the DVD, of course; on the international Special Deluxe Edition of *FIFA Fever* (2002), the summary of the game is wrapped up with praise for Geoff Hurst's hat trick in the game and with images of the English players celebrating, the voice-over stating, "Now the nation could rejoice."

The formatting work of highlights, scaling and adapting sports' special moments to different contexts and requirements, takes advantage of the rich mediatization of sports. Often many different media capture alternative versions of special moments, which can also be accounted for through more indirect means of representation: depictions of scoreboards

3   My translation.

in the stadium or of the audience cheering; testimonies of participants and eye-witnesses; and graphics, reenactments, and computer simulations. All of these exist for the 1966 goal. As a consequence, sports highlights are highly modular: images, sounds, voice-over, and additional footage can easily be replaced, augmented, and reedited. This makes "localization"—TV-formats' characteristic adaptability to cultural contexts and national broad-casters' needs (e.g., Chalaby 2005)—easily possible.

As I will show in the final two sections, the sports highlights' combination of condensation and scalability makes it both a productive machinery for managing reputation and attention and a well-protected yet contested commodity. Its formatting work allows sports to circulate across media, but it also allows for industrial and political strategies that harness sports through the formatting potential of highlights.

Promoting Sports/Managing Attention: Highlights as Cross-Media Strategy

The re-mediation and formal adaptation of sports highlights is shaped and fostered not only by the work they do for sports but just as much by the work they do for the media industries. Their modularity and scalability make highlights into versatile, strategically harvested instruments in the attention economy.

Because highlights condense and collect special moments that can easily be de- and recontextualized, they are open for additional layers of meaning, beyond the communication and evaluation of athletic perform-ances. Gamache argues that already in the 1920s and 30s the newsreels "helped to establish athletes as the heroes and heroines of a burgeoning consumer culture, comparable in stature to the Hollywood movie actors that followed the athletes onto the screen" (Gamache 2010, 67). The fragmentation of a game into outstanding moments, presented in slow-motion replays, fostered the connection between individual athletes and commodities or brands, which (more often than not) were based on a hegemonic concept of masculinity (Morse 1983) that is even more pro-nounced in highlight reels than in the coverage of entire games with all their contingencies. Later, highlights were key for the emergence of global megastars like Michael Jordan, Wayne Gretsky, and David Beckham, who had impacts far beyond their respective sports (Gamache 2010, 7).

The taming of contingency, as well as the modularity that allows for the aggregation of topical situations and their embellishment with music and voice-over, makes the highlight an ideal tool to establish a cultural identity for a particular sport or a sports organization (Gamache 2010, 10). Most famously, the American professional football league, the NFL, already in 1964 established a subsidiary film production company NFL Films. Travis Vogan has shown in detail how the careful selection, curation, editing, and embellishment of highlights, realized by NFL Films on a comprehensive scale for decades, shaped the cultural memory, meaning, and affectivity of the sport, making "pro football into a spectacle that exceeds its position as a sports organization and becomes a corporate site of cultural production" (Vogan 2014). Needless to say, highlights, far from being limited to summarizing competitions in hindsight, have thus also themselves become commercials announcing and creating expectations for upcoming events.

Next to this general commercial work for the wider sports and cultural industry, the scalability and modularity of highlights allows them to do invaluable "convergence work." Format TV, like *Big Brother*, *Survivor*, or *Idols*, not only enable global flows of content ideas but also organize—through online quizzes, additional backstage footage, and the like—the herding of audience attention across different media platforms (Bignell 2005; Ouellette and Wilson 2011).

Similarly, sports highlights are a key tool, as Victoria Johnson (2009) has shown, for the implementation of new media technologies and for their entanglement with the traditional media industries. They foster a smooth transition from the liveness economy of broadcast media to the access and click economy of social media; they can be fragmented, parceled, de- and recontextualized. This enables traditional media companies to expand to online culture where they can offer extra highlight reels. Additionally, it allows social media companies to harness sports to create buzz and clicks. Nowadays, Twitter, Facebook, YouTube, and other social media giants are in competition to win contracts with the major sport leagues and the "sport mega events" (like the Olympics and World Cups) for posting highlights. On Twitter, sponsored highlights are posted while a game is still ongoing (Kantrowitz 2018).

Sports highlights allow for connecting and bridging different media while pointing out their differences, and they combine watching (mass audience) with participation (individual users). The often unanimous agreement on what are the decisive (or awe-inspiring) moments of a game combined with the structural disagreement concerning the evaluation of a situation guarantee a stable core for the frantic multiplication and variation of sports highlights. The work of giving an account of events through selection and condensation and the work of scaling and adapting to different historical, cultural, and technological circumstances are closely interdependent. This makes the sports highlights also one of the prevalent formats of user generated content and on social media platforms more generally. Spawned by (and overlapping with) the success of lists and rankings online, sports highlights get de- and recontextualized into compilations, such as "Top 33 Unexpected Goals in Football" (2018), "Top 100 Goals Scored by Legendary Football Players" (2018), and "Best Humiliating Goals 2019" (2018)—not so different from what the *FIFA Fever* DVD already offered in 2002.

Against this background one can conceive of sports highlights not only as TV formats but also as memes avant-la-lettre. In 1976 Richard Dawkins used the concept to describe cultural units that are easily and reliably copied; the actual online memes—somewhat contrary to Dawkins original definition—circulate not because of identical reproduction but because of certain patterns of transformation that appropriate the differences of media and the tension between isolation and re-contexualization (Shifman 2013). Similar to sports highlights, memes are often based on a recognizable form (e.g., the image macros), but their circulation dynamic results from modularity and adaptability. Contrary to memes, however, which are shaped by a click-economy, sports highlights owe their quality as formats mainly to a copyright-based economy. Sports highlights' formatting potential allows for and is intensified through their appropriation as industrial strategies. They offer a machinery to adapt the form to different media and different commercial strategies. Their formatting of diffusion is inseparable from their dual character as property and public good.

Protection and Obligation: Highlights as Contested Commodity

The power of sports highlights to herd audiences and organize attention across different media makes them a valuable commodity. As I will show in this final section, they are a highly contested and therefore conceptually ambivalent product. The surge of TV formats introduced a new form of commodity, whose legal status remains vague because in most countries a "program idea"—the "paper format"—is not protected by copyright law. The sports highlight, as a derivative format that summarizes an original event to foster its diffusion, is even fuzzier as a commodity. Contracts and laws struggle in formatting the highlights into an economically and politically efficient entity. As is often the case with sports, though, the ongoing technical transformation also provokes ongoing renegotiations of what sports highlights are and who is allowed to use them in which way. The formatting potential of highlights, the way they condense and diffuse sports, is closely interrelated with ongoing conflicts about access to events and the reuse of event coverage.

When filmic documentation of boxing first became a commercial success in the later 1890s, the organizers started to sell exclusive rights to film producers. Already then, competitors tried to smuggle in cameras to "pirate" the events (Streible 2008, 106–108). Over the following decades, with varying patterns in different countries and for different sports, it became increasingly common for film companies (and later TV broadcasters) to be charged for access to major sports events.[4] In the case of the Olympics, for example, the local organizers of the London games in 1908 were the first to grant exclusive filming rights to one company; the organizers of the 1928 games in Amsterdam created outrage for selling the rights to an Italian producer, who offered a better deal than the Dutch companies (McKernan 2011); the BBC was the first TV broadcaster to pay a small allowance for the 1948 London games.

For Olympic highlights, though, the 1956 Melbourne games became a watershed moment. For the first time, the IOC asked for $500,000 from the US networks for broadcasting the event. As a consequence, media from all over the world threatened to boycott the games (Gajek 2013, 322). The press, after all, was granted free access because sports organizers knew very well that without press coverage few people would be interested in sporting events. The filming of events, however, and their transmission via radio and TV was considered to be a replacement for the real event that might trigger a decrease in actual visitors. In this context, highlight reporting had an ambivalent status: film and TV companies, not least with reference to sports' widespread coverage in newsreels, argued that sports highlights would be news, even more so because the Olympic Games (more than the commercial exploits of US baseball or boxing) were considered events of general public interest.

This conflict led to a formal recognition of the specific legal and economic status of highlights, when the IOC, in its official Olympic Rules, replaced an older paragraph on "Photographs and Films" with a newer, much longer one on "Publicity." Alongside granting free access to staff from the press,

---

4   In the 1920s, for example, "[i]n England, companies routinely paid for the rights to film important sporting events; however, securing the rights to an event of public importance was not common practice in America." (Gamache 2010, 62) Until today, some minor sports pay TV stations to broadcast their events to create attention.

movies, radio and television, the local Organizing Committee was now explicitly tasked with both selling the "Live Television Rights" and providing newsreels for general circulation. For broadcasters that did not pay for live transmission rights, however, the use of this newsreel footage was highly specified:

> Newsreel showing, whether cinema or television, shall be limited to regularly scheduled shows, where news is the essence of the program, of networks or individual stations. No individual program may use more than 3 minutes of Olympic footage a day. No network, television station or cinema may use more than three sections of three minutes of Olympic footage in all news programs combined within twenty-four hours, and there shall be at least four hours between each showing. In no case can these newsreel films be used for the compilation of any kind of special. (International Olympic Committee 1958, §49)

The granting of highlights without charge was less a concession to "public interest" than an acknowledgment of the work highlights do in creating a public that is interested in the ongoing evaluation and admiration of sports performances. From 1930 on, the IOC obliged the local organizers to "make the necessary arrangements for making a record of the Games by means of photography and moving pictures" (International Olympic Committee 1930, 30).

Maybe even more tellingly for the indispensable function of highlights, until today broadcasters that pay for the live transmission of an event are bound by contract to include summaries in their schedules too. For the 2014 World Cup, for example, the rights holders were "obligated to provide a roundup program that lasted at least 30 minutes and included daily highlights of the World Cup" (Rampazzo Gambarato et al. 2017, 285).

With the success of social media platforms, the ambivalent status of high-lights as prized commodity and promotional tool only became more pro-nounced. Often, user-generated highlight films are taken down because of the infringement of intellectual property rights.[5] There are other occasions, though, when fan contributions (infringement notwithstanding) are tol-erated or even encouraged because of their potential to attract a broader audience (Corrigan 2014, 48). While the NFL forced Twitter to suspend the accounts of reputable publications because they posted highlight videos

---

5   This quite probably happens to the YouTube videos I referenced above. They are quickly replaced though by similar compilations with very similar titles.

there, the NBA has accepted fan highlight channels on YouTube considering them as marketing (Winkie 2016).

Because of their potential to create a public different from the audience of the live event, sports highlights additionally became objects of political and legal concerns. In the context of the establishment of commercial broadcasters and their Pay TV channels in Europe, for example, the appeal of sports highlights was supposed to ensure that issues of public and national concern would be accessible to wide audiences (and for public service broadcasters). In 1991 Germany augmented its broadcast law with a paragraph regulating the right of news and highlights coverage, the so-called "Kurzberichterstattungsrecht," which was later implemented on the European level too. In the current installment, this law, more flexibly than the IOC's, determines the acceptable lengths of highlights compilations as being dependent on the duration necessary to cover the news-related aspects of the event, which, generally, are supposed to be no longer than 1.5 minutes ("Staatsvertrag Für Rundfunk Und Telemedien" 2016, §5).

The rationale behind the new paragraph, which covered all kinds of events and news, was to prevent against football being covered only by commercial stations. Sports highlights have thus become a format meant to guarantee the diffusion of content across the public service–commercial divide. Additionally, sports highlights are used to create competition on the otherwise monopolistic market for sports rights. In the 2000s, the European Commission forced the German football league to split the rights into nine packages.

> The packages include: two live rights packages, available to free-to-air and pay broadcasters; three highlights packages, two of which must be on free-to-air, including one that contains the rights for a minimum of two live matches a season; one live internet rights package; and one live or near live package of mobile phone rights. (Gratton and Solberg 2007, 161)

These are only more or less random examples. Each league, country, sports event, broadcaster, and platform develops its own highlights strategy. The cases discussed here might suffice to show how the diffusion potential of sports highlights is intensely shaped by—often conflicting—legal and economic practices that, at the same time, have constantly been adapted to the transformative potential of highlights over the past 100 years.

Conclusion

This chapter has shown that sports highlights are a relevant example for a general theory of cultural diffusion. They transform the events of sports into a highly spreadable form. They do this, first, through a process of selection and condensation that aims at compiling the most decisive and spectacular moments in a comprehensive and appropriate manner—their epistemological function. Second, highlights enable circulation by offering this compilation in a scalable and modular way, that allows for adaptation to different technological and cultural circumstances; that they "refuse to hold still in transit" (Katz 1999, 144) accommodates the ongoing debates about the appropriate evaluation of performances that have characterized sports culture for more than a century. However, highlights do not circulate because of what they do for sports culture alone; rather, their diffusion is fostered through industrial and political strategies that harness the scalability of highlights also to scale up audiences and manage their attention. The volatility of highlights becomes an economic and legal concern and is thus connected to a number of different dynamics.

Understanding the sports highlight as a format thus forces us to pay attention to the uneven entanglement of textual elements, technologies, regulations, and practices. Formats govern the circulation of culture by combining a number of heterogeneous elements that undergo dynamic, yet patterned, transformation in their adaptation to different media systems and cultural contexts. Importantly, formats negotiate the relationship between the circulating content and the infrastructure it circulates in. Sterne (2012) conceives of infrastructure as the water "in which the MP3 fish swim" (15); in this context, sports highlights, rather amphibian, move between water and land, provoking changes in the coastal line. The constitutive transformability of sports highlights allows for integration of and adaptation to different media technologies and media industries; simultaneously, the technologies and industries are entangled with the volatile formats and thus undergo change themselves.

The sports highlight is not just a standardized form to account for the results of sports but also contributes to the formatting of sporting practices. Similarly, as sports highlights adapt to different media infrastructures, such as film newsreels, television, and online meme culture, they shape the industrial, technical, and legal environment. Sports highlights *are* a format that allows for certain modulations and contributes to the formatting of reality, but they also *become* formatted through strategies that aim to constrain and harness their volatility.

As an admittedly marginal example of a format, finally, the sports highlights could direct the attention of format studies toward patterned
flexibility as a key aspect of formats' productivity. While formats are
often understood as forms geared toward one specific infrastructure or
the creation of compatibility, it might be worth analyzing how formats
structure the transformative and mutual adaptation of content and
infrastructures.

References

Allgemeine Sport-Zeitung. 1881. "Das Große Wiener Billard-Turnier," January 27.
Assfalg, Jürgen, Marco Bertini, Carlo Colombo, Alberto Del Bimbo, and Walter Nunziati.
2003. "Semantic Annotation of Soccer Videos: Automatic Highlights Identification."
Computer Vision and Image Understanding 92 (2–3): 285–305. doi:10.1016/j.cviu.2003.06.004.
Bale, John. 1996. *Landscapes of Modern Sport*. London: Leicester University Press.
BBC Match of the Day: The Best of the 60s, 70s and 80s. 2004. DVD. Produced by Ian Finch, Niall
Sloane, Paul Armstrong, and Phil Bigwood. London: 2 Entertain Video.
Bennett, Tony. 2016. "Mind the Gap: Toward a Political History of Habit." *The Comparatist* 40
(1): 28–55. doi:10.1353/com.2016.0002.
"Best Humiliating Goals 2019" 2018. YouTube video. Posted by "Shatta Wale," December 22.
https://www.youtube.com/watch?v=zwgfKW3Ob1w.
"Big Brother (Franchise)." 2018. Wikipedia. July 23, 2018. https://en.wikipedia.org/w/index.
php?title=Big_Brother_(franchise)&oldid=851611840.
Bignell, Jonathan. 2005. *Big Brother: Reality TV in the Twenty-First Century*. Basingstoke, UK:
Palgrave Macmillan.
Chalaby, Jean K., ed. 2005. *Transnational Television Worldwide: Towards a New Media Order*.
London and New York: I.B. Tauris.
———. 2015. "The Advent of the Transnational TV Format Trading System: A Global
Commodity Chain Analysis." *Media, Culture & Society* 37 (3): 460–78.
———. 2016. "Drama without Drama: The Late Rise of Scripted TV Formats." *Television & New
Media* 17 (1): 3–20.
Corrigan, Thomas F. 2014. "The Political Economy of Sports and New Media." In *Routledge
Handbook of Sport and New Media*, edited by Andrew C. Billings, 43–54. London:
Routledge.
FIFA Fever: Celebrating 100 Years of FIFA. 2002. DVD. TWI/FIFA.
FIFA Fever: Celebrating 100 Years of FIFA. Special Deluxe Edition. 2002. DVD. TWI/FIFA.
Gajek, Eva Maria. 2013. *Imagepolitik im Olympischen Wettstreit: Die Spiele von Rom 1960 und
München 1972*. Geschichte der Gegenwart, Bd. 7. Göttingen: Wallstein.
Gamache, Raymond. 2010. *A History of Sports Highlights: Replayed Plays from Edison to ESPN*.
Jefferson, NC: McFarland.
Genette, Gérard. 1997. *Paratexts: Thresholds of Interpretation*. Translated by Jane E. Lewin.
Cambridge: Cambridge University Press.
Gratton, Chris, and Harry Arne Solberg. 2007. *The Economics of Sports Broadcasting*. London:
Routledge.
Grosz, Elizabeth. 2013. "Habit Today: Ravaisson, Bergson, Deleuze and Us." *Body & Society* 19
(2–3): 217–39. doi:10.1177/1357034X12472544.

Hao Tang, Vivek Kwatra, Mehmet Emre Sargin, and Ullas Gargi. 2011. "Detecting Highlights in Sports Videos: Cricket as a Test Case." In *Proceedings of the 2011 IEEE International Conference on Multimedia and Expo*, 1–6. doi:10.1109/ICME.2011.6012139.

Heintz, Bettina, and Tobias Werron. 2011. "Wie ist Globalisierung möglich? Zur Entstehung globaler Vergleichshorizonte am Beispiel von Wissenschaft und Sport." *KZfSS Kölner Zeitschrift für Soziologie und Sozialpsychologie* 63 (3): 359–94. doi:10.1007/s11577-011-0142-5.

International Olympic Committee. 1930. "Charte Des Jeux Olympiques." https://www.olympic.org/olympic-studies-centre/collections/official-publications/olympic-charters.

———. 1958. "The Olympic Games. Fundamental Principles, Rules and Regulations. General Information." https://www.olympic.org/olympic-studies-centre/collections/official-publications/olympic-charters.

Jenkins, Henry, Sam Ford, and Joshua Green. 2013. *Spreadable Media: Creating Value and Meaning in a Networked Culture*. New York: New York University Press.

Johnson, Victoria E. 2009. "Everything New Is Old Again: Sport Television, Innovation and Tradition for a Multi-Platform Era." In *Beyond Prime Time: Television Programming in the Post-Network Era*, edited by Amanda D Lotz, 114–37. London: Routledge.

Kantrowitz, Alex. 2018. "How Twitter Made the Tech World's Most Unlikely Comeback." *BuzzFeed News*, June 21, 2018. https://www.buzzfeednews.com/article/alexkantrowitz/how-twitter-made-the-tech-worlds-most-unlikely-comeback.

Katz, Elihu. 1999. "Theorizing Diffusion: Tarde and Sorokin Revisited." *The Annals of the American Academy of Political and Social Science* 566 (1): 144–55. doi:10.1177/000271629956600112.

Keane, Michael, and Albert Moran. 2008. "Television's New Engines." *Television & New Media* 9: 155–60.

Keinonen, Heidi. 2017. "Television Format as Cultural Technology Transfer: Importing a Production Format for Daily Drama." *Media, Culture & Society* 39 (7): 995–1010. doi:10.1177/0163443716682076.

Levine, Caroline. 2016. *Forms: Whole, Rhythm, Hierarchy, Network*. Princeton, NJ: Princeton University Press.

Magder, Ted. 2004. "The End of TV 101: Reality Programs, Formats, and the New Business of Television." In *Reality TV: Remaking Television Culture*, edited by Susan Murray and Laurie Ouellette, 137–56. New York: New York University Press.

McCarthy, Anna. 2006. "From the Ordinary to the Concrete: Cultural Studies and the Politics of Scale." In *Questions of Method in Cultural Studies*, edited by Mimi White and James Schwoch, 21–53. Malden, MA: Blackwell.

McKernan, Luke. 2011. "Rituals and Records: The Films of the 1924 and 1928 Olympic Games." *European Review* 19 (4): 563–77. doi:10.1017/S1062798711000196.

Mikos, Lothar. 1995. "Internationale Fernsehformate Und Nationale Sehgewohnheiten." In *Kommunikationsraum Europa*, edited by Lutz Erbring, 169–80. Konstanz: UVK.

Moran, Albert. 1998. *Copycat TV: Globalisation, Program Formats and Cultural Identity*. Luton: University of Luton Press.

———. 2009. *New Flows in Global Television*. Chicago: Chicago University Press.

Morse, Margaret. 1983. "Sport on Television: Replay and Display." In *Regarding Television: Critical Approaches*, edited by E. Ann Kaplan, 44–66. Los Angeles: American Film Institute.

Ouellette, Laurie, and Julie Wilson. 2011. "Women's Work." *Cultural Studies* 25 (4/5): 548–65. doi:10.1080/09502386.2011.600546.

Radhakrishnan, Regunathan, Isao Otsuka, Ziyou Xiong, and Ajay Divakaran. 2005. "Modelling Sports Highlights Using a Time Series Clustering Framework and Model Interpretation." In *Proceedings of the SPIE, 5682, Storage and Retrieval Methods and Applications for Multimedia*, 269–76. doi:10.1117/12.588059.

Rampazzo Gambarato, Renira, Geane Carvalho Alzamora, Lorena Peret Teixeira Tárcia, and Amanda Chevtchouk Jurno. 2017. "2014 FIFA World Cup on the Brazilian Globo Network: A Transmedia Dynamics?" *Global Media and Communication* 13 (3): 283–301.

Shifman, Limor. 2013. *Memes in Digital Culture*. Cambridge, MA: MIT Press.

"Staatsvertrag für Rundfunk und Telemedien (Rundfunkstaatsvertrag - RStV)." 2016. http://www.ard-werbung.de/fileadmin/user_upload/media-perspektiven/Dokumentation/2016-1_Rundfunkstaatsvertrag.pdf.

Stauff, Markus. 2018a. "The Pregnant-Moment Photograph: The 1908 London Marathon and the Cross-Media Evaluation of Sport Performances." *Historical Social Research* 43 (2): 203–19. doi:10.12759/hsr.43.2018.2.203-219.

———. 2018b. "Non-Fiction Transmedia: Seriality and Forensics in Media Sport." *M/C Journal* 21 (1). http://journal.media-culture.org.au/index.php/mcjournal/article/view/1372.

Sterne, Jonathan. 2006. "The MP3 as Cultural Artifact." *New Media & Society* 8 (5): 825–42. doi:10.1177/1461444806067737.

———. 2012. *MP3: The Meaning of a Format*. Durham, NC: Duke University Press.

Streible, Dan. 2008. *Fight Pictures: A History of Boxing and Early Cinema*. Berkeley, Los Angeles: University of California Press.

"Top 100 Goals Scored by Legendary Football Players." 2018. YouTube video. Posted by "Notelicioux," July 17. https://www.youtube.com/watch?v=g94QgTwpXQk.

"Top 33 UNEXPECTED Goals." 2018. YouTube video. Posted by "Wizzer," November 15, https://www.youtube.com/watch?v=zynSRSGp5bA.

Vogan, Travis. 2014. *Keepers of the Flame: NFL Films and the Rise of Sports Media*. Urbana: University of Illinois Press.

Waisbord, Silvio. 2004. "McTV: Understanding the Global Popularity of Television Formats." *Television & New Media* 5 (4): 359–83. doi:10.1177/1527476404268922.

Werron, Tobias. 2009. *Der Weltsport und sein Publikum: Zur Autonomie und Entstehung des modernen Sports*. Weilerswist: Velbrück.

———. 2010. "World Sport and Its Public: On Historical Relations of Modern Sport and the Media." In *Observing Sport: System-Theoretical Approaches to Sport as a Social Phenomenon*, edited by Ulrik Wagner and Rasmus Storm, 33–59. Schorndorf: Hofmann.

———. 2014. "On Public Forms of Competition." *Cultural Studies ↔ Critical Methodologies* 14 (1): 62–76. doi:10.1177/1532708613507891.

Whannel, Garry. 1991. "'Grandstand,' the Sports Fan and the Family Audience." In *Popular Television in Britain: Studies in Cultural History*, edited by John Corner, 182–96. London: BFI.

Winkie, Luke. 2016. "The Quasi-Legal World of NBA Highlight Videos." *Sports Illustrated*, February 9, 2016. https://www.si.com/extra-mustard/2016/02/09/nba-highlight-videos-clips-youtube-legality.

Young, Liam Cole. 2017. *List Cultures: Knowledge and Poetics from Mesopotamia to BuzzFeed*. Amsterdam: Amsterdam University Press.

6

Viewer's Digest: Small-Gauge and Reduction Prints as Liminal Compression Formats

Alexandra Schneider

In one of the major culinary innovations of the 15th century, "chefs began to learn about the benefits of reducing sauces to concentrate flavors by simmering them on the stove" (Culinary Pro 2019).[1] As a terminus technicus of culinary art, "réduction" first appears in Viard's *Le cuisinier impérial* at the beginning of the 19th century. First published in 1806 and widely circulated in French and other languages in the 19th century, Viard's book adapted its subtitle to the shifting political landscape from each edition to the next, underscoring the role of the culinary fields as one area of continuity in French culture through the great revulsions of the postrevolutionary era. While the original edition referred to the reign of Napoléon Bonaparte, the ninth edition changed its title to *Le cuisinier royal,* and from the 22nd edition in 1852, it was published as *Le cuisinier national.*

Less common than the term "reduction" for gravy is the notion of a "reduction print," which describes small-gauge versions of films marketed over decades in the 20th century for domestic and nontheatrical exhibition. "Reduction" here can refer to both the film's gauge and duration, with reduction prints often shortening full-length feature films to the essential 3–20 minutes necessary to screen them in programs alongside home movies and other short films. What some consider mutilated copies of

---

1   See also the definition of "reduction" in the *Oxford English Dictionary*: "*Cookery.* A condensed sauce made by boiling a liquid to reduce and concentrate it; the action or process of reducing a liquid in this way."

presumably "original" theatrical versions, others appreciate as condensed versions of concentrated "flavors," similar to a culinary *réduction*.

My own interest in reduction prints arose from my research on home movies of the 1930s, given that in many private collections, home movies appeared alongside mass-market reduction prints of theatrical films (Schneider 2007).

In recent years reduction prints have become increasingly relevant for archival and restoration purposes, as reduction prints are often the only available copies or fragments of otherwise lost films.[2] However, the question of reduction prints has so far not been addressed in either archival studies or home movie research.

This chapter uses format studies as a framework to present some preliminary research on reduction prints as a historical practice for the distribution of films. Like contemporary compression formats, small-gauge reduction prints had a key purpose: to facilitate the circulation of moving images—in schools, at home, and in alternative screening venues. As I have suggested elsewhere, substandard or small-gauge reduction prints might be understood as a pre-digital compression format of sorts (Schneider 2014). Before the advent of electronic and digital storage formats, size (and format) actually mattered, as "smaller" prints would make film copies cheaper.

At the same time, the historical practices of producing, circulating, exhibiting, and consuming reduction prints can also be considered to occur in complex sites of negotiation: between industrial and artisanal production practices; professional and nonprofessional (amateur) film cultures; niche and mainstream audiences; so-called standard and sub-standard formats; economic and aesthetic concerns; and other considerations, such as copyright issues, cinephilia, news, entertainment, and education. As Haidee Wasson (2015, 58) observed in her article "Formatting Film Studies," drawing on Jonathan Sterne's format theory, the concept of format offers "a productive instrument to move beyond an ahistorical, unchanging and thus rather expansive concept of a medium."

---

2   Citing a report from the Library of Congress by Pierce (2013), Hoyt puts in perspective the number of films lost from the silent period: "Pierce determines that 70 percent of American silent features are lost, 14 percent survive in complete form in American 35mm prints, 11 percent survive in 35mm foreign-release prints or small-gauge prints, and 5 percent are incomplete—'a few reels in 35mm, a shortened Kodascope edition in 16mm, and several cut to a third or less of the original in 9.5mm.'" (Hoyt 2014, 223)

Rather than treating reduction prints as a mere oddity in the history of cinema, or as a "threshold format," to use Kit Hughes' (2016) term, I propose to consider them as a "liminal format," where liminal is used in the sense of being not there yet or transitional, a kind of *format de passage*, if you will. I draw on the anthropological concept of liminality as proposed by Arnold van Gennep ([1909] 2011) and further explored by Victor Turner (1969). I am particularly interested in the idea of the liminal as a period of "passing through an adjacent, often marginal space characterized by a dissolution of established social order and hierarchy" in order to secure broader structures (Taylor-Alexander 2016, 154). For Turner (1969, 7), there is a "peculiar unity of the liminal: that which is neither this nor that, and yet is both." In that sense, liminality is understood here as a figure of thought for understanding pre-electronic compression practices of moving image cultures.

Through a discussion of reduction prints as a liminal format, this chapter aims to further our understanding of the complex historical dynamics of formats and particularly of the continuities and discontinuities between analog, electronic, and digital media. It is divided into five sections: A first section engages with the disambiguation of the notion "reduction print" and briefly discusses the state of research. The second section reconstructs the work of Castle films, a company that played an important role in the US reduction print market. Though economically marginal from an industry point of view, small entrepreneurs and movie practitioners producing and marketing reduction prints, such as Castle films, provide an important angle on film and media histories more broadly speaking. Using a philological, text-based approach, the third section proposes a typology of reduction prints. The fourth section raises questions of media theory around the concept of compression. In conclusion and with a view to further research, the final section discusses the Pathé Baby 9.5mm format to provide a synthesis of the historiographical, typological, and media-theoretical challenges presented by the liminal format of the reduction print.

Taxonomies

Film historian Simone Fabio Ghidoni defines reduction prints as "sub-standard editions [of] film strips printed between 1912 and the early 1980s in the 28, 22, 17.5, 16, 9.5, 8, Super 8 mm gauges."[3] Possible domestic uses

---

3   Ghidoni's (2016, 2) unpublished master thesis in film archiving, *Reduction Prints: A Casuistry*, from the University of Bologna, co-supervised by Paolo Caneppele from

of film had been discussed since the beginning of the history of cinema (Schneider 2004, 56). According to Ben Singer (1998, 37), "manufacturers launched more than two dozen portable projectors designed specifically for the home and other small group uses between 1896 and 1923 alone." Standardization began when Kodak and Pathé released their first non-theatrical projectors for domestic use in 1912 (Kodascope and Pathé Kok, respectively, with Pathé favoring a 28mm format). Both systems were more successful than other "threshold formats" of their time. However, it was only with 9.5mm and 16mm in the early 1920s that sustainable small-gauge formats entered the market, followed by the 8mm standard format in 1932.

Reduction prints of 35mm theatrical films quickly became an important part of film catalogues for nontheatrical screenings. Apart from just reducing the gauge from a 35mm copy to a smaller format, reduction often also entailed a shortening of the film. In his *History of the Pathé Exchange*, Richard Lewis Ward (2016) uses the terms "abridgement," "abridged version," and "feature abridgement" for this practice. These were not technical terms at the time, however. Neither was the concept of "con-densed version." A search in the trade press of the late 1910s and 1920s suggests that "condensed version" was a standard term in the field of per-forming arts for operas with shortened playing times. In the trade press of the time, most discussions refer to the gauge, i.e., the size of the storage material, by differentiating between standard and substandard or small-gauge formats. "Substandard" and "small gauge" are terms used for all gauges smaller than the standard cinematic distribution format of 35mm. In French, the most current term is *formats réduits* (reduced formats), while in English, "reduction" mostly appears in technical reports, particularly in discussions of optical printing. While optical printers were first developed in the late 1910s to facilitate titling and visual effects, they were also used to produce versions of the same film in different gauges, whether through what is now known as "blow up" or downsizing the original format.[4]

An early report in the *Moving Picture World* highlights the uses of optical printing for reformatting: "The ingenious device illustrated below is a printer for printing from a standard size motion picture negative on to a smaller film used by one of the many small home projecting machines on the market" ("An Optical Printer" 1918, 1660).

the Austrian Filmmuseum in Vienna, so far seems to be the only academic research on the materiality of historical reduction prints.

4   The history of optical printing remains as yet to be written. There is some research in the context of advertising (see Hediger 2001) and for special effects and exper-imental film of the 1960.

An article in the "Transactions of the Society of Motion Picture Engineers" from 1922 states: "The necessity of the industry required an optical printer for making direct reduction prints from professional standard negative" (Mees 1922, 159). Reduction prints were later also referred to as "library prints": "LIBRARY PRINTS: 8 and 16mm. printed by reduction from original 35mm" ("Library Prints" 1937, 132).

In her seminal article on the role of 16mm and cinema's domestication in the 1920s, Haidee Wasson (2009, 21) retraces "how the seeing and saving films at home was linked to the function of reading and collecting books, and listening music." Wasson studies the trade discourse with a focus on the hardware, in particular advertisements for portable devices such as projectors. Wasson concludes that the "the 16mm home theater was more an imagined ideal than a reality, an ideal that prominently migrated to other technologies" (12). Although 16mm found a way into wealthy homes, "it eventually became the primary gauge for schools, churches, libraries, and universities from the mid-1930s onward, a function that spread and was thus secured during and after World War II" (12). The Kodascope Library offered 16mm prints between 1924 and 1939 and 8mm editions from 1932 onward (Wasson 2009). However, the Kodascope library, a catalogue of reduced prints for sale and rent, was only a modest success with private consumers. Eric Hoyt attributes the "the lack of significant consumer adoption" to the high price of the equipment, noting that the Kodascope Library "failed to deliver a profit center for Hollywood's vault" (2014, 53) The high cost can partly be traced to the production process. As Ghidoni explains, the prints for the

> Kodascope and Cine Kodagraphs Libraries of the 1920s and 1930s 'directly derived from appositely edited, first-generation interneg-atives.' They were reduced on positive 'sunshine'-tinted 35mm stock, where two 16mm (or four 8mm) strips fit parallel to each other in order to be later cut and perforated. The process resulted in sought-after crisp, high-quality prints; the costs being the extreme wear of the internegatives and the slowness of the procedure (two copies for each passage in the optical printer). (Ghidoni 2016, 3)

As with their later reaction to home video, the studios took an ambivalent stance toward reduction prints. Nontheatrical distribution opened up additional markets but also "represented a threat to both the studio's core business and the more important side business of theatrical reissues" (Hoyt 2014, 71). But the number of available small-gauge prints suggests that smaller companies perceived the reduction print as a potential business model. Pathé is of particular interest here, as the company was still one of the leading content providers in the global film industry of the 1920s. As we will see later, Charles Pathé was not scared of the non-theatrical circulation of his film library. Another instructive example is companies specializing entirely in the production and sale of nontheatrical reduction prints.

Castle Films

Castle films was a "a nontheatrical producer and distributor that specialized in compiling short films into packages and selling them to churches, schools, and home viewers" (Hoyt 2014, 135). In Hoyt's study on film libraries, Castle films earns its first mention when a larger, studio-affiliated competitor, United World Pictures, buys the company for the considerable sum of $2.25 million in 1946. United World was, in fact, created in the same year as the nontheatrical subsidiary of Universal studios, one of the smaller studios in search of new revenue streams in the postwar era. Castle Films' specialty was outright sales to home viewers and collectors, a market "Hollywood studios had previously shunned" (135). Not since the transition to the rental distribution system in the early 1900s had film producers sold prints to exhibitors and other users outright, let alone to nontheatrical end users. As the success of the video store would show in the 1980s, rentals were a much more profitable business model for the home viewing market than sales. According to Hoyt, the acquisition of the Castle film library in the end "proved to be a costly mistake" for Universal (135). Nonetheless, Castle films (later rebranded as Universal 8) released over one thousand titles during the almost forty years of its operation, from 1937 to 1984. Every year, new titles were added to its catalogue.[5]

Eugene W. Castle (1897–1960), the company's founder, had entered the movie industry in 1914 at the age of 17, working as a stringer and freelance photographer in San Francisco (MacGillivray 2004). He spent the war years as a United States Marine Corps publicity man and worked for Gaumont newsreels for several years ("Gaumont News to Issue West Coast Edition," 1919, 119). In 1918, at the age 21, Castle started his own company, Industrial Castle Films, which was geared toward the theatrical exhibition market. He first specialized on educational and industrial films and served schools and community groups (MacGillivray 2004, 2). In the early 1920s, Castle held an editorial position in newsreels at Fox while establishing himself as

5   For a full list of titles, see MacGillivray (2004).

a producer of industrial films on the West Coast. As the trade paper *Moving Picture World* reports, Castle went on a 10-month road trip to Europe in 1921:

> [Eugene Castle], a well-known Pacific Coast industrial film producer, sails for Europe on April 30 in order to be away for 8 to 10 months. Castle, accompanied by a cameraman, will visit eleven European countries for the purpose of completing industrial contracts that require European scenes. (Tidden 1921, 58)

It remains unclear when and how exactly Castle decided to enter the distribution of small-gauge prints for private homes. As Ward (2016, 160) writes, in 1937 Castle "decided to try his hand at the growing eight-millimeter and 16-millimeter home-movie market." Pathé Exchange had started to sell 16mm single-reel subjects "at some point in the late 1920s . . . under the trade name 'Pathegrams.'"[6] But as "the Great Depression set in Pathegrams' business fell off. Its output consisted largely of highly abridged versions of the Pathé Exchange's shorts and features of the 1920s" (Ward 2016, 160). But in May 1937 Pathé apparently revived its home-movie division and teamed up with Castle to market its films under the Pathegrams label through Castle's distribution network. Castle started selling small-gauge reduction prints for the home movie market with the release of a 16mm Pathegram edition of *Hindenburg Explodes!,* a one-reel news special. But the Pathegram–Castle cooperation was short-lived. In July 1937 Castle terminated the agreement and started his own company. All the later films launched with Castle Films "were offered for 16mm and 8mm projectors; in sound and silent, complete editions (9 minutes in sound, 12 minutes at silent speed)"; there were also three-minute silent editions for toy-projectors, called "headlines" (MacGillivray 2004, 4). Castle films used a successful, fine-grained and multi-layered mail-order and retail distribution system. The prints were available via direct-mail sales and they could also be found in department stores, camera shops, and neighborhood drug stores. By carefully harnessing this capillary distribution network, Castle Films became the most successful distributor of home movies and an attractive buyout target for Universal in 1946.[7]

After the merger with Universal subsidiary United World Film, Castle's distribution system became a point of contention with theatrical exhibitors, who protested against what they perceived to be unfair competition from one of the big Hollywood studios (see Hoyt 2014). Castle continued

---

6   See Wasson (2009, 9): "Pathegrams, newsfilms marketed to the home user."
7   In the mid-forties Pathé Industries bought the two other home movie distributors: Official Films and Pictorial films (Ward 2016).

to operate, however, and quickly adapted to the introduction of Super 8 in 1971. Castle privileged prints in the new substandard format alongside 16mm prints in its catalogue presentations. The 1976 catalogue still mentions regular 8mm prints, but only lists the prices for Super 8 and 16mm prints. Celluloid-based home entertainment reached its peak with Super 8 in the 1970s, and Castle continued to be the market leader for reduction prints. In 1977, nearly twenty years after the death of its founder in 1960, the company name Castle Films disappeared (MacGillivray 2004, 15). Universal rebranded its home movie retail division under the label Universal 8 Films, but the rapid spread of VHS home video soon made reduction prints obsolete. As MacGillivray writes, "the Universal 8 abridgements were now pointless: people wouldn't spend money for 17 minutes of clips from a favorite movie, when they could have the *entire* movie on a tape" (19). In 1984, Universal shut the Universal 8 division down, bringing the age of the commercially marketed small-gauge reduction print version of theatrical films to an end.

Several things are striking about Castle films. First of all, it is interesting to note how the nontheatrical circuit was created and shaped by an independent practitioner and entrepreneur. Eugene Castle had been in business for nearly twenty years before he founded Castle films, a company he then turned into a valuable brand in less than ten years. He was a seasoned and polyvalent industry professional who, like many others of his era, explored and thrived in niches which Hollywood studios considered to be of little or no interest. What remains to be understood is how Castle built his library and how the editorial choices for the abridged small-gauge editions were made. Castle must have been sufficiently well-connected to be able to obtain rights for reduction print versions of studio films and secure funding for his company. What is certain, however, is that Castle and others like him saw in the reduction print a business opportunity afforded by Hollywood's lack of interest in either its libraries or what would later become known as "ancillary markets," which are now Hollywood's main source of revenue.

Typology

Hollywood has always made it a point to standardize exhibition practices in the theatrical markets. For instance, to reduce transaction costs, the major studios founded a trade association, the Motion Picture Producers and Distributors of America, to preempt state censorship and limit the number of versions of a given film in circulation to one. By comparison, the market for reduction prints was far less standardized and homogeneous. There were many different types of reduction prints, both in terms of film gauge and reduction rationale. On August 31, 2009, the Harvard Film Archive published on its blog the following program note on the Northeast History Film Symposium:

> We presented film on 3 small gauge formats common to the US home cinema market: 16mm, 8mm, and super 8. First, an 8mm reduction print of a silent Mack Sennett comedy, *The Campus Carmen* (1928). Next up, *New England Holiday!*, a 16mm short, silent travelogue from the 1940s about vacationing in New England. In keeping with tradition, we moved to a cartoon, *Farmer Gray in English Channel Swim* (1925), shown in 16mm. The 'feature' finale was a super 8 condensed reduction print of *Taxi Driver* (1976), with mag sound.

While we have seen that the interest of studios in this marginal market was limited, it was far from unusual for studios to release condensed versions of feature films for the home market. Most common were the 8mm or Super 8 silent versions that reduced a feature film to a selection of the five best minutes, using intertitles to explain the story.

> The version of *Taxi Driver* screened in the program was a little different. The tale was cut down to the story of Travis, the pimp, and Iris (the teenage prostitute). A narrator is employed to describe some gaps in the story. "Travis Bickle has decided to take revenge against the pimp." The original sound from the film is retained. "You lookin' at me?" Using only the scenes of sex and violence, the film is reduced to an exploitation version of itself.

The program included "condensed versions," "silent versions," films that were reduced to "exploitation versions" of themselves, or, to refer back to the culinary term *réduction*, versions that were reduced to their best.

Simone Ghidoni distinguishes two types of reductions: those made by printing copies to a smaller gauge and those made by abridging the running time of the film. Both processes reduce the amount of material needed for a film copy. A standard 8mm copy requires only a quarter of the material of a 35mm copy, and a three-minute version of a feature film requires only a small percentage of the film stock needed for a theatrical version. However, information is lost not only through abridgment but also through copying down, as a smaller image surface means less data on the print (fig. 1). Unlike the aspect ratio or size of a specific format, the resolution can be considered as a secondary reduction effect. Losing resolution does not make a copy cheaper. While unabridged small-gauge editions exist, most reduction prints are also abridged, not least for copyright issues. Reduction prints were edited down "in line with requirements generally (but not exclusively) ascribable to commercial needs," as Ghidoni observes. The abbreviation changed "the textual structure, the figural-narrative dimension and the audiences' experience of movies. The extent of the alterations was largely dependent on the style and target audience of the publishing company" (Ghidoni 2016, 4). For a single title different reduction editions were produced for different target audiences and through successive re-issues.

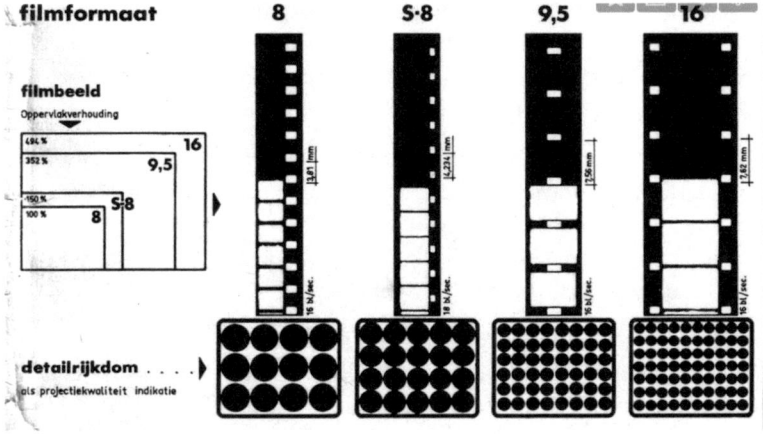

[Figure 1] Various film formats and resolutions. Source: Chasseur d'Images Forum, https://www.chassimages.com/forum/index.php?topic=264204.

Ghidoni also proposes to differentiate between an "abridged" and a "digest" version. The abridged version is a "classic reduction, where the movie has been significantly shortened without heavily affecting its narrative structure" (2016, 4). Usually, the beginning and end of sequences are short-ened, a practice often used for Kodascope prints. By contrast, editions with more radical and evident changes, as in the *Taxi Driver* version of the Harvard program, are "digest-editions" (5). The German-based Piccolo Film specialized in digest versions, as did Castle Films. Taking into account the professional background of Eugene W. Castle we can assume that he relied on his experience in the production of short news items in preparing digest versions of feature films.

Reduction meant lowering prices and thus also lowering the threshold for prospective buyers. Reducing the gauge and condensing the film to its presumably essential scenes saved footage, while turning a color film into a black-and-white film or a sound film into a "silent" film created further economies. In the latter case, titles were added to soundless versions to sustain the narrative, with the savings on the soundtrack offsetting the cost of the additional footage. With the shift from academy to widescreen ratio in the 1950s then, most reduction prints edited widescreen films back down to a 4:3 ratio, raising the problem that Jacob Burckhardt (1919) described for etchings of famous paintings and anticipating similar issues with VHS video versions of widescreen films in the 1980s and 1990s, which used so-called "pan-and-scan" procedures to keep the focus of the action in the center of the screen in video versions adapted for TV screenings. Widescreen systems for substandard formats did exist, but they were expensive and therefore mainly marketed as special editions for collectors and connoisseurs. Reduction prints were also used for home sales of pornography, and it remains to be determined to what extent this subsegment of the market may have contributed to the development of reduction prints and their distribution.

Reduction as Compression?

In his discussion of paper formats, Marek Jancovic argues that "formatting has always been a compression" in that "the folding of the sheet shrinks the dimensions of paper and simplifies its transport and storage" (see Jancovic in this volume). But if every format is already a form of compression, then what is a compression format? Is there a categorical or a gradual difference between a format and a compression format? For Jonathan Sterne (2012, 2), formats are a "technique of removing redundant data."[8] However, Sterne does not specify what distinguishes a compression format, such as MP3, from a non-compression format, such as WAV or HD-CD. We must infer that for Sterne the opposite of a compression format is high definition, but the distinction between "high" and "low" remains blurry, perhaps intentionally so. Sterne writes: "A general history of compression also connects contemporary practices that are self-consciously understood in terms of compression with a broader history of practices that share the same morphology" (2012, 6). In the case of the reduction print I would argue that it is indeed a set of practices that share "the same morphology" with other processes of compression. Small-gauge formats as such are based on compression, as we have seen. For the time being, I propose to understand compression according to a gradual and common-sense use of the notion: in such an understanding, MP3 is indeed always a compression format, not

8   Relatedly, the *Oxford English Dictionary* defines compression in the context of computing as "the process of reducing the amount of space occupied by data that is being stored or transmitted, by minimizing redundant information." First mentioned in Russian in 1957.

least for being a kind of wide-bodied aircraft of pop music and vehicle of global data tourism.

As we all know, the MP3 compression standard is a compromise, the result of an allocation of available data and the physiological conditions of human perception. The latter are also relevant for the standards in film history. The illusion of movement occurs at frame rates above 16 images per second. And those images become sharper and more luminous with increases in image size, or changes in the image format. A 70mm frame contains four times the amount of data of a 35mm frame. Similarly, increases in running speed, such as moving to 48 frames per second, produce even better, more data-rich moving images. In requiring more data, however, higher image resolution and faster frame rates also increase the price of the product. The standard rate of 24 frames rate per second was established in the 1920s as a compromise between the human physiology of perception and the economic and technical affordances of the circulation and projection of movies. It solidified into a world standard with the introduction of optical sound after 1928. Small-gauge formats were standardized at speeds between 16 and 18 frames per second, i.e., just above the threshold where human perception synthesizes separate successive frames into the illusion of movement.

Compression can thus be understood as the reduction of data to the threshold of comprehensibility. A standard 8mm reduction print of *A Gentleman's Gentleman*, a well-known Mickey Mouse cartoon directed by Roy William Neill and released in 1941, can illustrate this point. Mickey sends Pluto downtown to fetch the paper, but Pluto loses the coin he was supposed to trade for the paper. His effort to retrieve the coin with bubble gum only makes things worse. The reduction print starts about two and a half minutes into the original film and ends before the original ending. The reduction covers about half the running time of the 1941 release print and omits all scenes with Mickey Mouse, focusing on Pluto's adventure instead. The substandard version is also a black-and-white silent version of a Technicolor cartoon with music, dialogue, and sound effects. But because only Mickey talks in the original version and he has been eliminated from the reduction, the lack of the soundtrack does not really impair the comprehensibility of the film.

The reduction print is copyrighted by Disney Films, but it was made and distributed by Hollywood Films Enterprises, a company specializing in Walt Disney cartoons, which "resorted to an even less considered procedure, exploiting the original camera negative for every single reduction" (Pierce

1989, 40, as cited in Ghidoni 2016, 3). The small-gauge version ends as it began: with a title card. The card suggests that this is not a fragment or a reduction, but a "complete" film. In terms of data it is a much smaller version: both frame and run time are reduced, and color and sound information are omitted. Which raises the question: was the data that was eliminated in the reduction process redundant? In terms of narrative comprehensibility, the answer would be yes. The resulting silent, black-and-white film of a dog losing and trying to retrieve a coin in an urban setting is a self-contained narrative that can stand on its own and needs no further aids to be accessible to an audience. Yet if we assume that comprehensibility is not just a matter of passing the threshold of the perceptibility of movement set by human physiology and of mapping narrative events onto a basic story schema, but a matter of aesthetics, which means that the difference between silence and sound and black and white and color matters, then the data eliminated in the reduction process was not redundant at all.

Then again, compression practices and standards vary over time. What qualifies as comprehensibility is, to a certain degree, historically contingent. In the case of this Disney film, neither the lack of color nor the sound was considered to be an obstacle for its commodification and circulation in nontheatrical venues. Which means, among other things, that the acceptability and the success of reduction formats is always a function of the lack of alternatives. Absent an easily accessible version of the complete movie, even as radical a reduction as that of the color, sound, and Mickey-less Disney film would be deemed sufficient and acceptable by distributors and their audience.

The Pathé Baby Filmathèque

Pathé, the first fully vertically integrated producer of moving image equipment and films before Sony's acquisition of Columbia Studios and Matsushita's temporary ownership of MCA Universal, played a groundbreaking role in making movies portable and mobile, certainly outside of Northern America. In 1912 the Pathé Frères introduced their first nontheatrical substandard gauge, the 28mm Pathéscope home cinematograph, more commonly known as the Pathé KOK. Charles Pathé "comprehended the potential behind a well-conserved back-catalogue ready to be capitalised whenever a new technological advancement would allow it," as Ghidoni (2016, 3) writes. Pathé considered even the 28mm-system as a carrier for reductions, and an extensive catalogue of small-gauge prints, the

Descriptive Catalogue of Pathéscope Films, was made available for rental.[9]
But it was the next substandard format developed by Pathé, which was
even smaller and easier to handle, the Pathé Baby 9.5mm format, that
finally hit a cord and became a mass-market success. The library for the
Pathé Baby was called the *Filmathèque Pathé Baby* in French (using the
library and art gallery as a model and reference almost a decade before
the Cinémathèque Française was founded) and the *Catalog of Pathex:
Motion Pictures for the Home* in English.[10] In a departure from the rental-only
catalogue of the KOK system, the Filmathéque 9.5mm prints could also be
bought. The prints came in closed boxes (a kind of VHS cassette avant la
lettre) which made the handling easier. Ghidoni (2016, 3) observes:

> Even though the filiation-line behind the Pathé-Baby prints was in
> many ways comparable to the Kodascope procedure, a fundamental
> difference was the gauge of the shortened internegative, here a 3 x
> 9.5mm matrix allocated on specially perforated 35mm stock. This
> meant that the reduction process had to be carried out only once, in
> the passage from the lavender material to the internegative. All the
> projection copies could then be contact-printed three at a time. This
> method was undoubtedly faster, and, moreover, did not involve the
> exploitation of the precious standard-gauge intermediates, while it
> also proved less expensive, requiring a minor amount of stock.

In terms of the material costs of image size and resolution, 9.5mm was an
elegant solution because it offered nearly the resolution of 16mm with a
smaller gauge. This was achieved by placing the sprocket holes not at the
margin but between the frames. Another innovation that allowed for compression without a major loss of quality was so-called notched titles.

A cinephile and amateur film critic and historian explains on his blog:

> nine years ago, I bought four bobbins of the 9.5mm Pathé Baby version
> of *J'accuse* (1919). Since then, I've been picking up more when and wher-
> ever I could find them. At last, I've assembled the entire film. . . . At 840
> feet, it's considerably abridged from the theatrical release . . . If it was
> run straight, 840 feet works out to around 28 minutes, but *J'accuse* has

9   For the US nontheatrical market and Pathéscope, see Ward (2016) and Hoyt (2014).
10   Pathé Baby made its American debut in 1925, two years after Kodak introduced
     16mm film, being sold "under the trade name 'Pathex,' an abbreviation of Pathé
     Exchange" (Ward 2016). As we will learn later, Pathé Exchange had been forced to
     market the home movie format Pathé Baby in the US by the French head of office
     from 1925 onward. Sold under the name Pathex, the small-gauge system, which
     would become a decades-long success in the European and Southern markets, did
     not sell well in the US, though.

notched titles so it's actually a bit longer than that. . . . To save film, the Baby had a unique system whereby a little arm feels along the edge of the film as it passes through the projector. When it encounters a notch, it stops advancing the film for a few seconds—holding the picture on the screen. This way, titles could be reduced from several feet down to just a couple frames. . . . so [*J'accuse* is] probably closer to 45 minutes long. (Those Awful Reviews 2016)

J'accuse was released by Pathé in 1919 with an original length of about 156 minutes. It remains unclear when it was first released as a Pathé Baby reduction print, but it is listed in the extensive catalogue in the 1931 edition of the Pathé Baby Filmathèque under the category "comedies and dramas." Besides the information that the reduction print is about a third of the length of the theatrical release, the blog post offers a good description of the so-called notched title or stop notch mechanism that Pathé had introduced for its system to save film material, increase the comprehensibility of its prints, make copies cheaper, and improve the operation of a small-reel system (first using reels of 30 and later 60 feet). At the same time, the system had disadvantages in comparison to 16, 8, and later Super 8mm film systems, as the light source for obvious reasons could not be too strong lest it melt the film strip.[11]

Notched titles were used not only for intertitles but also for photographic images, such as portraits, landscapes, and other pictures that were turned into freeze frames. This is particularly interesting because it thus turned film into a composite medium of moving and still images. The compression process of Pathé Baby is somehow in between the two models of reduction printing that I have described before. Marking the titles for notching required a conscious selection process, but it was much simpler than creating a condensed version of a film narrative selecting entire sections of the film for elimination. I concur with Ghidoni when he argues that

it appears true to me that small-gauge editions testify to a fluid, shifting concept of cinematographic work. They indicate that the boundaries, the support and the text of a film can change, adapting to the times, the places and the functions which (r)evolve around them. Their existence implicitly supports the idea that cinema is an art (and

11   Or as Richard Ward writes: "Auto stop was only possible because the Pathé-Baby projectors came with low-wattage lamps that could only produce an acceptably bright image in a completely darkened room and a screen size that did not exceed three feet by four feet. While a higher-wattage lamp would have generated more light, permitting a brighter and larger image, it would also have produced enough heat to melt the film during a prolonged freeze-frame." (Kindle-Positions 3505-3510)

industry) where there is limited space for the concept of 'original', ide-
alistically intended as an unchangeable, untouchable model. (Ghidoni
2016, 8-9)

From today's perspective, the practices of reduction offer a perspective on
what is clearly a very extensive history of watching movies in fragments
and low-resolution or at speeds at variance with the original projection
speed (Alexander 2016). This history stretches from the earliest reduction
prints to present-day clip shows on YouTube. Film historical research of
the past decades has shed light on the many movie-watching practices
that question the idea of a closed text of a single work as the predominant
mode of the exhibition and reception of moving images. For instance, Ross
Melnick's (2012, 14) work on the exhibition practices of the 1920s and his
notion of the "unitary text" of the film program highlights the fact that even
in theatrical exhibition, the feature film was only one element in a larger
ensemble. Thus the individual work can no longer be the primary frame of
reference.

As Vinzenz Hediger argued in a text on film restoration a few years ago, the
original version of a film is always lost. What film historians and archivists
have to contend with is instead a multiplicity of prints and versions, or
the "original as a set of practices" (2005, 147) As Hediger writes, "Historical
research must always come to terms with the one fact that a complete set
of facts does not exist. A film historiography that defines the original as a
set of practices would have to take this limitation into account" (2005, 145).
The study of reduction prints complicates this question even further. Not
only does considering the histories of communication and representation
shift our attention from media to formats, as Sterne argues, but once that
shift happens, we can no longer limit ourselves to a film historiography that
is based on an abstract notion of the work as isolated from the conditions
of possibility of its existence. As Burckhardt knew, format is what keeps a
work from dissolving into infinity. A historiography that does not account
for "poor images," to quote Hito Steyerl (2009), for images that "lose matter
and gain speed" and "are poor because they are heavily compressed and
travel quickly," such as the Mickey cartoon stripped of color, sound, and
Mickey, cannot fully account for the work of which the reduction print is a
seemingly lesser version.

In that sense, format cannot be reduced to the protocol that defines what
a medium is, or what function it performs. For the foreseeable future, the
question of format will be one of the questions that defines what media
historiography is.

References

"An Optical Printer." 1918. *Moving Picture World*, March 23, 1918, 1660.

"Gaumont News to Issue West Coast Edition." 1919. Motion Picture News, January 4, 1919, 119.

Burckhardt, Jacob. (1886) 1919. "Format und Bild." In *Jacob Burckhardt: Vorträge*, 4th ed., edited by Emil Dürr, 252–60. Basel: Schwabe.

Culinary Pro, The. 2019. "About Sauces." Accessed August 9, 2019. https://www.theculinarypro.com/sauces/.

Ghidoni, Simone Fabio. 2016. "Film Archiving Reduction Prints: A Casuistry." Unpublished English Summary of his Master's thesis Reduction Prints of Standard Gauge Films. Sources for an Italian Casuistry, University of Bologna.

Harvard Film Archive. 2009. "NHF Summer Symposium." *Harvard Film Archive Collections*, August 31, https://blogs.harvard.edu/hfacollections/2009/08/.

Hediger, Vinzenz. 2001. *Verführung zum Film: Der amerikanische Kinotrailer seit 1912*. Marburg: Schüren.

———. 2005. "The Original Is Always Lost." In *Cinephilia: Movies, Love and Memory*, edited by Marijke de Valck and Malte Hagener, 135–49. Amsterdam: Amsterdam University Press.

Hoyt, Eric. 2014. *Hollywood Vault: Film Libraries before Home Video*. Berkeley: University of California Press.

Hughes, Kit. 2016. "Record/Film/Book/Interactive TV: EVR as a Threshold Format." *Television & New Media* 17 (1): 44–61.

"Library Prints."1937. *Movie Makers*, March 1937, 132

MacGillivray, Scott. 2004 *Castle Films: A Hobbyist's Guide*. Indianapolis: iUniverse.

Mees, C. E. K. 1922. "Color Photography." *Transactions of the Society of Motion Picture Engineers* 6 (14): 137–56.

Melnick, Ross. 2012. *American Showman: Samuel "Roxy" Rothafel and the Birth of the Entertainment Industry, 1908–1935*. New York: Columbia University Press

Oxford English Dictionary, s.v., "Reduction." Accessed October 7, 2019, https://oed.com/.

———. s.v., "Compression." Accessed October 7, 2019, https://oed.com/.

Pierce, David. 1989. "Silent Movies and the Kodascope Libraries." *American Cinematographer* 70: 36–40.

———. 2013. *The Survival of American Silent Feature Films: 1912–1929*. Washington, DC: Council on Library and Information Resources and the Library of Congress.

Schneider, Alexandra. 2004. *Die Stars sind wir: Heimkino als filmische Praxis*. Marburg: Schüren.

———. 2007. "Time Travel with Pathé Baby: The Small-Gauge Film Collection as Historical Archive," *Film History* 19: 353–60.

———. 2014. "Ta-ta Ta-ra Ta-ta Ra-Ra: 1991 – Kompressionsformate und Memoryscapes." *Memoryscapes: Filmformen der Erinnerung*, edited by Ute Holl, 301–20. Zürich: Diaphanes.

Singer, Ben. 1998. "Early Home Cinema and the Edison Home Projecting Kinetoscope." *Film History* 2: 37–69.

Sterne, Jonathan. 2012. *MP3: The Meaning of a Format*. Durham, NC: Duke University Press.

Steyerl, Hito. 2009. "In Defense of the Poor Image." *E-Flux* 10 (November): 1–9.

Taylor-Alexander, Samuel et al. 2016. "Beyond regulatory compression: confronting the liminal spaces of health research regulation." *Law, Innovation and Technology*." 8 (2): 149–76.

Tidden, Fritz, 1921. "Keeping in Personal Touch." *Moving Picture World*, May 7, 57.

Those Awful Reviews (blog). 2016. "*J'accuse* (Pathé, 1919)," May 6, https://thoseawfulreviews.wordpress.com/2016/05/03/jaccuse-pathe-1919/.

Turner, Victor. 1969. *Ritual Process: Structure and Anti-Structure*. Ithaca, NY: Cornell University Press.

van Gennep, Arnold. (1909) 2011. *The Rites of Passage*. Chicago: University of Chicago Press.

Ward, Richard Lewis. 2016. *When the Cock Crows: A History of the Pathé Exchange.* Carbondale: Southern Illinois University Press.

Wasson, Haidee. 2009. "Electric Homes! Automatic Movies! Efficient Entertainment!: 16mm and Cinema's Domestication in the 1920s." *Cinema Journal* 48 (4): 1–21.

———. 2015. "Formatting Film Studies" *Filmstudies* 12 (1): 57–61.

7

Formatting Faces: Standards of Production, Networks of Circulation, and the Operationalization of the Photographic Portrait

Roland Meyer

Every picture has a format. Indeed, one could even say that having a format, i.e., measurable dimensions and technical specifications, is what distinguishes a picture from an image. As W. J. T. Mitchell and Hans Belting have argued, images float freely across different media while changing their formats, sizes, and material qualities; even more, images can be merely verbal or mental, and not materialize themselves in visual form at all. Pictures, on the other hand, have traditionally always been bound to specific media like painting, sculpture, photography, and film, or technical *dispositifs* like screens and displays—material image carriers that determine the physical dimensions and visual qualities of images as pictures (Mitchell 1994, Belting 2014). Thus, if format matters are central to defining what images and pictures are (and as I argue, even more so to what they *do*), then it comes as no surprise that the idea of "format" as a theoretical concept has gained some prominence recently, not only in media studies but also in visual studies and image theory.

Focusing on contemporary art, David Joselit has proposed a notion of "format" that aims to replace the traditional concept of the work of art. According to Joselit, the most relevant current artistic practices today no longer focus on the aesthetic production of singular works and original content but rather on the appropriation and reformatting of images circulating as endless streams of data in networked media. From the 1960s on, artists began developing new formats for dealing with these preexisting images, "dynamic mechanisms for aggregating content," as Joselit defines his notion of a "format." Such new aesthetic formats, whether they materialize as multimedia installations, performative spaces, or conceptual practices, can be understood as aggregators or assemblies that establish new patterns of connections within vast populations of images—nodes emerging from the endless network of contemporary visual culture (Joselit 2013, 55). Thus, for Joselit, formatting becomes "as much a political as an aesthetic procedure" because the question how to assemble and connect the images appropriated from the endless streams of networked media "introduces an ethical choice about how to produce intelligible information from raw data" (Joselit 2015, 268).

Taking their lead from David Summers's (2003) analysis of the relationship between images and "real spaces," Wolfram Pichler and Ralph Ubl propose quite a different, more phenomenological notion of "format" in their recent introduction to image and/or picture theory (*Bildtheorie*). Pichler and Ubl's extended concept of "format" not only covers the material substrates of pictorial media and the physical properties of image carriers, e.g., measurements, dimensions, materialities, surface qualities, and technical specifications; it also includes established conventions of representations, e.g., linear perspective, and ultimately all "culturally specific conditions of presentation" that mediate between the real-spatial situation of an image carrier and the "image objects" depicted on it (Pichler and Ubl 2014, 147). Thus, "format" for Pichler and Ubl more or less replaces the idea of "media": whatever an image needs to become visible, i.e., materialize itself in time and space, can be called its "format."

What both of these definitions—despite their obvious differences—seem to have in common is that they reflect a model of sovereign aesthetic production in which the question of format is more or less subject to an individual decision, which can be made based on mainly aesthetic (or ethical) considerations. These broad notions of "format" thus do not seem to address what is to me the most salient aspect of formatting: the idea of repetition and standardization. Unlike media studies, art history has never been very interested in the idea of standards, focusing rather on the unique, singular, and exceptional—a predilection that it passed on to its offspring in visual studies and picture theory, at least in their German version called *Bildwissenschaft*. But as I would like to argue, the notion of format can only be made productive as a basic term for analyzing visual culture if we take into account that formats are meant to be repeatable and binding, if not universal, and that they become formats by being applied not only to singular artifacts but also to vast numbers of different, albeit comparable, items. Formatting is, almost by definition, a practice of specification, regulation, and restriction (Krajewski 2007). Formats manifest themselves in rules, protocols, and technical apparatuses, in hardware and software, in juridical specifications, bureaucratic processes, and social arrangements. "Format," media scholar Jonathan Sterne writes, "names a set of rules according to which a technology operates" (Sterne 2012, 7). Although these rules and standards may at some point have been the contingent effect of a sovereign decision, once they are established, they become encoded in physical and symbolic infrastructures that become extremely difficult to change (Bowker and Star 1999, 34–39). In visual culture, such infrastructures specify the conditions for the production and distribution of images and other visual "content"; regulate what can be stored, trans-mitted, and processed; determine how these items are handled; and in doing so establish standards for what becomes visible and remains invis-ible (Bruhn 2003, 8–18; Heidenreich 2004, 7–26).

In the following, rather than proposing my own definition of what a format *is*, I would like to ask what formatting as a repeatable and standardizable pictorial practice *does* and how it becomes productive in the field of visual culture. Unlike Joselit or Picher and Ubl, I won't focus on (contemporary) art, but on much more mundane visual practices that have nevertheless completely changed the way pictures are used, in everyday culture as well as in more specialized fields of knowledge such as police identification.[1] Thus, in what follows, I will present three small case studies, three "primal scenes" of formatting, which, rather than adding up to a continuous history, should be read as distinct but related stories of beginnings: the beginnings of popular portrait photography in the 1860s, the beginnings of stand-ardized police photography in the 1880s, and the beginnings of Facebook as a platform of image circulation in the 2000s. In each case, the introduction of a new pictorial format not only changed the conditions of pictorial production but also helped to establish new practices of distributing and connecting pictures, thus fostering new logistics of images.

It is no coincidence that the focus of these three case studies is on images of the face. After all, the history of photographic portraiture has been determined by technical, commercial, and institutional formats almost

---

1   On how the notion of formatting as a repeatable and standardizable pictorial practice can be made productive for an analysis of artistic production, see Meyer 2019b.

since its beginnings. More important, unlike any other field of pictorial production, photographic portraiture involves formatting that not only influences pictorial practices, modes of production, and means of distribution but also in doing so informs our notions of individual identity. Thus, formatting faces also means establishing new formats of identity. What follows, then, can also be read as a short and incomplete visual history of identity and identification, focusing on three paradigmatic shifts in the modern history of photographic portraiture: mass production, systematic operationalization, and networked datafication.[2]

Disdéri: Increasing Production, Unbounding Circulation

Mass photographic production literally begins with the introduction of a new standard format, namely Adolphe-Eugène Disdéri's carte-de-visite format. "In order to render photographic prints practical for commercial needs," Disdéri stated in his patent application of November 1854, "it would be necessary to diminish greatly the costs of production, a result which I have obtained by my improvements" (quoted in McCauley 1985, xviii). The formulation is as precise as it is telling: Disdéri does not claim a technical invention, but rather some "improvements" (*perfectionnements*) on an already established technology, namely the collodion wet plate process. The focus of his "improvements" is on the efficient use of storage space: A camera with four lenses exposes one half of a photosensitive plate with four images; the plate is then moved by means of a cassette so that the second half can be exposed. After the prints have been made, they are cut up and mounted on cardboard, with each individual portrait measuring around nine by six centimeters, almost the size of a contemporary calling card, hence the name "carte de visite" (fig. 1). With this measure of standardization, Disdéri could offer a dozen portraits at a price for which customers previously would not have gotten even a single one. The patent, however, was of little use to Disdéri. He set a new industrial standard that would soon be copied by others, and after an unprecedented career he died impoverished and forgotten, while his format lived on until after 1900 (McCauley 1985; 1994).[3]

2   The case studies are based on my PhD dissertation *Operative Portraits*, HfG Karlsruhe 2017, published as Meyer 2019a, which gives a more nuanced and detailed account of what can only be sketched out here.

3   My presentation of Disdéri is very much indebted to Elizabeth McCauley's groundbreaking and still fundamental work on the subject. But while McCauley mainly focuses on the social and economic history of early portrait photography, as well as

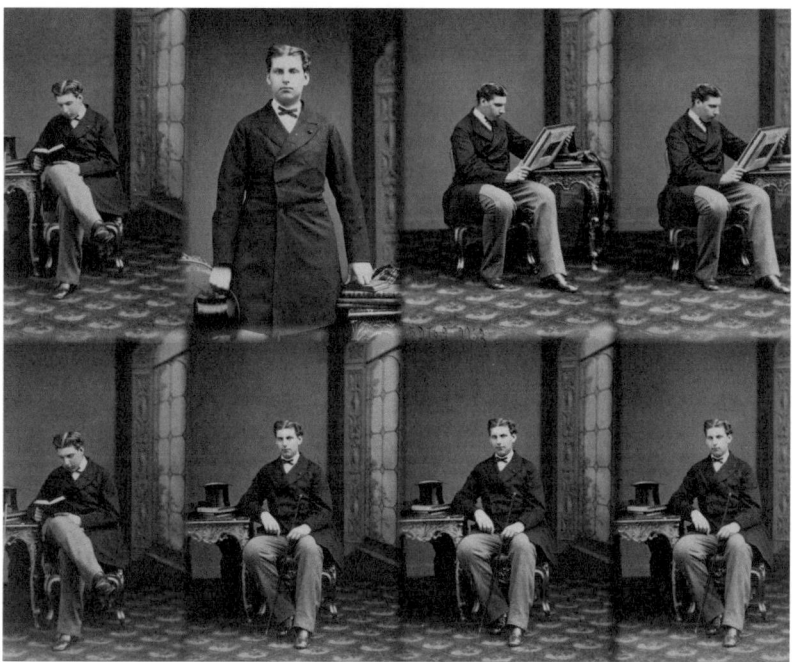

[Figure 1] Adolphe-Eugène Disdéri, uncut Carte-de-Visite sheet, around 1860. Source: George Eastman House Collections.

Formats, as is evident in Disdéri's standardizing operation, always presuppose a certain interpretation of preexisting technical media, their possibilities, affordances, and limitations. Before Disdéri, hardly anybody conceived of the photographic plate as a limited storage space whose efficiency can be multiplied by division and subdivision. And something else becomes apparent in Disdéri's economical view of picture production: formats in a technical sense are the effect of formatting procedures and are based on repeatable operations of division and partitioning, of establishing, specifying, and standardizing material and symbolic frames, arrangements, and dispositions that structure (visual) media.[4] Because the formatting of an image carrier limits the contingency of possible images, formats provide predictability and comparability. Thus, the standardization of pictorial formats proves to be an essential prerequisite for establishing the connectivity of image operations in large institutions and networks,

    its relations to portrait painting, I would like to develop in the following some of the more general implications of Disdéris practice for a history and theory of pictorial formats.

4   See also Jancovic in this volume.

meaning that formats, as Axel Volmar (2017) has convincingly stated, can be understood as "media of cooperation" (12).

The standardization of operations and predictability of their results also characterized the modes of production in Disdéri's studio, as well as those of other early portrait photographers in general. With the standardization of photographic formats, the large portrait studios, which were founded around 1860 in Paris and elsewhere, were able to establish a strict division of labor and thereby pioneer the commercial mass production of pictures (Kempe 1982; Tagg 1988, 34–59; Lalvani 1996, 66–68). In its best days, Disdéri's studio employed around 60 people, most of them doing routine tasks in pre- and postproduction, e.g., preparing the plate, producing the prints, cutting the cartes. But pictorial production itself became largely standardized as well, in that Disdéri personally went behind the camera only for very prominent customers, while employed "operators" did the day-to-day business according to his style specifications. The portrait photo thus became the standardized product of an aesthetic-technical apparatus in which a limited set of poses, a selection of interchangeable backgrounds, and a fixed repertoire of props could be continuously rearranged and recombined. And the existence of this apparatus became preliminary to every single photographic act. Before any image was taken, its essential coordinates had already been specified and determined. Rather than being individually chosen according to aesthetic (or ethical) considerations, a universal pictorial format now preceded the whole process of photographic production, thus determining what could become an image in the first place.

Formatting limits the contingency of possible images—and that's what makes it productive. The carte-de-visite format not only allowed for the mass production of photographic pictures based on the division of labor but also set in motion new social practices of images distribution. Technical images were becoming media of social communication for the first time. Since the cartes were designed for reproduction, and a minimum purchase of 25 pictures was not unusual, a portrait was hardly ever produced for oneself or one's own core family alone. Rather, the pictures were meant to circulate in more or less loose networks of friendship. Thus, they inherited older printed calling cards not only in respect to their physical measurements but also concerning their social function (McCauley 1985, 23). Calling cards as well as photographic cartes de visite were to be exchanged during visits and festive occasions, and they became sought-after collector's items, as they allowed a visible demonstration of the network of kinship and friendship of which one was part.

The place where this network manifested itself and became truly visible for the first time was the bourgeois family photo album—and this too, at least in its most popular format, was an effect of Disdéri's formatting (Maas 1977). The standardization of image sizes allowed for the production of pre-fabricated albums with standardized sections in which to put the cards (fig. 2). Sold in large quantities and integrated into a developing media economy of image exchange, these albums served as repositories that brought the circulation of photographic portraits to a temporary standstill and at the same time sped it up, as they were waiting to be filled with images of relatives and friends as well as of prominent personalities (Bickenbach 2001).

[Figure 2] Photo album, 1860s. Source: The Elisha Whittelsey Collection, The Elisha Whittelsey Fund, 1969.

In addition to the private production of portraits, the mass production of collectors' pictures in the 1860s became the most important source of income for the large photographers' studios. Statesmen, aristocrats, clergy members, military heroes, prominent figures from the arts and sciences, and stars of the vaudeville and theatre stage were called upon to sit as models, and their portraits, for which they usually granted the photographer all rights of commercial exploitation, were now "easily purchased and passed from hand to hand" (McCauley 1985, 86). Prominent and anonymous faces, in private portraits and commercial pictures, thus circulated through the same networks of exchange, and they became often mixed together in the same private albums. This new visual economy was mainly an effect of the preexistence of a universal format. Disdéri's standardizing operations decoupled the picture format from the specific image object and thus created a market in which portraits of almost any person could circulate under standardized conditions (Starl 1989, 12–18).

Bertillon: Controlling Capture, Universalizing Comparison

The history of the photographic portrait is a history of not only formats and formatting but also, through its standardization, increasing instrumentalization and operationalization. From its earliest years, photographic portraiture enabled individual representations that made it possible also to classify and identify individuals. One of the "primal scenes" of this operationalization of photography can be traced back directly to the new private culture of collecting and exchanging cartes de visite. Soon after the brutal suppression of the Paris Commune in 1871, a flourishing trade in collectible carte-de-visite portraits of leading communards began, which were sold individually or in entire albums. In order not to endanger the fragile "public peace," the sale of these pictures was soon forbidden by the police, who at the same time began to use them for their own purposes. Confiscated studio portraits of prominent communards were used to identify captured suspects and also sent to border posts to hunt down those who fled the capital. The success of these measures was limited but sufficient enough to politically enforce the police plans of photographing all prisoners and arrested suspects, which had been debated for years but could only now be put into practice (English 1984, 54–70).

Initially, the police commissioned commercial portrait photographers to photograph the arrested; it was not until 1879 that the Préfécture de Police set up its own photo studio. According to a statement by the Préfécture budget rapporteur in 1883, the photographic service had in only four years produced 75,000 images of suspects. But it was precisely this vast number of pictures taken that rendered them basically useless. To find out the true name of a suspect, one would need a photograph for comparison, but to find the photograph in the registers, which were sorted alphabetically, one would first need to have the name (Phéline 1985, 34).

Finding a single entry in an extensive collection is basically a problem of information retrieval, of indexing files, addressing data, and specifying metadata. Alphonse Bertillon's anthropometric system of identification, or "Bertillonage," which he developed in the 1880s as an answer to the problem just described, can be understood as an early attempt at devising a bureaucratic protocol for information retrieval. Moreover, Bertillon developed a new medium of photographic storage that could replace the older medium of the album, which was used by the police as well but had reached the limit of its efficiency due to photographic overproduction. Albums, be they bourgeois family albums or criminal mug-shot albums used by police, assemble mobile—or rather, mobilized—pictures into physically stabilized, materially limited, and visually assessable arrangements and constellations. Finding a picture in an album always needs a subject able to recollect and identify the order of the album and its contents. Basically, in an album, you more or less only find what—and whom—you already know. However, if the sheer number of pictures to be stored and collected becomes so huge that individual subjects are overwhelmed with their sorting and management, new media of access are required.[5]

This new medium developed by Bertillon, as Allan Sekula (1986) has classically analyzed it, is the archive, an expandable symbolic structure, in which every single image becomes a standardized and interchangeable element within a structure of relations and differences. All the protocols of information production, storage, and retrieval that Bertillon devised follow precisely specified standards, and their main goal was to disconnect the process of identification from the individual memory of the police officer, his ability (or inability) to recollect the physiognomic features and bodily marks of a suspect. The central element of his system was thus not the photograph or any visual representation at all, but a set of bodily measurements, a collection of numerical data that could be discretely notated and unambiguously sorted and compared. These anthropometric data formed the basis of a system of metadata that allocates to every single body, i.e., its photograph and the file card it is mounted on, a unique position within the structure of the archive. By measuring an anonymous body and comparing its data to the statistical mean (that was Bertillon's basic idea), one could calculate a stable and unforgeable code of identity, supposedly much more reliable than a name or a face.

In devising his system of identification, Bertillon undertook a double formatting of the police photograph. First, with his anthropometric file card

---

5   My account of Bertillon's operationalization of the photographic portrait is very much indebted to the classical studies by Phéline (1985) and Sekula (1986) as well as as Ellenbogen's detailed (2012) interpretation of Bertillon's theoretical stance toward the photographic image. In focusing on Bertillon's procedures of formatting, though, I hope to shed some light on the specific productivity of his system of identification: Bertillon not only standardized police photography but also combined the production of images and (meta)data in a way that in some respects prefigures today's digital culture.

or fiche, he created a hybrid storage format that combined photographic and written records, integrated visual data into numerical data sets, and made pictures as data retrievable using measurements as metadata (fig. 3). On the other hand, the pictures themselves were also being reformatted: not in terms of their external dimensions, but in terms of their internal organization. As far as the physical dimensions of his mug shots were concerned, Bertillon adopted the commercial carte-de-visite format, by then a commercial standard for over 20 years, out of "habit," as he writes (Bertillon 1895, 20). However, he used the limited space of the carte de visite in a fundamentally different way than the commercial portrait photographers did. Whereas Disdéri and his contemporaries used the carte-de-visite format vertically, for staging the individual in full figure in some kind of imaginary bourgeois interior or garden setting, Bertillon switched the format by 90 degrees, divided it into two segments, and used each print for two separate shots, *en profile* and *en face*, in front of a neutral background, a standard that had its model in ethnographic photography (Phéline 1985; Ellenbogen 2012).

[Figure 3] Alphonse Bertillon on one of his his anthropometric file cards, 1891. Source: Frizot 1985.

As stated before, formatting always presupposes a certain interpretation of existing media, their possibilities, affordances, and limitations. Disdéri interpreted the photographic plate as a limited storage space for pictures, and pictures as commodities that could be distributed more profitably the cheaper they were produced. Bertillon, on the other hand, interpreted photography as but one structural element in a system of capture or data acquisition (Meyer 2016a). Photographing becomes a form of measuring the body, a way of recording visual data. Accordingly, the photographic standards Bertillon devised are marked by their unconditional will to transform the photographic act into a repeatable "experimental situation" (Rheinberger 1997, 21), and controlling the conditions of capture as completely as possible is supposed to guarantee that comparable results are achieved regardless of the location and time of the recording. To this end, Bertillon designed a complex technological apparatus, meticulously arranging bodies and cameras, chairs and instruments, places, directions and distances (fig. 4). As Bertillon (1909) stated himself, this photographic "dispositif" was intended to force the "operateur" into "uniformity" and "precision," namely through the "material impossibility" of deviating from the standardized picture format (quoted in Phéline 1985, 13).

[Figure 4] Photographic studio of the Paris Préfécture de Police, around 1900. Source: Frizot 1985.

With this combination of data capture and picture production, Bertillon indeed established a new format for photographic portraits. And this format was not supposed to be limited to suspect identities and deviant subjects. On the contrary, as far as Bertillon was concerned, his system was a way of making all bodies comparable and thus providing each and every person with a uniquely defined and scientifically determined identity (Bertillon 1890). Perhaps the most notable example of this "inclusive" approach to identification is Bertillon's portrait of Émile Zola, which was created in 1896 as part of a comprehensive medical-psychological examination of the author (Hagner 2004, 192–93). Under the direction of the psychiatrist Edouard Toulouse, a team of scientific experts subjected Zola to a series of psychometric tests to determine his memory and his responsiveness to stimuli, they prepared graphological and hereditary reports, and examined his fingerprints as well as his urine. Zola himself saw the result as a document of his "physical and moral individuality," which presented his brain to the public "like in a glass skull" (Toulouse 1896, v–vi). Bertillon was responsible for recording Zola's anatomy and physiognomy and determining possible deviations from the statistical norm. Somewhat disappointingly, given the extraordinary significance of his subject, he concluded his report by stating that the anatomical characteristics of Zola "do not exceed the limits of normal variation" (Toulouse 1896, 142).

The example shows how Bertillon's new format of the photographic portrait went far beyond a mere "means of surveillance" (Jäger 2001). Rather than being only intended to make recidivist criminals identifiable, the interweaving of photographic production and data acquisition aimed to make any "ordinary" body comparable with any other "ordinary" body, to record its deviations from the mean and locate them in a distribution of differences. Individual identity thus becomes relational and structural, based as it is on the acquisition and comparison of large sets of anthropometric data (Meyer 2016b). A quite similar project was undertaken by Francis Galton at the same time. Since 1882, Galton had been promoting the establishment of "anthropometric laboratories" in England, "where a man may, when he pleases, get himself and his children weighed, measured, and rightly photographed, and have their bodily faculties tested by the best methods known to modern science" (Galton 1883, 40–41). Unsurprisingly, being "rightly" photographed for Galton also meant according to anthropometric standards, i.e., in a format combining two headshots *en profile* and *en face*.

Formatting creates the means for comparison— and not only between individuals. The standardization of the means of recording also makes visible the changes of a body and a face in the course of time. Both Bertillon and Galton saw this form of biographical (self-)recording as a valuable enterprise. From the birth of his nephew François through François's youth, Bertillon regularly made anthropometric photographs of him documenting his development (Meyer 2016a). Similarly, Galton propagated a *Life History Album* with which parents could record the physical changes of their off-spring from year to year until they themselves would be able to continue their self-tracking autonomously (Galton 1902).

In a sense, projects such as these drew a radical consequence from Disdéri's formatting, standardization, and serialization of the photographic portrait: if the classical individual portrait was based on the idea of the uniqueness of the person, represented in an equally unique picture, the standardization of formats created spaces of comparability that preceded every individual act of pictorial production. The photographic picture ceased to function as the representative double of a unique individual; instead, it became a serialized document of the always repeatable confrontation of a random subject with an anonymous apparatus of data acquisition.

Facebook: Unbounding Access, Distribution, and Comparison

Neither the history of mass portrait production nor that of police identification ends with the formats of Disdéri or Bertillon. One could, for example, draw a line from Disdéri's cartes, across the photo booth portraits popularized in the 1920s, to today's selfie culture, or from Bertillon's fiches past the invention of fingerprinting around 1900 and the introduction of obligatory passport photographs during World War I to their biometric standardization after 9/11.[6] But all of these examples, in a way, still follow one of the two logistics of the image introduced earlier, falling rather neatly into the spheres of either commercial pictorial production and private exchange or bureaucratic data acquisition and institutional identification. With my third example, though, I would like to show that the boundary between these spheres has become quite blurry during the last two decades.

With the beginnings of Facebook in the early 2000s, we once again witness a kind of "primordial scene" of appropriation and reformatting. As is well known, not least through David Fincher's movie *The Social Network* (2010), the story of Facebook started in autumn 2003 with a legendary hack, through which Mark Zuckerberg illegally gained access to the Harvard

6   These and other episodes are discussed in Meyer 2019a.

servers and thus to the digital image data of the university's college year-books, the so-called face books. These official collections of freshman portraits, which had a decades-old tradition as printed albums or "Freshman Registers," were by then already online, but only available within the social limits of Harvard's dormitories. Zuckerberg took these portraits and used them to launch a website he called Facemash, which allowed visitors to view and compare the photos of their fellow students, without any limitations. The site was inspired by the then very popular—and quite misogynistic—photo rating site hotornot.com, and featured a telling motto: "Were we let in for our looks? No. Will we be judged on them? Yes." (Mezrich 2010, 49).

Again, we are dealing with a practice of reinterpreting an existing pictorial format—whereby the images themselves remain unchanged, but their status is redefined by their embedding in a new data structure. The result was a new logistics of access to an already existing population of images. What previously remained a common, informal social practice, namely leafing through the yearbooks and spitefully comparing the portraits, now became technically implemented and socially unbounded. Although Zuckerberg only sent the link to his site to a few friends to test it, it got more than 22,000 hits within a few hours. But protests arose almost as quickly; not least, complaints from feminist campus groups eventually led to Facemash being taken off the net and Zuckerberg being warned by the university. Obviously, he didn't let himself be discouraged for long. Less than half a year later, thefacebook.com went online, and regardless of its infamous prehistory, within just one month half of the Harvard under-graduates registered and voluntarily uploaded their images and profile data (Kirkpatrick 2011, 23–25).

In its early years, Facebook allowed only a single image in its otherwise largely text-based interface: the standard "profile picture." However, some users soon started changing their profile picture several times a day—and thus assigned a new function to it: what was meant to be a static rep-resentation became a dynamic status update. Facebook responded quickly to this development, and in autumn 2005 launched the Photos feature, which in a very short time made it the largest photo sharing platform ever (Kirkpatrick 2011, 153–57). The history of Facebook Photos shows once again how formatting can become productive by being restrictive. Compared to photo sharing platforms such as Flickr, which were already established at the time, Photos' usability was extremely limited. Where Flickr allowed freely chosen categories to tag motifs, genres, and camera types, Facebook used a tagging function that allowed nothing else but to link a face with a name and a profile. Showing private photos to friends, pointing to faces, and naming names is as old as the photo album. But with Facebook's technical implementation, this largely innocent social practice changed its character completely. If someone is marked on a photo in Facebook, then the friends of this person get to see these pictures as well. Identification between friends thus becomes the key mechanism of an almost uncontrollable logistics of images in which labeling and distribution are merged into a single operation (Hand 2012, 173–78).

What Facebook still anachronistically calls an "album" has thus largely changed its function. What once was a material medium for the storage and arrangement of photographic prints has become a database function, serving less to stabilize collections than to mobilize mass image flows. These digital albums channel digital data streams (the size of which would exceed any physical album or institutional archive), regulate their visibility as images, and link them to data profiles and communication networks. In turn, the maintenance and growth of these profiles and networks become by and large functions of the constant circulation of images as data.

By limiting tagging to facial identification, Facebook Photos not only sets in motion a new logistics of distribution but also creates a huge database of individual faces identified by name and linked to personal profiles. It is no coincidence that in recent years Facebook has become one of the leading developers of face recognition algorithms. Today's facial recognition algorithms are increasingly based on machine learning: instead of analyzing faces according to fixed rules and comparing them using predefined features, as was the rule until a few years ago, new algorithms optimize their parameters and criteria autonomously. They learn how to discriminate faces by searching for patterns in vast populations of images. By analyzing many different photographs of the same person, they become better and better at identifying the particular patterns specific to that individual's face (Alpaydin 2016). With its endless series of tagged photographs of known individuals, taken in different circumstances, under varying lighting conditions and over large spans of time, Facebook's databases offer an optimal testing ground for this form of machine learning. Thus, it came as no surprise when Facebook's research department proudly announced in 2014 that its DeepFace software had (almost) successfully closed the "performance gap" between human and machine face recognition (Taigman et al. 2014).

DeepFace is interesting not only because it would probably never have been created without the globally distributed participation of millions of

Facebook users but also because it shows how today the production of comparability by means of formatting has moved from production to post-production. Since the beginnings of automated face recognition around 1970, one thing has remained largely unchanged: optimum comparability presupposes strict frontality (Gates 2011, 25–61; Kammerer 2014). However, this frontality, which is still required for "biometric" ID-cards, can now be produced by retrospective simulation. Before the artificial neural networks begin to analyze digital face images, DeepFace first rotates them in virtual space (fig. 5). Based on individual feature points, a grid-shaped 3D model of the face is created, onto which the digital pixel image is then projected. Even semi-profiles can be "frontalized" in this way (Meyer 2018). Thus, in a certain way, pictorial formats have become flexible and preliminary under the digital conditions of elementary addressability and complete computability, as formal standards can always be algorithmically superimposed in postproduction.

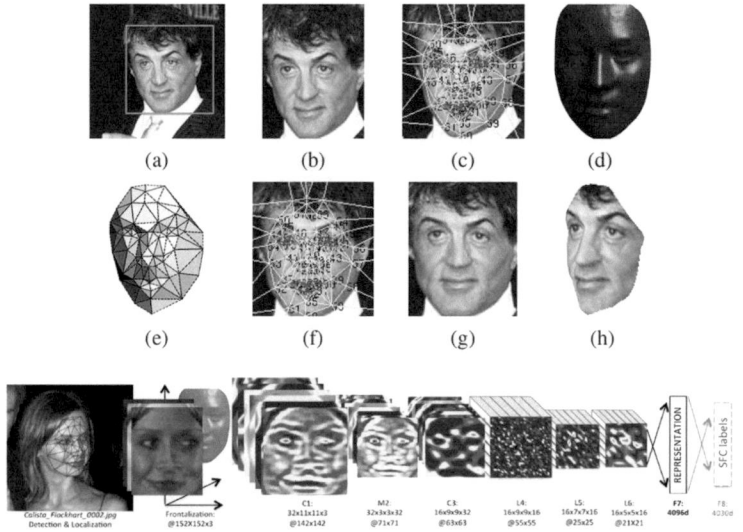

[Figure 5] Facebook's *DeepFace* facial recognition algorithm, 2014. Source: Taigman et al. 2014.

Facebook and similar platforms realize what can be characterized as a digital short-circuit of the two logistics of the image I have described in the first parts of this essay: the mass circulation of private portraits and the institutional instrumentalization of photographic documents as sets of data. Furthermore, with these platforms, we witness what could be called the preliminary endpoint of a history of (photographic) portraiture in which operationality increasingly replaces representation. Rather than re-presenting a supposedly stable identity that prefigures its pictorial representation, the billions of digital portraits circulating on social networks contribute to the continuous and never-ending production of digital identities. As digital portraits become elements in operational processes of connecting and comparing them to each other and aggregating them to data profiles, identity turns into an ever-expanding network of images and data, held together by processes of algorithmic comparison. Although social media platforms like Facebook do everything they can to stabilize online identities and prevent their proliferation, the profiles they aggregate are not fixed entities but rather fluid processes, the continuously updated products of operational chains involving large populations of images. And characteristically, these operational chains no longer require the prior formatting of the visual or pictorial form of the image—rather, under the digital condition, the data structures in which image files are embedded and the resulting possibilities of relating images as data sets to other data sets prove to be the decisive format specifications.

Coda: What Formatting Does

While the short case studies I presented in this essay may not lead us to a precise theoretical definition of what a "format" is, they provided us with some preliminary theses on what formatting pictures *does*, which I hope can prove useful in studying the role of pictorial formats in visual culture:

1. Formats are always the product of formatting. Rather than simply having a format, pictures are subjected to repeatable and standardizable processes of formatting: of establishing, specifying, and standardizing material and symbolic frames, arrangements, divisions, and dispositions. Such processes of formatting organize and structure pictures as products of media technologies and embed them within larger technical ensembles such as albums, archives, and databases.

2. As a cultural and economic practice, formatting always requires a certain interpretation of media technologies, their possibilities, affordances, and limitations. Formatting can be seen as a form of investment: it analyses the opportunities already latent in technological apparatuses and tries to systemize their usage, optimize their use of resources, and maximize their effects.

3. Formatting is thus more often than not some kind of re-formatting: new formats are generally based on existing formats, which they further specify, differentiate, supplement, and extend.

4. Most important, formatting becomes productive because and in so far as its effects are mostly restrictive: formats channel, accelerate, and intensify modes of production and networks of circulation; they create expectability and thus the possibility of new practices, apparatuses, and formats of collecting, comparing, and connecting; and in doing so, they change the way we not only deal with images but also think about ourselves, about who we are, what constitutes our identity, and how individuality can be determined with and through images.

References

Alpaydin, Ethem. 2016. *Machine Learning: The New AI*. Cambridge, MA: MIT Press.

Belting, Hans. 2014. *An Anthropology of Images: Picture, Medium, Body*. Princeton, NJ: Princeton University Press.

Bertillon, Alphonse. 1890. *Das anthropometrische Signalement: Neue Methode zu Identitäts-Feststellungen, Vortrag am internationalen Congresse* für Straf- und *Gefängnisswesen zu Rom*. Berlin: Fischer's Medicinische Buchhandlung.

———. 1895. *Die Gerichtliche Photographie: Mit einem Anhange über die anthropometrische Classification und Identificierung*. Halle a. S.: Knapp.

Bickenbach, Matthias. 2001. "Das Dispositiv des Fotoalbums: Mutation kultureller Erinnerung. Nadar und das Pantheon." In *Medien der Präsenz: Museum, Bildung und Wissenschaft im 19. Jahrhundert*, edited by Jürgen Fohrmann, Andrea Schütte, and Wilhelm Vosskamp, 87–128. Cologne: DuMont.

Bowker, Geoffrey C., and Susan Leigh Star. 1999. *Sorting Things Out: Classification and Its Consequences*. Cambridge, MA: MIT Press.

Bruhn, Matthias. 2003. *Bildwirtschaft: Verwaltung und Verwertung der Sichtbarkeit*. Weimar: VDG.

Ellenbogen, Josh. 2012. *Reasoned and Unreasoned Images: The Photography of Bertillon, Galton, and Marey*. University Park: Pennsylvania State University Press.

English, Donald E. 1984. *Political Uses of Photography in the Third French Republic 1871–1914*. Ann Arbor: UMI Research Press.

Frizot, Michel, ed. 1985. *Identités: De Disderi au photomaton*. Paris: Centre National de la Photographie.

Galton, Francis. 1883. *Inquiries into Human Faculty and Its Development*. London: MacMillan.

———. 1902. *Life History Album: Tables and Charts for Recording the Development of Body and Mind from Childhood Upwards, with Introductory Remarks*. London: MacMillan.

Gates, Kelly. 2011. *Our Biometric Future: Facial Recognition Technology and the Culture of Surveillance*. New York: New York University Press.

Hagner, Michael. 2004. *Geniale Gehirne: Zur Geschichte der Elitegehirnforschung*. Göttingen: Wallstein.

Hand, Martin. 2012. *Ubiquitous Photography*. Cambridge: Polity.

Heidenreich, Stefan. 2004. *FlipFlop: Digitale Datenströme und die Kultur des 21. Jahrhunderts*. Munich: Hanser.

Jäger, Jens. 2001. "Photography: A Means of Surveillance? Judicial Photography, 1850 to 1900." *Crime, History & Societies* 5 (1): 27–51.

Joselit, David. 2012. *After Art*. Princeton, NJ: Princeton University Press.

———. 2015 "What to Do with Pictures" [2011]. In *Mass Effect: Art and the Internet in the Twenty-First Century*, edited by Lauren Cornell and Ed Halter, 267–84. Cambridge, MA: MIT Press.

Kammerer, Dietmar. 2014. "Die automatische Zukunft der Kameraaugen." In *Phantombilder: Zur Sicherheit und Unsicherheit im biometrischen Überwachungsbild*, edited by Ulrich Richtmeyer, 149–59. Munich: Fink.

Kempe, Fritz. 1982. "Atelier und Apparat des Photographen." In *Lichtbildnisse: Das Porträt in der Fotografie*, edited by Klaus Honnef, 26–40. Cologne: Rheinland.

Kirkpatrick, David. 2011. *The Facebook Effect: The Real Inside Story of Mark Zuckerberg and the World's Fastest-Growing Company*. London: Virgin Books.

Krajewski, Markus. 2007. "In Formation: Aufstieg und Fall der Tabelle als Paradigma der Datenverarbeitung." *Nach Feierabend* 3: 37–55.

Lalvani, Suren. 1996. *Photography, Vision, and the Production of Modern Bodies*. Albany: State University of New York Press.

Maas, Ellen. 1977. *Die goldenen Jahre der Photoalben. Fundgrube und Spiegel von Gestern*. Cologne: DuMont.

McCauley, Elizabeth Anne. 1985. *A.A.E. Disdéri and the Carte de Visite Portrait Photograph*. New Haven, CT: Yale University Press.

———. 1994. *Industrial Madness: Commercial Photography in Paris, 1848–1871*. New Haven, CT: Yale University Press.

Meyer, Roland. 2016a. "Operative Porträts: Formate und Protokolle erkennungsdienstlicher Bildproduktion um 1900." In *Wie Bilder Dokumente wurden*, edited by Renate Wöhrer, 121–39. Berlin: Kadmos.

———. 2016b. "Augmented Crowds: Identity Management, Face Recognition, and Crowd Monitoring." In *Social Media–New Masses*, edited by Inge Baxmann, Timon Beyes, and Claus Pias, 101–16. Chicago: University of Chicago Press.

———. 2018. "False Positives: Operative Bilder der Gesichtserkennung 1970/1991/2014." In *Visualität und Abstraktion. Eine Aktualisierung des Figur-Grund-Verhältnisses*, edited by Hanne Loreck, 144–59. Hamburg: Materialverlag.

———. 2019a. *Operative Porträts: Eine Bildgeschichte der Identifizierbarkeit von Lavater bis Facebook*. Konstanz: Konstanz University Press.

———. 2019b. "Gesichtsbildformate 1860/1960: Disdéri, Warhol und der Primat der Zirkulation." In *Politiken des Formats*, edited by Magdalena Nieslony and Yvonne Schweizer. Bern: Lang (in print).

Mezrich, Ben. 2010. *The Accidental Billionaires: The Founding of Facebook*. London: Arrow Books.

Mitchell, W. J. T. 1994. *Picture Theory: Essays on Verbal and Visual Representation*. Chicago: University of Chicago Press.

Phéline, Christian. 1985. *L'image acusatrice*. Paris: Les Cahiers de la Photographie.

Pichler, Wolfram, and Ralph Ubl. 2014. *Bildtheorie zur Einführung*. Hamburg: Junius.

Rheinberger, Hans-Jörg. 1997. *Toward a History of Epistemic Things: Synthesizing Proteins in the Test Tube*. Stanford, CA: Stanford University Press.

Sekula, Allan. 1986. "The Body and the Archive." *October* 39: 3–64.

Starl, Timm. 1989. "Der Faden des Gedächtnisses: Über Fotoalben im 19. Jahrhundert." In *Welt-Geschichten. Fotoalben aus der Sammlung Herzog*, edited by Martin Heller, 9–41. Zürich: Limmat.

Sterne, Jonathan. 2012. *MP3: The Meaning of a Format*. Durham, NC: Duke University Press.

Summers, David. 2003. *Real Spaces: World Art History and the Rise of Western Modernism*. New York: Phaidon.

Tagg, John. 1988. *The Burden of Representation: Essays on Photographies and Histories*. New York and Houndmills: Palgrave Macmillan.

Taigman, Yaniv, Ming Yang, Marc'Aurelio Ranzato, and Lior Wolf. 2014. "DeepFace: Closing the Gap to Human-Level Performance in Face Verification." In *Proceedings of the IEEE Conference on Computer Vision and Pattern Recognition*, 1701–08.

Toulouse, Edouard. 1896. *Enquête médico-psychologique sur la supériorité intellectuelle: Émile Zola*. Paris: Societé d' Editions scientifique.

Volmar, Axel. 2017. "Formats as Media of Cooperation." *Media in Action* 2 (2017): 9–28.

8

Instant Failure: Polaroid's Polavision, 1977–1980

Erika Balsom

"An Instant Dud for Polaroid": the title of the April 16, 1979, *Newsweek* article captured the prevailing sentiment about Polavision, the instant motion-picture format introduced only two years earlier after more than a decade in active development (Langway and Malamud 1979). With a camera using cartridges containing Super 8mm film and a 12-inch rear-projection playback device that doubled as a developing chamber, Polavision was a proprietary system for shooting, processing, and exhibiting film—a resurrection of the triple functionality of the Lumière Cinématographe—that was first made available to the amateur arena in 1977 for an introductory list price of $699 ($2,785 in 2016 dollars).[1] The cartridges held silent "phototape" (as Polaroid called it), which could be edited only in-camera, producing a color image through an additive process recalling the Dufaycolor process used by Len Lye in the 1930s. When popped into the top of the viewer, the rewinding of the exposed film punctured a reagent pod, releasing developing chemicals. In only 90 seconds, two minutes and 35 seconds of film was ready to be played at 18 frames per second.

Polavision promised instantaneity, simplicity, and efficiency; it significantly limited the variables involved at each stage of the filmic process in the hope of enabling virtually anyone to make and exhibit movies. User participation was encouraged not by offering flexibility and customization but by

---

1   According to the US Bureau of Labor Statistics' Consumer Price Index inflation calculator, http://www.bls.gov/data/inflation_calculator.htm.

severely curtailing the need for skill and decision making. To appropriate the language of computer coding, Polavision operated at a higher level of abstraction than a typical film system in that it automated processes that would otherwise require manual operation. Polavision offered a complete and closed ecosystem and embraced reduced functionality in an attempt to democratize production. Its constraints asserted themselves aggressively. But through this, the format courted the impression of immediacy, as the user would not be nagged by the many questions that habitually accompany film production and exhibition, such as how long the film should be, what lens to use, where to develop the film, how to edit it, or where to project it.

Despite Polavision's simplicity and its anticipation of a prosumer user experience that has since become widespread, Louis Lumière's declaration about his short-lived Cinématographe would prove true of its late-20th-century descendant too; it was an invention without a future. The *Newsweek* reporters canvased for reactions. "'This is an all-time turkey,' grouses the manager of a large photo-products store in Chicago. 'It's a real dud'" (Langway and Malamud 1979, n.p.). Marvin Saffian, a Wall Street analyst, was no less forgiving, matching Polavision's triple functionality with a triple condemnation: "Polavision is just the wrong product for the wrong market at the wrong time" (Langway and Malamud 1979, n.p.). After costing an estimated $200 million in research, development, production, and marketing, the commercial failure of Polavision culminated in September 1979 with a $68.5 million write-down to a nominal value of the remaining inventory and standing commitments to Eumig, the Austrian manufacturer of the hardware. By the end of the year, some retailers had cut prices by as much as 60 percent (Fanelli 1979). However, during its brief life, Polavision would draw interest from experimental filmmakers such as Stan Brakhage, Morgan Fisher, and Andy Warhol—figures whose engagement with the format would both makes claims as to its specificity and take it far beyond Polaroid's anticipated uses.

Polavision could easily be consigned to the media-historical dustbin, seen as little more than a passion project of Polaroid founder Edwin Land that ill-advisedly came to market two years after the introduction of Betamax. Instant film was a doomed product in the age of video; in this regard, Polavision appears as a prolepsis of the fate met later by Polaroid's still cameras at the hands of the digital. But unlike Polaroid photography, which has recently received significant attention, Polavision has been overlooked aside from a pioneering consideration by Elizabeth Czach (2002).[2] Yet there is ample reason to reconsider the quirky episode of instant movies, and not simply because new research materials have become available since Czach's 2002 article. Polavision's reappraisal chimes with the archaeological interest in failed media—what Bruce Sterling called in 1995, "media that have died on the barbed wire of technological advance, media that didn't make it, martyred media, dead media" (n.p.)—due to their ability to question hegemonic logics of innovation by raising the specter of untaken paths and unfulfilled futures. But pursuing such a variantology of the media, to use Siegfried Zielinski's phrase, must do more than simply produce a catalog of curiosities. Turning to Polavision resonates, too, with what Jonathan Sterne (2012) calls "format theory"; namely, an approach that "ask[s] us to modulate the scale of our analysis of media somewhat differently" (11), paying attention to the technical systems, infrastructures, and standards that constitute formats rather than emphasizing content or the larger category of the medium.

The idea of format is closely aligned with the study of digital media. Sterne, for instance, develops the concept in the context of his book on the MP3. Why this heuristic would be useful for the analysis of digital devices should be clear: such devices throw into crisis traditional conceptions of the medium by accommodating numerous platforms and file formats within a single machine. And yet, format theory is tremendously useful for the study of analog media, as it entails adopting a more granular level of analysis than is conventional, breaking apart an entity such as "photochemical film"—often erroneously discussed as if it were a single thing—to reveal the varied technologies encompassed by this category and the diverse experiences and ecologies to which they give rise. Polavision is a particularly fascinating object in this regard, as it rejects many of the characteristics often thought of as fundamental to photochemical film and is thus especially well positioned to respond to the pressing imperative to recover the historical heterogeneity of cinema. As Haidee Wasson (2015) writes, "The cinema we have long loved and often naturalised in our theories and histories is a highly specific one, utterly dependent on a normative industrial ideal that belies the contingency shaping one particular, persistent technological settlement" (58). What is dominant is too often misrecognized as what is essential. This naturalization occurs in numerous fashions, but today the construction of a monolithic notion of cinema often takes shape as the long-standing stability of its historical material support

2   On Polaroid photography, see Bonanos (2012), Buse (2016), Hitchcock (2009) and Lombino (2013).

(photochemical film) and normative exhibition situation (the movie theater) are invoked in opposition to the manifold formats, traveling images, and flexible apparatuses of the digital. As this narrative would have it, the analog-to-digital transition is one from the singular to the multiple, from a sole cinema to many multimedia environments. However, as Wasson emphasizes, there has long been more than one cinematic apparatus, and the cinema has long been "reconfigured, rearticulated and recombined" across diverse technical supports and locations (58). Considering a marginal format like Polavision allows one to illuminate these processes, to unsettle received ideas and install in their place a more nuanced and historical account of the non-self-identity the cinema has always possessed. Following Wasson's call for "understanding cinema as a family of formats" (61), Polavision emerges as that odd cousin twice removed: a family member quite different from the rest of the clan and usually forgotten but whom it would be rude not to invite to a major gathering.

I.

The dream of Polavision is as old as instant photography. When Land first demonstrated Polaroid's one-step still cameras in February 1947, the idea that the same technology might be deployed to make instant movies was already on his mind. He emphasized that his process was "inherently adaptable" and might be used "for making motion pictures" (Laurence 1947, 15). According to Peter C. Wensberg (1987), senior vice president of marketing at Polaroid from 1971 to 1982, Polavision was "developed by [Land's] fiat"; "The *why* was never examined" (223). Land (1977) described the system as "one of our earliest and most challenging dreams," which "in coming to maturation has utilized all of our own accumulated understanding" and "issues not only from the persistent vision of a few people, but also from the enthusiastic efforts of hundreds" (225). Polavision would be both Land's last significant undertaking after decades of invention and his greatest failure.

Following years in development under the code name "Sesame," the system became public knowledge without Polaroid's approval in the March 1974 issue of *Popular Science*. Reporter Robert Gorman, having researched recently filed patents in an effort to speculate on what Polaroid's next major offering would be, produced a remarkably accurate picture of the system that would be named Polavision one year later, including a detailed diagram of what the cassette's interior workings might look like (Gorman 1974). In response, Polaroid's Eelco Wolf (1974) issued a memorandum to all publicity managers on March 7, setting out the company's position in case of any press inquiries: the as-yet-unnamed product was part of the corporation's ongoing research into instant transparencies, still in the development stage, and did not yet possess "any marketing dates or timetables."

Polavision's public launch occurred three years later on April 26, 1977, in the presence of some 3,800 stockholders and 200 members of the press at Polaroid's 40th annual meeting in Needham, Massachusetts. Attendees were given cameras and encouraged to film the jugglers, mimes, and members of the Boston Ballet Company who had been called in to perform. They could then instantly develop their cartridges and view the results. Following this carnivalesque demonstration, Land addressed the crowd. "The new system," he said, "is a way to relate ourselves to life and each other" ("Shareholders Astounded" 1977, 6). In subsequent promotional copy, this social dimension was repeatedly emphasized, with Polavision trumpeted as producing "living pictures." A memorandum produced to accompany the European introduction of the system is representative:

> Polavision offers besides home entertainment, real opportunities to be creative, active, and to stay away from the tube, which is eating into so much of people's leisure time. . . . It activates people, brings social involvement, stimulates family-life, and opens communication. (Polaroid Corporation Amsterdam 1978)

Unlike the supposedly passive reception of television, Polavision offered active creativity in the home and, through the feedback mechanism of its (near-)instant playback, the possibility of collapsing the stages of production and exhibition into a single, shared encounter of intimate sociality.

The idea that the specificity of Polavision might reside in its relational possibilities emerges as particularly significant when one compares how radically different these are from those of more conventional film formats. What one might call the cinema's circulatory reproducibility—that is, its ability to be distributed to diverse publics through the production of multiple copies—has long been held to be one of its central attributes as a medium and is inextricably tied to its social function. Polavision performs a double withdrawal from what Walter Benjamin (2002) discerned as the tremendous exhibition value of cinema, understood dialectically as both the reservoir of its utopian potential (mass culture as collective enervation) and the harbor of its most dystopian possibilities (mass culture as mass deception). First, like many other small-gauge formats, Polavision relocated the film experience into the domestic realm, thus taming its potential to act as an alternative public sphere and opening onto other forms of relationality, in this case closely tethered to the act of filming and viewing with friends and family. But second and perhaps more important, Polavision produced a unique object. Like Polaroid photographs, Polavision cassettes could not be duplicated (short of scanning or rephotographing them on another format), distinctly tying the format to private ownership and situating it far outside the economy of the multiple that the cinema has historically inhabited.[3] Though the film inside the cassette was the same size as Super 8mm, it was unable to be projected on Super 8mm projectors due to the thickness and opacity of the filmstrip, which resulted from its additive color process.

While Polaroid photographs can be easily given away and thus circulate far from the apparatus of their production and its owner, Polavision depended absolutely on the playback apparatus to be viewed. While one could trade cassettes with another owner, the strong likelihood was that Polavision films would remain closely bound to their producer, making it in some sense a proprietary format twice over. Polaroid fabricated the system hardware to be incompatible with any existing film technologies, giving the corporation end-to-end control. But such a notion is also an apposite description of the user's relationship to the apparatus, as within Polavision's limited parameters the entire production-distribution-exhibition complex occurs without the intervention of any external agents, in a tightly bound circuit. This restricted circulation suggests that Polavision's investment in nurturing relatedness had little to do with advancing any notion of a democratic public sphere of shared media experience. Rather, it suggests a privatized sociality that might serve as a remedy to an increasingly fragmented family unit. Understanding Polavision as a wholesome domestic activity resulting in the production of lasting memories was to conceive of it as reparative technology, a form of social glue.

Polavision sacrificed circulatory reproducibility so as to emphasize film's referential reproducibility—the image's intimate closeness to the pro-filmic scenes it captures. While this closeness has often been under-stood according to the notion of the indexical trace, Polavision made its claims for proximity to the profilmic not simply through this spatio-material relation of touch but via the temporal category of the instant.

3   Though Polavision footage can now be transferred to video, as of March 1979 Polaroid reported being incapable of duplicating its cassettes (von Thuna 1979).

Instantaneous development enabled the reception of Polavision cassettes to function as immediate feedback, offering a reflective experience of a situation perhaps still ongoing, which might then be rethought, modified, or otherwise acted upon depending on what one witnessed onscreen. This temporality was understood as a key element of the specificity of the then-emerging medium of video and has since become a major feature of vernacular uses of digital video, particularly as circulated on social networking platforms. Polavision broke from film's firm alignment with pastness to instead approach these looping circuits. Its closing of the inter-val between exposure and exhibition was given graphic metaphorization in Polaroid's promotional images depicting a movement on the Polavision screen exceeding the frame to occupy the surrounding "real" space as well, as if to suggest that the movement occupies the profilmic and filmic realms simultaneously, temporally proximate as they are. In one such image, a white bird's wing breaks through the right of the frame while its body is onscreen; in another, the image onscreen shows a boy holding a beach ball, while three more such balls extend above the top of the frame, as if to suggest a trajectory of movement that breaches the picture plane. "Living pictures," indeed.

II.

In the summer of 1977, Charles Eames and Ray Eames began work on a promotional film for Polavision, continuing the relationship with Polaroid that had commenced in 1972 when they were commissioned to make a film about the SX-70, the instant camera Polaroid introduced that year to great success. Ted Voss, vice president of marketing, began to discuss the Polavision project with the Eameses as early as January 1976. By the time Polavision launched in California in November 1977—five months before it was available nationally—the 10-minute *Polavision* was finished, and the Eames Office in Venice, California, served as the location for three days of press visits.

Polaroid's objectives in branding Polavision are nowhere as clearly articulated as they are in *Polavision*. The film reinforces the emphasis on privatized sociality that runs through Polaroid's corporate literature, staging its uses of the system primarily within a suburban, nuclear family context and suggesting that "perhaps in the long run the greatest value" will not be the films themselves but "will be something that grows out of th[e] experience" of making and watching them together. Polavision was a social medium *avant la lettre*, albeit one of intimate circulation. Contrary to the cinema's unidirectional reception, Polavision's sociality was overtly participatory and marked by multiple vectors of interaction between what would today be called "prosumers." Polavision was not something to watch; it was something to *do*. This experience, rather than the quality of the filmic product, was its locus of value.

Like *SX-70* (1972), *Polavision* employs voice-over narration and a whimsical soundtrack by Elmer Bernstein to stress the ingenuity and creativity of Polaroid technology, while offering basic instructions for use. Key differences between the two films, however, index Polaroid's under-standing of the respective marketing needs of each product. *SX-70* devotes a substantial portion of its 10-minute duration to an in-depth explanation of the intricacies of the camera's functioning and shows many possible methods and purposes for producing photographs without advocating in favor of one over another. *Polavision* presents the system as a technology about which it is unnecessary to know much, if anything, of its inter-nal workings, while advancing a particular prescription for how to use it successfully. *Polavision* thus addresses the user of the system as a barely competent amateur—indeed, children are extensively featured—positioned at some distance from the technologically curious photographer addressed in *SX-70*. This might be due to the relative rarity of proficiency in filmmaking when compared with still photography, but it also suggests a concerted strategy to transform Polavision's limitations into benefits for the user. Polaroid and the Eames Office decided to avoid indulging power users' interest in the complexities of hardware and instead forged an analogy between Polavision's absence of complication and the simple happiness of idealized family interaction.[4]

The pedagogical thrust of *Polavision* prescribes a single strategy for success not emphasized in Polaroid's own copy: planning. In a 1981 draft for an article on the Eames Office's involvement with Polaroid, staff member Jehane Burns wrote,

> The "limitations" of Polavision—the short tape, the need to edit in the camera and not afterwards—were more than half the magic. Immediate reward for good planning—that was the first moral, and it

---

4   This black-boxing may be understood as prefiguring the more recent tendency in user experience design to mask complexity and offer a surface simplicity at the level of the interface. Today, this constitutes a dominant ideology in the design of consumer hardware and software, but Polavision embraced this strategy long before it was fashionable, at a time when many technologies operated at a lower level of abstraction. Exemplary of this approach are Krug (2014) and Raskin (2000).

made Polavision one of the most powerful learning—self-educatiing? [*sic*]—devices that ever came into the office.[5]

Here the emphasis is again placed not on the value of Polavision's material outcomes—that is, the notion that it might result in quality films—but on its ability to produce a particular experience for the prosumer: not only family interaction but self-education through feedback. Burns's notion of "good planning" pervades *Polavision*, as the film prescribes strategies for vanquishing the capturing of contingency that one might think of as central to the home movie. Since footage shot on Polavision could not be edited later, it became all the more imperative that the processes of selection and sequencing be displaced from postproduction to preproduction.

Polavision opens with a man and a woman shooting a production of *Macbeth* performed by children, with each scene storyboarded on paper. Later, a brief interview with animator William Hurtz, "one of the great storyboarders," reassures the viewer that no skill in drawing is needed to create a successful storyboard—just an aptitude for parsing the main elements of a scene. The chase is suggested as a suitable narrative for the format, and the production of a clear beginning, middle, and end is deemed a "satisfaction" and "challenge." *Polavision* also showcases how in-camera editing can be used for stop-motion animation, time-lapse, and trick effects—all techniques that rely on taming the potential spontaneity of recording and that serve to break the flow of real time. In short, Polavision is presented as a tool that might help one to develop skills of organization and systematization—aptitudes of significant value in grappling with life in the electronic age. In this regard, the Eameses' approach to the format is very much in line with their established interest in training the sensorium to operate successfully in information-rich environments, particularly through forms of media pedagogy that turn to cinematic practices beyond the standard apparatus.[6] As much as *Polavision* wistfully partakes in a nostalgia for the simple joys of the family and the wholesome hobbyist (woodworking and knot tying are featured), it equally asserts a distinct contemporaneity in its rhetoric of self-improvement through feedback. The film proclaims the necessity of segmenting intractable phenomena

5   The article appeared as Burns, Jehane R. 1981. "Did You Get Pictures? Charles Eames' SX-70 Designs." *Polaroid Close-Up* 12 (3): 6–11. In the published version all references to Polavision have been excised, perhaps due to the recent, widely publicized write-down.

6   On this topic, see Colomina 2001. As Colomina notes, for the Eameses, "Spaces are defined as arrays of information defined and constantly changed by the users. This is the space of the media. . . . The reader, viewer, consumer constructs the space, participating actively in the design" (22).

into discrete units to facilitate management and intelligibility—processes that Seb Franklin (2015) argues are constitutive of a digital logic of control even when pursued through means that do not depend on digital media technologies. By situating the instillation of these new forms of organization within the family unit, the Eameses suggest a wholly administered existence: the totality of life, even seemingly private experiences far from the domain of wage labor, is taken to be open to modulation in the interests of efficiency and productivity. Here, one finds an understanding of Polavision that supplements Polaroid's notion of the format as a reparative technology that might rehabilitate and restore an imperiled family idyll. At stake is a late version of what Justus Nieland (2015) calls the "Eamesian happiness" that emerged at midcentury: a contradictory, liberal happiness requiring calculation, one that is instrumentalized within a "coercive, postwar technocracy" so as to remove the "hap"—the unpredictable contingency—that might seem to be a constitutive part of happiness.[7] In the place of such capricious pleasures, one finds a normalizing modulation of behavior tied to planning and predictive models.

This proposed development of highly contrived scenarios went against predominant practices of home moviemaking, as noted in a document entitled "Summary of Home Moviemaking Behavior," produced by Davida Carvin (1977), a member of the marketing research department at Polaroid. Dated December 15, 1977, and forwarded to the Eames Office, the document summarizes Richard Chalfen's 1975 article, "Cinema Naivete: A Study of Home Moviemaking as Visual Communication," in which the author reports that home moviemakers regularly ignore the advice of instructional manuals to plan before shooting. Carvin suggests that in order to remedy this problem, Polaroid might offer free workshops to Polavision owners to help them develop their filmmaking skills. Though this initiative was never pursued, the Eameses' promotional film fulfills a comparable function, instructing its viewers how to take control over the profilmic, make optimal use of the cassette's limited duration, and cope with the impossibility of postproduction editing. Carvin also finds in Chalfen's research a justification for Polavision's lack of editing and its denial of circulatory reproducibility. She reports that home moviemakers rarely edit their films, even when the opportunity is available to them, and that in both the production and exhibition of home movies, one tends to encounter "a *select*

---

7   The Eameses possessed, in Nieland's words, "a hostility to any model of agency predicated on total freedom, spontaneity or the will to original self-expression, which is also, of course, an ideology of happiness" (2015, 205–206)—and a position that resonates deeply with the in-built limitations of Polavision.

group of family and intimate friends" (Carvin 1977, emphasis in original).
Home movies tend not to engage in the ordering and condensation of time
typical of fictions but are instead made up of real-time recordings that
reside outside a narrative frame. The focus on planning attempted to bring
actually existing forms of home moviemaking closer in line with professional norms, to promote conformity to conventions that rely on a notion
of capture as an operation of control based in selection and exclusion. And
yet, Polavision's retreat from montage approaches a second, very different
idea of capture, one typical of home movies: a form of capture found in
the revelatory capacity of brute recording, an operation closely wedded
to the contingency that might be vanquished by the Eameses' cybernetic
happiness. Polavision's lack of postproduction editing, like its denial of
circulatory reproducibility, thus demands to be understood not simply as
a failure to meet a desired standard, an obstacle to be overcome, but as a
form of stripping down cannily tailored to the format's anticipated uses.

III.

The Eameses were far from the only notable figures to work with
Polavision. While the use of obsolete domestic imaging technologies
such as Fisher-Price's PixelVision (1987–1988) and Kodak's Carousel slide
projector (1965–2004) by artists such as Sadie Benning and James Coleman,
respectively, has received considerable attention, the lesser-known
Polavision also figures as a technology closely tied to the home context and
of interest to prominent figures. But unlike PixelVision and the Carousel,
which were appropriated by artists after their commercial lives had either
ended or at least begun to wane, Polavision's experimental uses are con-
temporaneous with the height of its commercial prominence and are the
result of marketing efforts on the part of the Polaroid Corporation. This
departs from the well-established narrative of the artistic recuperation
of obsolete technologies that might release what Benjamin called "the
revolutionary energies that appear in the 'outmoded'" to instead intersect
with discussions of collaborations and between artists and industry, such
as the episodes of Lillian Schwartz at Bell Labs, Stan VanDerBeek at the US
National Aeronautics and Space Administration, or Peter Campus at WGBH-
TV—that is, a scenario much more closely associated with the development
of professional televisual and computing technologies than with photochemical filmmaking and devices made for use in the family home.

Polaroid had an established tradition of working with artists through its
Artist Support Program, begun in the 1960s to supply artists with free

film and equipment in return for valuable feedback, their assistance in branding efforts (by creating favorable associations between Polaroid and creativity), and donations to what would be formalized in 1968 as the Polaroid Collection. But even before this, the corporation actively sought out the consultancy of artists. Ansel Adams began his work in this capacity in November 1949 for a retainer of $100 per month; he would stay on the Polaroid payroll for the rest of his life, filing more than three thousand reports (Bonanos 2012, 45). Adams shot footage of horses and stables with the Polavision system, but the company realized its first motion picture product called for an engagement with filmmakers, a group with which it had hitherto established few ties. An outreach effort similar to the Artist Support Program, though more informal, took shape. Polaroid asked for nothing in return save for feedback on the system. No contracts were signed, and Polaroid made no effort to begin a collection of films, as it had with photographs. As Sam Yanes, the corporate product publicity manager who worked with Polavision, said, the engagement with filmmakers was intended "on one hand to push the limits of the products far beyond the imagination of the technical staff, and secondly to create an atmosphere of creativity, quality, and panache—whatever artists bring to the game" (Yanes, interview with author, November 9, 2015). The corporation aggressively pursued the dissemination of Polavision in the independent and experimental filmmaking communities, directly or indirectly getting it into the hands of important practitioners, including Warhol, Brakhage, Robert Gardner, Alfred Guzzetti, and Morgan Fisher.

Warhol—well known for his use of Polaroid photography and his eagerness to try out new media technologies—attended the New York launch party for Polavision in early 1978 and was photographed there with a Polavision camera in hand ("Film Maker with New Film Maker" 1978). From January 16, 1978, to October 18, 1979, Warhol and his associates shot 46 cassettes, largely directionless recordings of comings and goings at the Factory, featuring celebrities such as Phyllis Diller, Lou Reed, Liza Minnelli, and John Lennon (who, not incidentally, also used Polavision).[8] In these films, many people address the camera, speaking to it as if unaware that it is incapable of recording sound. Scarcely any of the Warhol cassettes fit the Eameses' imperative of "good planning": the camera roams among groups of people who often are in the midst of having lunch or socializing, filming without any clear itinerary. One three-cartridge series stands as a

---

8   Excerpts of the Lennon home movies shot on Polavision are included near the end of Andrew Solt's 1988 documentary *Imagine: John Lennon*, where they are identifiable by their exceptionally grainy quality.

notable exception, somewhat recalling the process-based observations of Warhol's early filmmaking and gesturing to his interest in pop iconography. While most cassettes have hand-written descriptions such as "Montauk—Halston #2" (part of a hauntingly voyeuristic three-part series shot on October 18, 1979) or "Blizzard, Second Day" (filmed out the Factory window, looking down at skiers on Manhattan streets on February 2, 1978), *Burgers on Parade* (1978) is the sole instance of a proper title, indicated as such by the presence of quotation marks on the cassette label and box. Over the course of three cassettes shot on September 15, 1978, a man eats six McDonald's hamburgers lined up in front of him on a table, occasionally pausing to take swigs of a large drink and to wipe his mouth with a red napkin. The use of in-camera editing deprives this nearly eight-minute sequence of the durational record offered by a film such as *Eat* (1964), in which Robert Indiana eats a mushroom over some 39 minutes (when projected at silent speed). Whereas *Eat* took the 100-foot reel of 16mm film as its basic unit of construction, *Burgers on Parade* fails to do the same with the Polavision cassette. In-camera edits elide time and thereby weaken the impact of the gross spectacle of consumption depicted onscreen, since the eater's progress cannot be as surely pegged to any determinable profilmic duration.[9]

Though by no means a major work in Warhol's filmography, *Burgers on Parade* gestures to another feature of Polavision's brief existence: in addition to making home movies, the format also served as a means of making art. After gaining access to Polavision through Polaroid's outreach efforts, filmmakers put the format to uses far beyond those anticipated by the corporation during its development and marketing, "pushing the limits" as Yanes hoped they would, using Polavision to stage the moving image within the gallery space. Brakhage came across Polavision through the School of the Art Institute of Chicago (SAIC), where he was working as a visiting lecturer and where systems had been sent due to a preexisting con-nection between Polaroid and SAIC professor Barbara Jo Revelle. Through Fred Camper, a system was sent to Brakhage in Rollinsville, Colorado—a census-designated place naming a small cluster of dwellings in the mountains about 50 miles northwest of Denver. Brakhage seems to have discussed the format with Kenneth Anger, since Anger sent him several clippings about Polavision, annotated with his handwritten comments. An advertisement from the April 13, 1978, issue of the *New York Times* bears the

9   Nonetheless, *Burgers on Parade* is notable as a prefiguration of Jørgen Leth's five-minute document of Warhol eating a single Burger King Whopper, included in Leth's film *66 Scenes from America* (*66 scener fra Amerika*, 1982).

inscription "PROGRESS? *Look ma, no splices!" On a second ad, this time for the sale of Polavision at Macy's, Anger expressed his position on the system more definitively: "ITS ALL SO *EASY* TO—SPEND MONEY IN U.S.A. IN$TANT MOVIE$: JUNK FOOD PICTURES INC" (Anger, n.d., emphasis in original).[10]

Contrary to Anger's skepticism that Polavision was a high-priced way of deskilling the labor of filmmaking, Brakhage was extremely enthusiastic about the format, putting it to use in precisely the family context of privatized sociality foregrounded by Polaroid and the Eameses. For a film-maker living in the mountains, Polavision was poised to provide a family activity, but it also offered Brakhage a means of making films that accorded with the values of intimacy and individual production he had long espoused and buttressed his conviction that the home should be considered a site of cinema as—or even more—important than the movie theater. Though the films Brakhage and his children made have been lost, surviving letters testify to his engagement with Polavision and his unfulfilled plans to use it in what would have been an innovative form of experimental film distribution. In a letter to Camper, Brakhage (1978a [1979]) lists the Polavision films he had previously shown to Camper, giving credit to his children's efforts where due.[11] These titles, absent from all existing Brakhage filmographies, including the catalogue raisonné published in 2016, are: *#4 Bear by Rare* (October 16, 1978), *#6* (Neowyn Brakhage, October 16, 1978), *#7 Room to Room* (October 19, 1978), *#8 In and Out* (date unknown), *#12 Night + Day* (October 22–23, 1978), *Tri Part-Something* (date unknown), *A Snow Night Parts I + II* (Bearthm Brakhage, date unknown), *Portrait of Forrest* (December 17, 1978), *Bob Benson's Madonnas #1 + #2* (December 22, 1978), *Memory Fog* (date unknown), *Dying Animal* (January 16, 1979), *February's Bloodstream* (Neowyn Brakhage, February 12, 1979), *Music #1* (March 18, 1979), *Little Poems* (anonymous, March 24, 1979), and *My Vision* (Crystal Brakhage, March 25, 1979). The numbering of these titles suggests that Brakhage shot additional cassettes beyond those he showed to Camper.

In January 1979, Brakhage (1978b [1979]) wrote to Yanes at Polaroid, giving a detailed account of his "most rewarding" experience with the "great

---

10   The source and date of the second clipping is not identified but is likely from April 1978.

11   This letter is dated 12 April 1978 but was in all likelihood written on 12 April 1979. All dates given for the films in the letter are without years, except for *Dying Animal*, which includes "79" underlined. The listing of the films in chronological order suggests Brakhage used Polavision from October 1978 to March 1979. The mention of films completed in 1979 leads one to assume that the letter's date of 12 April 1978 is a mistake by one year.

discovery" of Polavision.[12] "I have, at great and joyful labor, accomplished several complete films which are nearly as perfect (in my tough estimate) as one might reasonably expect from, say, a sketch or water-color technique." He calls it "a great pleasure to have Mr. Land's genius revolutionize [his] area of making" after already having done so for still photography. Brakhage notes that he would prefer a more flexible camera with the possibility of using a greater variety of lenses, and to this end he asks Yanes to keep him informed about new additions to the line. In general, Brakhage saw Polavision's so-called limitations as its greatest assets, for they advanced a conception of, as he wrote, "Film as an Art Object." Brakhage found in the specificity of Polavision implications wholly other than those imagined by Polaroid. First, he believed that the cassette's uniqueness made it an ideal way for film to become a collectable art object, since it made the moving image amenable to the symbolic and financial economies of art. Second, he saw the lack of postproduction editing as encouraging precision and artfulness, describing it as "the greatest incentive to *thoughtful* motion picture photography which has existed since the birth of Film" (Brakhage 1978b, emphasis in original). Unlike the "video mentality which is the greatest corrupter of thoughtful picture-taking," Polavision required and promoted a "discipline of photographic attention" (Brakhage 1978b).[13]

Czach (2002) argues that Polavision can be seen as "the missing link" (3) between film and television, given that it shares characteristics of both. Indeed, the format is often aligned with video despite its filmic substrate: its filmstrip is called "phototape," it is cataloged in the archives of the Andy Warhol Museum as part of the video collection, and it has even been

12   This letter is dated 19 January 1978, with an asterisk marked in pencil after the year, presumably to indicate that it had been misdated. The information in the letter and Yanes's reply date the letter to January 1979, thus pointing to the same error Brakhage made with his April 12 letter to Camper.
13   In this regard, Brakhage's interest in Polavision chimes with what filmmaker Joel Schlemowitz (2015) terms the "camera roll film," which uses a single roll of 16mm film with no postproduction editing. As Schlemowitz writes, in language echoing Brakhage on Polavision, "With editing there is something diluted from this raw power of the pure, unadulterated footage, no matter how masterfully the material is pruned and refashioned. Perhaps the phrase of Allen Ginsberg, Chogyam Trungpa, and others, 'First thought, best thought' expresses this energy present in the camera-roll film? From the perspective of a filmmaker there is exciting [*sic*] about this methodology of making a film—a sense of challenging oneself to try to accomplish a work 'perfect for what it is' lacking any of the cosmetics of the cutting room." I thank Josh Guilford for bringing this to my attention.

perplexingly referred to as "laserdisc" and "early DVD."[14] In "The Promise of
Polavision" (n.d.), Polaroid deemed the system "the video counterpart of
the now ubiquitous audio cassette tape recorder" (4). Polavision's instant
playback, domestic setting, and boxy, television-like apparatus served to
forge an association with video. And yet, Brakhage positioned Polavision
in clear opposition to video, as was usually the case for Polaroid. Notwithstanding the passing remark about Polavision as a "video counterpart,"
"The Promise of Polavision" (n.d.) casts video in an unfavorable light,
deeming it "bulky, expensive, and complicated to use" and "requir[ing]
a rather high degree of expertise and training" when compared with
Polavision (6).[15] One might diagnose this position as an opportunistic
way of targeting a specific audience—one invested in simplicity over
functionality—for a format that was in some sense already outmoded by
the time it appeared on the market. But for Brakhage, who most certainly
did not fall into this target group, the advantages of Polavision lay elsewhere. Compared to the videotape's surfeit of time and the increasing
complexity of video cameras, Polavision created an urgency and an
opportunity for a modernist confrontation with material limitation that
Brakhage believed led to thoughtfulness and discipline. As Charles Eames
(n.d.) had argued decades earlier, "All freedom is too big"; true creativity
would come from "knowing an objective and working within restraints."[16]
Contrary to Anger's notion that Polavision resulted in "junk food pictures,"
Brakhage, like Eames, saw the brief duration of the cassette as summoning
the filmmaker to be judicious in his or her use of it, to find freedom in
constraint. Brakhage did not advocate for planning in the manner of the
Eameses, instead understanding Polavision as a format able to spark the
filmmaker's powers of intuition and observation by concentrating the act of
creation in a single moment and disallowing any "second thoughts." Though
Brakhage's investment in the format had little to do with the possibility of
feedback, he shared with the Eameses an interest in creativity founded in a
productive relationship to limitation; yet unlike them, he was interested not
in taming the unruly field of the profilmic but in engaging with the specific
qualities of the medium in an immediate creative encounter.

14   Max Underwood (2005) describes Polavision as both laserdisc and early DVD.
     Polaroid's official term for the filmstrip was "phototape" (62).
15   Though the system sold for only one-third the price of a Sony video player in 1977, its
     cassette was $8 and ran less than three minutes, whereas a videotape cost $17 but
     lasted for two hours and could be recorded over multiple times. See McElheny (1998,
     422).
16   I thank Justus Nieland for drawing this citation to my attention and for his perceptive
     comments on this article.

Brakhage's endorsement of craft and his advocacy for a form of filmmaking that would be understood as possessing an artistic status comparable to the finest poetry or music will sound familiar to anyone who has encountered his writing or correspondence. But his interest in the notion that the Polavision cartridge might make film salable as a unique object in art galleries is surprising given the lack of interest in participating in the structures of the art market he otherwise displayed throughout his lifetime. Brakhage (1978b [1979]) told Yanes he planned to ask Gallery 609—a commercial space in Denver run by his high school friend Gordon Rosenblum—to offer "one or two" of his Polavision works for sale, along with their players, "the same as they are selling paintings or sculptures." Brakhage had long taken an active interest in trying to develop alternatives to the distribution and exhibition models that prevailed in experimental film, understanding the ephemerality of public exhibition as incompatible with the extended time necessary to appreciate artistic achievement. In the mid-1960s, he was interested in the possibility of using 8mm as a distribution format that would enable the sale of prints to home viewers for affordable sums. Though the initiative did not meet with widespread success, Brakhage advocated passionately for this home cinema on the grounds that it would allow films to be viewed repeatedly and intimately, just as a poem must be read multiple times to be truly appreciated.[17] But he was equally interested in the notion that 8mm reduction prints would allow for increased circulation through the production of cheap, possessable copies. His model in the 1960s was not the unique object of the art market but the publishing of books and records. His love of Polavision resurrected this dream but notably left behind the prioritization of access that marked his earlier investment in 8mm. The domesticity of Brakhage's experiments with Polavision was already firmly in line with the privatized sociality imagined by the Eameses, but in this distribution decision he took an additional step toward the fulfillment of the format's proprietary logic, producing works intended for sole private ownership. Though Brakhage did not quote a price range for the Polavision works, he would be selling a unique object *and* a playback system, and thus one can assume an amount orders of magnitude higher than the $30 ($20 for members) price for Grove Press's unlimited 8mm edition of *Lovemaking* (1967). Despite Brakhage's excitement, the exhibition at Gallery 609 never took place. When Yanes (1979) replied on January 30, 1979, he said he had still not heard from the gallery. And though Brakhage may not have known it, by that time Polavision's future was already beginning to darken. Nevertheless, his

17   On this topic, see Balsom (2017).

unfulfilled plan to sell Polavision cassettes as unique artworks is notable, for it inserts him into a sphere of activity and a trajectory from which he is generally understood to have otherwise abstained, if not outright opposed: the art context and its development of a commercial market for moving image artworks through the imposition of scarcity.

In his letter to Brakhage, Yanes mentions that he had "been considering an 'art' show of Polavision films for some time and hope[d] to pursue this in the near future." Just as the initiative to supply free Polavision products to filmmakers continued a culture well established at Polaroid in relation to still photography, so, too, was Yanes's idea a logical extension of the company's practice of holding exhibitions to showcase what amateur and professional photographers had accomplished with their cameras. In 1973, Polaroid opened the Clarence Kennedy Gallery at its main headquarters on 784 Memorial Drive in Cambridge, Massachusetts, to hold exhibitions, including presentations of employees' work and displays curated from the *Polaroid Collection*, which comprised some 16,000 pieces by the time of the company's 2008 bankruptcy. Though the Polavision art show would never take place, the format did feature prominently in one exhibition, on view precisely when Brakhage and Yanes were in correspondence: a retrospective honoring Josep Lluís Sert, the Catalan architect and director of Harvard University's School of Design from 1953 to 1969. Held at Harvard's Carpenter Center for the Arts from December 2, 1978, to February 1, 1979, *Josef Lluís Sert: Architect to the Arts* focused on three of Sert's major buildings—the Spanish Pavilion at the 1937 Paris Exhibition, the Maeght Foundation in Saint-Paul-de-Vence (1964), and the Miró Foundation in Barcelona (1975)—as well as his relationships with artists such as Alexander Calder and Alberto Giacometti. In addition to architectural models, photographs, slide projections, and artworks, the exhibition featured 17 Polavision players exhibiting cartridges shot by Guzzetti and Gardner, both Harvard faculty at the time. Polaroid contributed $9,000 in sponsorship to the exhibition, which took place a mere 1.1 miles from its offices.[18]

Gardner (1978) had originally planned on incorporating 16mm footage into the exhibition but was happy to use Polavision, finding it "very much more adaptable to exhibit use" than 16mm. He was also keen to benefit from Polaroid's largesse, telling Sert, "Polaroid has plenty of MONEY." Initially, Polaroid promised to modify the Polavision camera for Gardner and Guzzetti so as to offer them a greater diversity of lenses (particularly

18   This accounted for one-third of the exhibition's total committed costs of $26,747 ("January 3, 1979 projection, Sert exhibition summary," CFA).

a wide-angle lens), the ability to control the exposure, and the possibility of mounting the camera on a gyroscope stabilizer (Gardner 1978; Alfred Guzzetti, interview with author, December 8, 2015). Polaroid never delivered on the promised modifications, but the filming went ahead nonetheless, with Gardner shooting Sert's buildings in Cambridge, while Guzzetti went to France and Spain to shoot the architect's work there, demonstrating the system for Joan Miró during a visit to film his studio. For the exhibition, the Polavision players were adapted to play on loop, set on shelves, and recessed into walls with windows cut out to reveal the screen, hiding the player from view and preventing the possibility of visitor manipulation. Whereas Brakhage saw Polavision's amenability to the art context as lying primarily in its status as a unique object, the Sert installation shows a second affinity at the level of exhibition design: Polavision could be used to create an automated, spatialized, multiscreen *dispositif*. Lest one assume these two qualities together make Polavision an ideal format for gallery exhibition, recall that they are inherently in tension with each other: the looped display might be appealing in its ease but over time would lead to degradation of the image, with no ability to strike a new copy.

The Sert cassettes document the architect's work in an objective manner, giving precedence to the display of architecture over any experimentation with filmic technique. And yet, one's attention is frequently drawn to the format itself, not because of any choices made by Gardner and Guzzetti but because of the distinctive graininess of the image and its occasional dis-integration into a blotchy, colored surface. The images frequently appear to possess a skin of amoeba-like organisms that have been subjected to microscopic enlargement, a result of Polavision's unique color process and the at-times uneven application of developing chemicals. These visual characteristics of the format are amplified in what is perhaps the most fully realized extant work made in Polavision, Morgan Fisher's *Red Boxing Gloves/ Orange Kitchen Gloves* (1980). Never exhibited in its original format, it first showed at Raven Row in London in 2011 as a two-monitor video installation after having been transferred at Colorlab in Maryland. Since then, due to the artist's preference, it has been exhibited as a two-channel projection.[19] In 1980, Fisher was invited to take part in *Film as Installation*, an exhibition curated by Leandro Katz at the Clocktower Gallery in New York. Featuring artists such as Ericka Beckman, James Benning, and Jack Goldstein, its

---

19   According to Fisher, the monitor-based presentation at Raven Row was "not an arrangement [he] was crazy about but it was more or less a matter of necessity in view of how the space in the buildings was divided" (Morgan Fisher, email to the author, December 22, 2015).

title was somewhat deceptive: the show consisted of models, drawings, photographs, and so on, related to the idea of film as installation; that is, any form except film installation proper, which was deliberately excluded. Fisher, living in Cambridge, Massachusetts, at the time, booked an appointment in Polaroid's large-format studio with the plan of producing a diptych of stills using the compositional device of the pendant pair that would be exhibited at the Clocktower as preparation for an absent film. After taking these photographs, the Polaroid technician asked Fisher if he would like to shoot a film version with Polavision, and he agreed.

The resulting work partakes of a play of similarity and opposition that is at once strangely fascinating and amusing. Despite the fact that Fisher's encounter with Polavision was accidental, given the format's intended place in the home it is striking that the composition is in part marked by domestic iconography and might be understood as a subversive figuration of that perennial domestic theme, the battle of the sexes. On the left, hands massage zaftig boxing gloves against a green background; on the right, the same hands caress flaccid kitchen gloves against a blue background. The intensely grainy image possesses a haptic tactility that mirrors the work's subject matter. The chromatic contrasts are echoed by a semiotic antithesis: a violent and public spectacle of masculinity on the left, a mundane and homely femininity on the right. But a reversal is simultaneously at play: the gloves are touched in ways that transform them into graphic puns on body parts belonging to the gender opposite to the one with which they would generally be associated: the boxing gloves appear as breasts and the fingers of the kitchen gloves as limp phalluses.

Far from the expressivity Brakhage relished and felt was amplified by Polavision, Fisher had long engaged deeply with industrial norms and predetermined structures as part of an effort to eliminate subjectivity. These preoccupations stay strong in *Red Boxing Gloves/Orange Kitchen Gloves*. Fisher has always been a filmmaker of format rather than medium, as evidenced by films such as *Production Footage* (1971) and *Standard Gauge* (1984), which reflexively insist on the internal heterogeneity of the category of film by investigating its diverse industrial determinations. If Brakhage's modernism resided in a notion of creative freedom generated from material constraints, Fisher's is to be found in an interrogation of the diversity of material supports encompassed in the term *film*. Like many of Fisher's works, *Red Boxing Gloves/Orange Kitchen Gloves* takes the single reel as its basic compositional unit, but it attenuates the effect of this decision through its use of the loop. Nor does it engage with Polavision's instantaneity in any way. Rather, Fisher's reflection on Polavision qua format emerges in his use of color. In their rich saturation, tremendous density, and unique texture, the hues of *Red Boxing Gloves/Orange Kitchen Gloves* return one to a consideration of Polavision's anachronistic dependence on an additive color process.

Most color film processes are subtractive, reconstructing the color spectrum on the material of the film through stratified emulsions, each sensitized to a different color. Polavision, by contrast, resurrected a long-abandoned means of generating photographic color that dates back to James Clerk Maxwell's experiments of the 1850s: an additive process that resolves color in the eye of the beholder.[20] Polavision film consists of a silver halide emulsion covered by a fine array of lines of alternating colors—3,000–4,500 lines of red, green, and blue per inch. When shooting, these lines function as filters, resolving incoming light into its primary components and preserving a latent image of each on the emulsion. When the developed film is played back, light passes first through the black-and-white base image and then through the lines so as to reconstitute a color image. Like a pointillist painting—or, perhaps more apt given Polavision's affinities with video, like a cathode-ray tube television—color blends in the eye, not in the image. The layers involved in this process caused the filmstrip to increase in thickness and become so opaque that the image is scarcely visible on the strip when held up to light. The film looks almost like videotape. For projection, a tremendously bright light source and a plastic prism built into the cassette to concentrate the light are necessary to realize the image. Polavision was thus restricted to a small scale not because this was most suitable for home viewing but because it was simply not possible to produce an adequately luminous image at a longer throw.

By exhibiting *Red Boxing Gloves/Orange Kitchen Gloves* as a digital projection, Fisher moves away from the material specificity of the scalar confinement dictated by Polavision's additive color process. But in magnifying the image, he exacerbates its pointillist qualities, revealing its unique textures and pushing its alternating lines of color to the point at which their synthesis begins to falter. The lines remain invisible to the eye, but the film's colors cease to appear as solid planes, revealing their contingent precariousness. Each color shows its internal difference: the green background, for instance, appears not only as green but as inhabited by pulsating flecks

---

20   For an overview of additive film color processes, see Flueckiger (n.d.). Polavision is the last entry on this list of additive color systems using the screen process, and little information about it is provided. Prior to Polavision, the latest additive process on Flueckiger's timeline is Eastman Kodak's Eastman Embossed Kinescope Recording Film, released in 1956.

of pink, violet, yellow, and blue. This surface play, alongside palpable degradation, draws attention to the picture plane's double status as represented scene and flat surface. The array of colored lines on the filmstrip generates an unstable and subjective experience of only partially blended color. Fisher's deployment of complementary colors in his overall composition is thus important. In this brazen staging of chromatic confrontation, he offers a displaced figuration of the surface of the filmstrip itself, marked as it is by a clash of discrete hues that never fully resolve into a unity. The magnified movement of the grain and the enlarged lines of the color process endow the image with a vibrant and vibrating intensity that infuses Fisher's deadpan images with an erotic agitation, while also laying bare something of Polavision's uniqueness as a format.

*

By the time Fisher encountered Polavision, Polaroid had ceased to promote the system to the home market. The public was not much interested in a social medium that almost entirely lacked the capacity for circulation and sharing. In March 1979, a class action lawsuit was brought against Polaroid by stockholders, claiming the corporation had failed to disclose information regarding Polavision's poor performance at the time of a January 1979 stock sale by Land and Julius Silver, chairman of the executive committee. At the April shareholders' meeting, Land demonstrated a wide-angle screen meant to solve problems with oblique visibility, as well as a sound version of the system, but the latter was never brought to market. In June, a month after the first layoffs at Polaroid since the 1950s, another new version of the system was announced, this one equipped with stop-motion functionality enabling the analysis of movement. This was a last attempt to salvage investment in Polavision by rebranding its possible uses. While industrial applications had been promoted from the beginning, they had been resolutely secondary. But as evidence of failure in the home market became unimpeachable, Polaroid increasingly emphasized Polavision's more "useful" uses, eventually to the point of exclusivity. Endorsements from the United States Olympic skiing team and the Professional Golfers' Association of America promoted the stop-motion system's ability to replay and analyze performance immediately and thus serve as a new training aid. Polavision could be used by real estate agents as part of a "property preview center," by physicians for medical endoscopy, or even by police to catch drug smugglers.[21] After the September 1979 write-down, Polavision

---

21   See "Instant Replay: Police Capture Drug Smugglers on Instant Movie Film." 1980. *Law Enforcement Communications*, February (press clipping, in PCAR, box I.25, folder 4–7).

left the home market, and most attempts to engage artists and experimental filmmakers ended. As Yanes noted, "[w]e didn't have enough time
to do the kind of building with artists that we wanted to do. . . . It takes
a while to learn a medium" (Yanes, interview). The proposed industrial
applications met with no more success than the home market had, and
production on the Polavision line ceased. On March 7, 1980, Edwin Land
resigned as chief executive officer of the company he had founded 43 years
earlier, with coverage of the event regularly citing the failure of Polavision
as a significant contributing factor.[22] Polaroid would not be free of the
negative impact of Polavision until 1987, when it finally lost the class action
lawsuit filed in 1979 and was found liable for damages of $30 million.

Dead media trouble the logic of innovation that dominates our culture
because, perhaps counterintuitively, dead media tend to be new media—
that is, media that did not last long enough to become old. But not only
the obsolete gets cast onto the scrapheap. The failed format of Polavision
lasted barely three years, puncturing the spurious promise of novelty—a
putrid glow that shines on us today more than ever—differently but as
sharply as those much-loved media forms that live long lives before they
die. Moreover, Polavision asks us to question the very categories of old and
new, for despite being enduringly new—no prior or subsequent format
can be said to be precisely like it—it was simultaneously always already
old because it was film not video, silent not sound, and additive color not
subtractive. The format is a curiosity, belonging to the family of film and
yet characterized by its departures from it, best comprehended in its
affinities with its victorious opponent, video. But Polavision rests uneasily
in its child's grave, making good on Sterling's (1995) insistence that dead
media constitute the "spiritual ancestors of today's mediated frenzy"
(n.p.). Certain qualities of this instant failure, such as its prosumer sociality
and modulation of quotidian behavior, would succeed by other means in
the future. Yet what resonates most today about the quixotic enterprise
of Polavision is its profound and enduring idiosyncrasy, its challenge to
any notion of "film" as a unified object. Resurrected, it is recast as a lens
through which to glimpse the heterogeneity of a cinema ceaselessly in
transition.

Acknowledgements
This research was generously supported by the Danish Council for Independent
Research as part of the research project "The Power of the Precarious Aesthetic."
It was first published as Balsom, Erika. 2017. "Instant Failure: Polaroid's Polavision,

22   See, for instance, Schuyten, Peter J. 1980, "Polaroid's Land to Quit Chief Executive
      Position." *New York Times*, March 7. D1, D3.

References

Anger, Kenneth. n.d. Loose clippings sent to Stan Brakhage. Brakhage Collection, box 3, folder 2.

Balsom, Erika. 2017. *After Uniqueness: A History of Film and Video Art in Circulation*. New York: Columbia University Press.

Benjamin, Walter. 2002. "The Work of Art in the Age of Its Technological Reproducibility: Second Version." Translated by Edmund Jephcott and Harry Zohn. In *1935–1938*, vol. 3 of *Selected Writings*, edited by Howard Eiland and Michael W. Jennings, 101–33. Cambridge, MA: Harvard University Press.

Bonanos, Christopher. 2012. *Instant: The Story of Polaroid*. Princeton, NJ: Princeton Architectural Press.

Brakhage, Stan. 1978a [1979]. Letter to Fred Camper, April 12, in Brakhage Collection, box 7, folder 10.

———. 1978b [1979]. Letter to Sam Yanes at Polaroid, January 10, in Brakhage Collection, box 53, folder 2.

Burns, Jehane R. 1981. Draft of article on Charles Eames for *Polaroid Close-Up*, in Charles and Ray Eames Papers, box 86, folder 7.

Buse, Peter. 2016. *Polaroid: The Camera Does the Rest*. Chicago: University of Chicago Press.

Carpenter Center for the Arts (CFA) Files. Harvard University Archives, Pusey Library, Harvard University.

Carvin, Davida. 1977. "Summary of Home Moviemaking Behavior." Document forwarded to the Eames Office, December 15, in Charles and Ray Eames papers, box 86, folder 1.

Chalfen, Richard. 1975. "Cinema Naivete: A Study of Home Moviemaking as Visual Communication." *Studies in the Anthropology of Visual Communication* 2 (2): 87–103.

Charles and Ray Eames Papers, 1850–1989. MSS83006. United States Library of Congress. Washington, DC.

Colomina, Beatriz. 2001. "Enclosed by Images: The Eameses' Multimedia Architecture." *Grey Room* 2 (Winter): 5–29.

Czach, Elizabeth. 2002. "Polavision Instant Movies: Edwin Land's Quest for a New Medium." *The Moving Image* 2 (2): 1–24.

Eames, Charles. n.d. Unpaginated transcript of lectures delivered at University of California, Berkeley, School of Architecture, December 1953–April 1954, pt. 2, Charles and Ray Eames Papers, box 315.

Fanelli, Louis A. 1979. "Polavision Price Cuts Don't Deter Polaroid." *Advertising Age*, October 8. Press clipping, in PCAR, box I.115, folder 6.

"Film Maker with New Film Maker." 1978. *San Jose News*, February 2. Press clipping, in Andy Warhol Museum, Pittsburgh, PA.

Flueckiger, Barbara. n.d. "Timeline of Historical Film Colors." http://zauberklang.ch/filmcolors/cat/screen-processes/.

Franklin, Seb. 2015. *Control: Digitality as Cultural Logic*. Cambridge, MA: MIT Press.

Gardner, Robert. 1978. Letter to Josep Lluís Sert, June 6, in CFA.

Gorman, Robert. 1974. "Instant Movies from Polaroid?" *Popular Science*, March: 96–97.

Hitchcock, Barbara. 2009. *The Polaroid Book*. Cologne: Taschen.

James Stanley Brakhage Collection (Brakhage Collection). University of Colorado, Boulder.

Krug, Steve. 2014. *Don't Make Me Think, Revisited: A Common Sense Approach to Web Usability,*
  3rd ed. Berkeley, CA: New Riders.
Land, Edwin H. 1977. "An Introduction to Polavision." *Photographic Science and Engineering* 21
  (5): 225–36.
Langway, Lynn, and Phyllis Malamud. 1979. "An Instant Dud for Polaroid." *Newsweek*, April 16.
  Press clipping, in PCAR, box I.114, folder 8.
Lombino, Mary-Kay, ed. 2013. *The Polaroid Years: Instant Photography and Experimentation.*
  London: Prestel.
Laurence, William L. 1947. "One-Step Camera Is Demonstrated." *New York Times*, February 22.
McElheny, Victor K. 1998. *Insisting on the Impossible: The Life of Edwin Land.* Reading, MA:
  Perseus Books.
Nieland, Justus. 2015. "Making Happy, Happy-making: The Eameses and Communication
  by Design." In *Modernism and Affect*, edited by Julie Taylor, 203–25. Edinburgh: Edinburgh
  University Press.
Polaroid Corporation Administrative Records (PCAR). Mss 658 1905–2005 P762. Baker
  Library, Harvard University.
Polaroid Corporation Amsterdam. 1978. Publicity office memorandum, August 23, in PCAR,
  box I.179, folder 4.
"The Promise of Polavision." n.d. Draft document, in PCAR, box 179, folder 1.
Raskin, Jef. 2000. *The Humane Interface: New Directions for Designing Interactive Systems.*
  Boston: Addison Wesley.
Schlemowitz, Joel. 2015. "First Thought, Best Thought: A Compendium of Camera Roll Films,"
  Program notes for December 4, 2015, screening at Film-makers' Cooperative, New York
  City.
"Shareholders Astounded by First Public Polavision Demonstration." 1977, May 16. *Polaroid
  Newsletter* 22 (8): 6. Press clipping, in PCAR, box I.75, folder 8.
Sterling, Bruce. 1995. "The DEAD MEDIA Project: A Modest Proposal and a Public Appeal."
  http://www.deadmedia.org/modest-proposal.html.
Sterne, Jonathan. 2012. *MP3: The Meaning of a Format.* Durham, NC: Duke University Press.
Underwood, Max. 2005. "Inside the Office of Charles and Ray Eames." *Ptah*, no. 2: 46–63.
von Thuna, Cynthia. 1979. Correspondence to Rose Maria Malet, director of Fundació Joan
  Miró, March 12, in CFA Files.
Wasson, Haidee. 2015. "Formatting Film Studies." *Film Studies* 12 (1): 57–61.
Wensberg, Peter C. 1987. *Land's Polaroid: A Company and the Man Who Invented It.* Boston:
  Houghton Mifflin Company.
Wolf, Eelco. 1974. Memorandum to subsidiary publicity managers, March 7, in PCAR, box
  I.324, folder 6.
Yanes, Sam. 1979. Letter to Stan Brakhage, January 30, Brakhage Collection, box 53, folder 2.

FORMATS IN TRANSITION

9

Fold, Format, Fault: On Reformatting and Loss

Marek Jancovic

After the dissolution of the Intelligence Directorate of the Buenos Aires Provincial Police in 1997, a safe with 15 rolls of microfilm was found half-accidentally in its former headquarters in a room disguised as a supply closet (Vales 1999). The roughly 20,000 personal files recorded on these microfilms contained information about many *desaparecidos*—an estimated 20,000 to 30,000 "disappeared" who were secretly arrested, kidnapped, tortured, or murdered by the Argentine military dictatorship during the 1970s and '80s as alleged political enemies, criminals, dissidents, or suspected socialists.

The early history of microfilming in Argentina is closely tied to the military and public administration (Gionco 2016). The use of this medium, such as for microfilming cadaster records and patents or archiving the resolutions of dissolved state organs, was encouraged and in some cases mandated legislatively or by presidential decree in the 1970s. The transfer of the *desaparecidos'* paper records from one carrier medium to another was a reformatting, a compression. It was a schismatic gesture that, on the one hand, physically and symbolically diminished the significance of the past in shaping the present, and, on the other hand, preserved the traces of this past for a future yet to come.

It is in the nature of microfilm—its affordance or medium specificity, as we might say somewhat archaically—to easily hide large amounts of information. Over the years, its compressive property permitted the police and

secret agencies of Argentina and other previous South American dictator-
ships to conceal and deny the existence of hundreds of thousands of
documents and, by extension, the people that "disappeared" with them.[1]
The act of reformatting became the subject of an international political
scandal when, in 1997, *El Mundo* revealed that many thousands of further
files had been brought to Spain, microfilmed there and transported secretly
to Switzerland (La Nación 1997a). There, it was reported, in a lockbox in
an unidentified bank in Lugano, they anticipate their own discovery. The
reasons for this are a matter of speculation and although the existence of
still unseen *desaparecidos* records has been confirmed by several military
officials (Clarín 1997a, 1997b; La Nación 1997b; Ares 1999), to my knowledge,
they have never been found. "[T]hey remain in waiting, *about* to be *of history*," as Charles Wolfe wrote about the limbo in which knowledge lingers on
its journey from the past before it becomes history (2009, 98, emphasis in
original).

The past stored on microfilms can, of course, still be "lost"—that is to say,
incinerated in secret, as indeed happened with many of them (Bonnefoy
2017). Yet being the archival medium that it is, under the right conditions,
microfilm also accommodates the possibility to be found. When a fraction
of the films were recovered after 23 years, the painful but in many cases
intangible trauma of the Dirty War was finally formatted into evidence that
could be mourned—it became an archive of repression, as they are called.
The archives of repression, some of which remain undiscovered and some
already destroyed, symbolically link the memory of Latin American state
terror and genocide to others across the globe. The existence and sub-
sistence of the microfilms gradually discovered throughout the 1990s has
been and continues to be vitally important in the judicial and cultural recuperation from Argentina's dark past, or what Thomas Keenan (2014) calls
"counter-forensics": an unearthing of buried bodies and hidden archives in
the service of political struggle, in the search for justice for the victims and
their families, and in remembrance of their personal narratives.

The microfilms later underwent another reformatting. Around the year
2000, they were digitized and stored in *Tagged Image File Format* (TIFF)
by the Argentine Forensic Anthropology Team, the nongovernmental
organization tasked with the search for information about *desaparecidos*
(Hanson 2000).[2] This format migration, too, enabled (though not without its

1   Kahan (2007) gives a good historical overview (in Spanish) of the functioning of the
     Intelligence Directorate archive and its opening.
2   For a contemporary account of preservation challenges at the turn of the millennium
     in Argentina, Chile, and Uruguay, see also Bickford (1999). For a more recent social

own losses and difficulties) a rereading of the past. Digitizing the films into a lossless format meant not only preserving them as testimony, but also made possible the computer-assisted analysis of conserved fingerprints, thanks to which the remains of some missing people could be identified and located.

Let us thus, at least provisionally, assume that the Argentine case is not an aberration and that format changes are *always* an expression of a political will. This is not only because "format-making activities" often play out as political machinations in the arena of cartel-like consortia (Sebok 2009; see also Decherney 2013). Even after formats have formed and their wars have been won, the reformatting of old documents does not become a neutral procedure. The choice to store information in any particular format for a given purpose, even when this choice appears to be a disinterested effect of convention, always precludes some manipulations of the past while permitting others, whether the information is concealed in a closet, stored in a deposit box, or submitted to computer analysis. This supposition—that media formats are political characteristics of history—demands that we enter and interrogate a place where reformatting is performed on a grand scale: the audiovisual archive.

In this chapter, I wish to consider reformatting as a recurrent cultural practice and explore the ways it transforms our relationship with the past—that is, both curtails and multiplies the ways in which we can interact with it. What objects get reformatted, how, and why? What relationship exists between reformatting, loss, and history? In order to offer some possible answers to these questions, I will look at mechanisms of format standardization, identification, and migration. In the interest of capturing some of formats' overarching logics and simultaneously taking advantage of the many meanings of "format," I will do so across a number of different media and industries, but pay close attention to film archives in particular. My analysis will be conceptually informed by bibliography, as my starting point will be to develop a format theory—and a theory of reformatting—grounded in the study of paper and bookmaking.

An Epistemology of Loss

Many heritage institutions worldwide—but among them especially those influential European and North American archives whose preservation

science perspective on the forensic-anthropological work in South America, see Mazzucelli and Heyden (2015).

policies will significantly shape the future of audiovisual heritage for generations to come—are currently participating in international format standardization initiatives. These projects aim to reduce the diversity of analog and digital media formats, which is perceived to be chaotic and prone to error. Central in this undertaking are lossless digital formats. Audio and photographic archives have been making use of lossless formats for a long time, but for moving images, the lossless compression or uncompressed storage of large quantities of video material only recently became computationally viable and financially tolerable.

It is noteworthy that Jonathan Sterne (2012) fleshed out the outlines of what a format theory could be on the example of a *lossy* file format. Lossy compression has been called "the very foundation of computer culture" in some of the canonical works on new media (Manovich 2001, 55), and more recently also "imperative today for theories of media and mediation" (Galloway and LaRivière 2017, 143). Contrarily, lossless compression and uncompressed formats have received rather scant media-theoretical treatment. At first glance, this may seem like an issue of proximity. We experience the lossy, epoch-defining triumvirate of the post-television age (JPEG, MPEG, MP3) in interactions with devices we keep at intimate distance from our bodies and touch daily. Lossy compression's sensory qualities are familiar to us in form of manifold errors, glitches, and artifacts. Such faults make the materiality of formats and compression schemes media-historically palpable.

Lossless file formats, on the other hand, at first seem to fall into two categories. Those like FFV1 and LTO are niche instruments with specialist applications, or, like PNG, omnipresent but rarely noticeable in situ. Yet as I have argued elsewhere (Jancovic 2017), lossless compression, as part of the algorithmic infrastructure of the world and precisely because it operates in hiding and on glacial and mostly dormant strata of culture and knowledge (archived films, criminological records, genomic data), may be capable of exerting cultural forces much more insidious and unpredictable.

On closer inspection, though, there are actually plenty of quotidian file formats that utilize lossless compression: GIF, ZIP, and FLAC (familiar to music aficionados), to name a few. Additionally, even lossy formats like JPEG use multiple iterative levels of compression to reduce file size, only some of which are lossy. Other formats like camera raw (familiar to photography aficionados) exist in uncompressed, lossy, and lossless "flavors." And as might be objected at the mention of GIF, the contours of lossiness itself are unsharp: though GIF uses lossless encoding to compress data, its limited color palette still firmly places it on the spectrum of what we consider lossy formats (see also Strauven in this volume). These ambiguities show how imprecise our terminology is in naming "loss" and in discriminating between filtering, subsampling, quantizing, reduction (see Schneider in this volume), and other technocultural procedures for manipulating signals in order to condense them. But what, then, is the relationship between formats and loss?

On the Folding and Unfolding of Paper

The semantic reservoir of the word "format" is seemingly inexhaustible (see Volmar, Jancovic, and Schneider in this volume). I would like to offer an additional inflection, the oldest one. Bibliographer Thomas Tanselle (1971) explains that the science of books needs a word to describe the relationship between the physical structure of a book and the routines of a print shop that occasioned it.[3] Historically, the printing trade used "format" for this. Unlike its vernacular use, "format" refers not to size but to the folding of a book: a single folding of the paper sheet creates a folio, a double a quarto—the ancestor of today's A4—a triple an octavo, and so on. Writes Tanselle: "format is not one of the properties of paper but represents something done to the paper" (1971, 32). To format is to fold.

I return to this orthodox bibliographic definition not out of etymological puritanism. Rather, I am convinced that bibliography has much to offer to the study of many media besides books, both methodologically and conceptually, and that a look toward historical bookmaking practices can shed light on persistent and important media-technological notions such as compression and, indeed, format. Bibliography directs our attention to formats as practices, as actions done. A narrow interpretation of format as folding may seem limiting, but it already contains all of its later permutations and sets the stage for the subterranean links between media recognized by Sterne. Formatting has always been a compression in the contemporary sense: the folding of the paper sheet shrinks its dimensions and simplifies its transport and storage, while the imposition—the spatial arrangement of individual pages on the forme before printing—is fundamentally an encoding problem; it ensures that the compressed data is collated correctly and decodable in the right temporal order during reading (see also Seppi 2016, 38–42). We may think of the fold of a book as an early example of a compression artifact.

3   See also Needham (1994).

Thus, if format is not a description of what an object is but rather a trace of the material procedures that have called forth its outward form,[4] then identifying formats is not a matter of the Galilean techniques of measurement and categorization. Rather, it belongs to the domain of interpretation and inference, the domain of all those disciplines—history, archaeology, criminology, medicine—that, as Carlo Ginzburg (1989) has argued, share a distant lineage in divination and the reading of venatic clues. A format is not simply "there" but has to be deduced and teased out from traces in the paper. The placement of watermarks and the direction of chain lines (fig. 1) left behind by the mold are, fundamentally, just residue of the papermaking and therefore irrelevant to the philological essence of a book, the text. Bibliography reverses this semiotic hierarchy. To attain a bibliographically and bibliogenetically useful description of the format of a book, the preserved wave patterns have to be unfolded and made legible as inscriptions, and therefore as always already more than just a side-effect of a technological process.

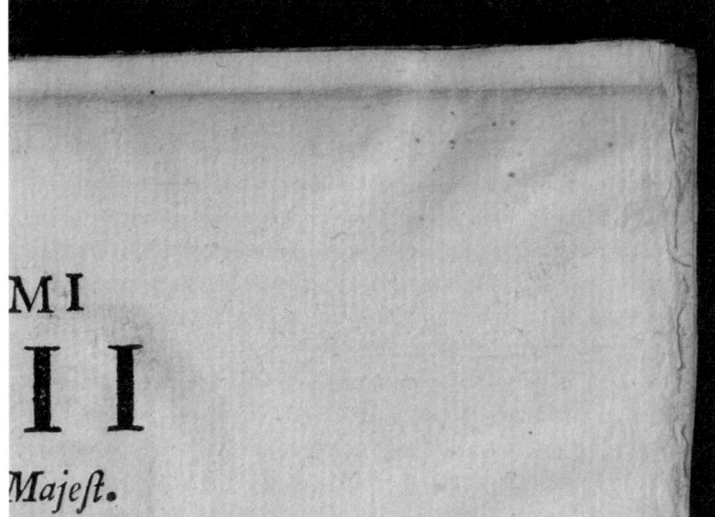

[Figure 1] Detail of the title page of *Gothofredi Guillelmi Leibnitii Opera Omnia*, a collection of Gottfried Wilhelm Leibniz's writings edited by Louis Dutens (1768), second volume, as scanned by and available from the Library of the Max Planck Institute for the History of Science (document ID MPIWG:U68MHQT3). Edge damage and faint vertical chain lines are visible.

4   On this point cf. also Niehaus (2018) who contrasts the philosophical category of "form," which can arise from inside, with "format," which only materializes as a consequence of being acted upon from outside. Also see Wiedemeyer's discussion of the German *Falte* vs. *Falz*, fold vs. hinge, in relation to Deleuze.

The mechanization of the printing industry in the first quarter of the 19th century enabled the production of much larger paper than was previously possible. As Tanselle (1971) notes, besides the tenfold increase in papermaking speed, this also led to a great multiplicity of book formats, much in the same way audiovisual archives have been experiencing it with video and digital files. With the introduction of wove paper in the mid-18th century and later automation of papermaking, chain lines disappear or become purely ornamental, ceasing to give an indication about the format—as a matter of fact, it is entirely possible to encounter books that do not have an identifiable format at all. But already prior to that, such markings were always only incomplete traces, a kind of circumstantial evidence that needs to be deciphered in order to be explained. As incunabulists know well, in the history of bookmaking, many ambiguous formats exist for which provisional terms like "octavo-form sextodecimo" have to be improvised (see Tanselle 2000, 1971).

Unruly Formats

Such unruly formats refuse to be contained by economies of *scale*. Things that are oddly formatted do not fit into standard envelopes, mass-manufactured picture frames or the time slots of broadcast programming. They stick out of folders, are awkward to carry, stubbornly resist being embedded in slideshows or opened with incompatible software. Few objects are as puzzling and productive to think about media-theoretically and epistemologically as an electronic file whose format is unidentifiable and whose contents are therefore illegible even though they can be read.

The identification of formats is of major concern for not only bibliography but also archives and the entertainment industry. Formats, whether book or broadcast, are more than the immediate appearance of the formatted thing. This is why the trade association FRAPA, Format Recognition and Protection Association, can offer services like the analysis and comparison of television formats to assist TV producers in copyright litigation. Archives, too, often need help identifying the format of electronic files. A number of format registries exist to aid with this, such as the UK National Archives' PRONOM, a database of technical information regarding the structure of file formats and software products that support them.

Format matters have thus been troubling heritage institutions for a while, film archives in particular due to cinema's international nature. Already in the late 1970s and early 1980s, when film archivists began using computers to assist their work, format standardization became an urgent goal of the archiving community. The format in question was not only the merry congeries of film gauges, magnetic tapes, and file types that cause preservation headaches today, but the format of catalog data. The development of a common computerized cataloging format—a WorldCat for film—would, so it was hoped, greatly facilitate international exchange, consistency, and discoverability, and was among the International Federation of Film Archives' major priorities. Despite widespread support throughout the 1980s, such initiatives often encountered difficulties at the level of technology as well as in administration, logistics, and politics (see, e.g., Smither 1987). We may compare this with the medieval standardization of paper sheet and mold sizes, or similar attempts in Republican France around 1800, or the thirty-odd years it took to somewhat standardize film camera and projector apertures, or the early 20th century efforts to create "world formats" for all everyday objects—all of which produced mixed or, to put it more mildly, very gradual and approximate results (Needham 1988; Schubin 1996; Kinross 2009; Niehaus 2018). Notably, however, Wilhelm Ostwald's international format standardization ambitions, which ultimately inspired the ISO 216 paper sizes in use today, were already fundamentally driven by a notion of losslessness: he advocated for the $1:\sqrt{2}$ aspect ratio for paper because it allowed reformatting without loss—that is, without waste (Krajewski 2006). Today's baroque cornucopia of formats and the associated question of lossless reformatting is therefore by no means a new set of problems, although each time it reappears in a different industrial, institutional, cultural, and technological climate.

During the 1990s, libraries and, later, photographic archives began to experiment with digitization (as opposed to microfilming) for preservation reformatting. Halfway into the decade, archivists for the first time carefully considered the prospect of using digital images as preservation master copies. Even before that, the notion emerged that for electronic records, "preservation means copying, not physical preservation" (Lesk 1992, 13). The issues then were nearly identical to those faced by film archives today, namely, the obsolescence of hardware and software, proprietary and therefore opaque technologies, incompatibilities between vendors, and lack of comprehensive and inter-institutional integrity verification methods (Graham 1994; Walters 1995).

The TIFF format into which the *desaparecidos* microfilms were digitized is notably the same format that many European film archives now use to store large portions of their born-digital (and in less common cases, digitized) collections. This is not a coincidence. TIFF is used commonly as a preservation or migration target format because it allows the lossless storage of image data, a trait both criminologists and archivists consider desirable. Archival format migrations are one specific manifestation of what Wolfgang Ernst has diagnosed as the "shift from an ancient European culture that privileged storage to a media-culture of permanent transfer" (2002, 14, my translation). Reformatting is what contemporary archives *do*: 35mm films are scanned into DPX images, DPX images compressed into MXF mezzanine files, mezzanine files transcoded into H.264 access files, QuickTime containers rewrapped into Matroska containers, JPEG2000 sequences converted into TIFF sequences, LTO-5 tapes migrated to LTO-7. The archive of the 21st century is like a book bindery where objects are endlessly folded, unfolded, and refolded. Behind all these formats is some technological promise, some standardizing authority, some hard-ware marketing department, some implicit or explicit policy on closed or open source, some formal and informal knowledge circulated between archivists, some weighing of preservation ideals against financial realities. Each format reveals a chain of aesthetic, political, and financial balancing acts that have led to its being chosen over others in a particular cohort of archival material.

Formatting as Cultural Technique

For Gilles Deleuze, the fold was a pluripotent instrument with which to think about and irritate, among other things, the distinction between interiority and exteriority (Deleuze 2006; O'Sullivan 2012). The fold is a fault line, a division that connects. In the fold, inside and outside, container and cargo, sea and ship, discrete and continuous touch. Deleuze's interest in folding (and its prehistory in Foucault, Merleau-Ponty, and so on) did not arise in a vacuum. In the year following the publication of his book on the fold and Leibniz, the first International Meeting of Origami Science and Technology was held in Italy. Folding has had a long but latent existence on the periphery of mathematics. As Michael Friedman (2018) observes, paper, usually a passive storage medium for mathematical inscriptions, exhibits the peculiar behavior of producing mathematical objects when folded: straight lines. Yet folding never, until recently, occupied the same position of prominence that other mathematizable cultural practices like knotting and weaving do. Folding was axiomatized only late in the 20th century (Friedman 2018), around the time of Deleuze's engagement with it, marking its inauguration into the mathematical sciences' arsenal of epistemically productive machines.

We may also notice how the gesture of folding was taken up shortly afterwards elsewhere; for example, by Bruno Latour (1999), who identified the folding of time and space, of human and nonhuman, as a property of all technical mediation; or recall that Donna Haraway (2007, 249) proposed *infolding* as an alternative to *interface*. In the years since, much like format theory, folding has taken off considerably, recently even warranting an edited volume (Friedman and Schäffner 2016) with the subtitle "Towards a New Field of Interdisciplinary Research." Like formats, folding is in vogue. These two distinct concepts, formats and folding, both of which have recently become major research paradigms, can thus be drawn together through a long, shared material history in the medium of paper.

Although the idea of a media history of folding has been broached previously by Nina Wiedemeyer (2014), folding, surprisingly, has rarely been counted among cultural techniques and considered as such.[5] Cultural techniques are a unit of analysis born in the interstice between German-speaking cultural science and historical media anthropology.[6] Harun Maye, Sybille Krämer, and Horst Bredekamp conceive of them in similar terms as "inconspicuous knowledge-techniques," "cyclical translation chains between signs, people and things" (Maye 2010, 121, 124) or bodily and habituated "operative procedures concerning the handling of things and symbols" (Krämer and Bredekamp 2008, 18; all translations mine). Often-given examples are enliteration processes (reading, writing, counting) or more primeval agricultural procedures like the demarcation of plots, boundaries, and enclosures in soil (Siegert 2010, 2013; Winthrop-Young 2014). Key to these operations is that they produce those primordial distinctions governing anthropic culture that are undone in Deleuze's fold: inside and outside, culture and nature, private and public, subject and object (see also Young 2015).

The formatting and reformatting of things—and I mean, in the first instance, the literal folding of paper—is a prime example of a cultural technique, not only since, as media scholar Susanne Müller (2014) argues, computers became ubiquitous. Children the world over learn how to fold paper, that is to say, they cultivate a habitual empirical understanding

---

5   Except perhaps for marginal mentions, e.g., in Siegert (1993, 2010) and for a treatment by Friedman (2018) and Wiedemeyer (2014) herself, both of whom deal primarily with highly specialized—i.e., mathematical or artistic—cases of folding.

6   This term, too, has been enjoying dramatic popularity in recent anglophone media research, due in no small part to the translation efforts of John Durham Peters, Geoffrey Winthrop-Young, and others. For its genealogy, see Geoghegan (2013) and Winthrop-Young (2014).

of the manipulation of planar surfaces in space without recourse to symbolical knowledge of topology. Ignoring for a moment Deleuze's metaphysical insights about the fold, the folding of paper as cultural technique operationalizes the boundary between a featureless plane of virtual possibility and actualized space and function: a "transition from nondistinction to distinction" (Siegert 2015, 14).

In its focus on process, cultural techniques research thus resonates with format theory. Format, after all, as bibliography teaches us, is always a doing. Bernard Dionysius Geoghegan (2013, 69) argues that cultural techniques encompass both the moment of emergence of new symbolical systems as well as their formalization, and can emerge prior to the media that form around them. The same could be said for many formats: the great multitude of early Kinetoscopes, Bioscopes, Biographs, and so forth anteceded the notion of cinema. In a description closely resembling the definitions of cultural techniques just mentioned, Liam Cole Young interprets format theory as a field interested in "how humans and their devices converge to establish ways of doing, hearing, seeing, and thinking that are the ground upon which concepts, desires, and institutions are built" (2015, n.p.). It is its genesis in the habituated gestures of paperfolding that explains why format studies finds so much agreement with the anti-ontological stance of cultural techniques research posited by Young.

The bibliographical identification of book formats requires a diachronic understanding of papermaking, printing, binding and trimming methods and tools, of the sequence of imposition, of the shape and weight and durability of the molds and deckles and wire facings, of the pressure and weight applied to various parts of the machines, and of the specific, precise directions, rules, and ways of grasping and handling them that papermakers, typesetters, and binders traditionally used. It is this type of haptic, material knowledge that we might seek when researching other kinds of formats, too.

To summarize, folding and formatting need to be thought concurrently as cultural techniques. I argue that folding must be studied by format theory as much as it is by philosophy and mathematics. In fact, there may be an entire genealogy waiting to be uncovered that connects the seemingly unrelated sciences that study folding: from mathematics, philosophy, stratigraphy, and bibliography to the physics and engineering of metamaterials or the biochemistry of peptides and DNA.

Fault Lines

Here, I return to the question posed at the beginning: what is the relationship between formats and loss? One consequence of the mechanization of
papermaking was a change in the bibliographical value of faults and losses.
The format of books from the 19th century onward can often only be
revealed through incomplete copies and damages. For example, the leading
edge of a printing forme receives the most stress, so examining damage on
the type can disclose clues about the imposition, and therefore also about
the format (Tanselle 2000). In newer books, the format/folding can at times
be determined if an untrimmed or even unopened copy has been preserved. Such an object, though it resembles a book, is, paradoxically, not
one yet because it cannot be opened and therefore also cannot be read.
It is only by irreversibly cutting open the folds, by creating an interface—
Schnittstelle—that the bookness of a gathering of paper begins.[7]

If Leibniz provided Deleuze with the folds that hold the universe together,
he also provided the history of mathematics with cuts in search of an
interface. At the Gottfried Wilhelm Leibniz Library in Hannover, Germany,
a reconstruction of Leibniz's notes has been underway since 2015. Leibniz
had the habit of filling sheets of paper with notes on different subjects,
from metaphysics to calculus, and then cutting the paper with scissors
and ordering the snippets by topic. In an effort to piece the preserved
fragments together, librarians and historians turned to forensic software
developed for the purpose of reassembling files of the East German State
Security Service that had been torn up by hand (Wehry 2017). The hope
is that by reforming the scraps into a whole—undoing the "losses" that
Leibniz intentionally introduced by severing the temporal relationships
within his writing and replacing them with thematic relationships—a well-
formatted chronological narrative might emerge.

Paper is an excellent storage medium for creases, it remembers every
fold. A fold is also a fault, a wrinkle, a pleat, *un pli*. To figuratively *apply*
something (like a framework or a concept, such as the concept of "fold"
to a theory of media formats) means to put it to work but also to ply it, to
bend, fold, and distort it. Reformatting—the applying of a new format—is
therefore never just a repackaging but always a refolding. As we know
since Matthew Kirschenbaum (2012), who applied methods of both bibliography and forensics to the study of electronic documents, every

---

7   Here, again, we hear a remote echo of agri-cultural techniques at work: the folded
     leaves are slit open with a tool called a plow.

migration is a mutation.[8] There are no lossless formats because formats are not transparent vessels but imprint the content they frame with scars, tears, and folds. When something is formatted and reformatted, it yields to the politics of the format. Cinema offers a most striking example: the awareness that their films might be reformatted for television and home video led cinematographers to develop techniques like "shoot and protect." This frame composition principle anticipates aspect-ratio alterations that have not yet taken place and subtly affects not only what appears in the picture and how but also the set design, lighting, sound recording, and, as Mark Schubin (1996) has demonstrated, also the plot, timing and dramaturgy. Formats can thus also shape and reformat cultural expressions preemptively and across different media.

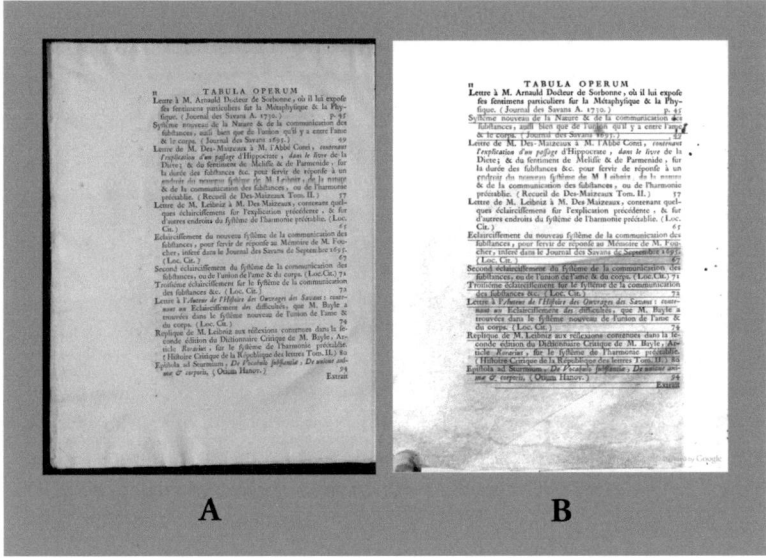

[Figure 2] Page II from the table of contents of *Gothofredi Guillelmi Leibnitii Opera Omnia* in two different online-accessible versions.
A: A copy held and scanned by the Library of the Max Planck Institute for the History of Science; digitization provenance unknown.
B: A copy held by the National Central Library of Rome, scanned on March 19, 2013 by Google (Archive.org identifier: bub_gb_zeDzFGJjWLIC).

Bibliography teaches us that loss and faults in their many forms are epistemically fertile: they can be read. Indeed, for certain modes of addressing the past, they are *desirable*. This is a critical realization for

8   See also Chun 2008.

any process of reformatting, especially for the institutional realities of preservation and digitization. Historical books, for example, are often—most prominently in Google's book digitizations—scanned and retouched in a way that prunes away the fuzzy and damaged edges of leaves. The examples in figure 2 demonstrate two very different approaches to book digitization on the same passage of text. Image A includes the fold and edges as well as faintly visible chain lines. In image B, contrast is increased, rendering all of them invisible. The former much better preserves historical information pertaining to the format as a material and sensory property of the book. But image B, too, is not without its own folds, faults, and marginalia that document the technical processes and labor of its own reformatting: some text is automatically turned into blue hyperlinks and underlined, and the scanner operator's presence is marked by the inclusion of a finger covered with a protective pink glove in the lower left corner.[9] These reformattings encode very different relationships to the past, and make very different forms of historical inquiry possible or impossible.

As far as knowledge practices go, the online accessibility and searchability of library and archive collections is one of the great achievements of the 21st century. But trimming off the edges and other traces of formatting means, in essence, presupposing that people accessing the digitized records will have an interest only in a select (although undoubtedly very important) aspect of the book, namely the text. Even when scanned in high resolution and saved in a lossless format, the—quite literally—marginal knowledge contained in the shape and structure of the book's folded leaves can thus be lost.[10] One could argue that for the vast majority of readers, such digitizations are good enough, since only the minuscule audience of the bibliographically inclined would be interested in examining the paper, and those should likely prefer to do so on the physical original. While that is hard to dispute, my point here is that all acts of reformatting express some limited and limiting ideology of use and utility, some opinion on what constitutes content or "essence" and what is secondary to it, and, as the hidden *desaparecidos* microfilms show most urgently, some politics of access and exclusion, visibility and secrecy, history and memory.[11]

9   On the relationship between Google's book scanning process and outsourced labor, see Bergermann 2016.
10   Wiedemeyer (2014, 145–48) makes a similar criticism of digitizations.
11   Siegert (1993) compellingly delineates the separation between public and secret in the late medieval period as a difference of medium, of (rigid) parchment against (foldable and sealable) paper. One could rephrase this as the difference between a capacity to be reformatted and resistance to it.

Even lossless formats are "lossless" only in a narrow and transitory sense bound by historical contingencies. TIFF, for instance, carries the affordances and constraints of 32-bit computing: it can only reference addresses 4 gigabytes away from beginning of file. For image sequences in digital film preservation, this is not yet a problem because a single frame is orders of magnitude smaller. But if we venture to the periphery of what might still be considered visual culture—astronomical and medical imaging, for example—it quickly proves to be an insurmountable limitation. In response, these fields develop image formats of their own (like DICOM or BigTIFF), and they often do so fully aware of the need to standardize them. But as imaging practices and hardware change and the needs of particular communities (clinical vs. research imaging, for instance) diverge, the formats tend to mutate and multiply (see, e.g., Larobina and Murino 2014; Kitaeff et al. 2015).

Deleuze's reading of the Baroque was closely tied to an uproar of formats, a Great Reformatting:

> the painting exceeds its frame and is realized in polychrome marble sculpture; and sculpture goes beyond itself by being achieved in architecture; and in turn, architecture discovers a frame in the façade, but the frame itself becomes detached from the inside, and establishes relations with the surroundings so as to realize architecture in city planning. (2006, 141)[12]

Our age industrialized Deleuze's Baroque into the bedrock of cultural production. Not just in the archive, reformatted audiovisual objects surround us everywhere; in fact, most images, texts, and recorded sounds we encounter undergo dozens of format changes throughout their existence. Documents born as InDesign files are reformatted for e-readers and exported as PDFs, printed and then scanned as DjVu files; online videos are downscaled for mobile devices and upscaled for 8K television sets; films metamorphose from raw video to intermediate editing formats to DCPs or XDCAM or VP9 files. Our messaging apps convert all the animated GIFs we send into MP4 videos, since we would otherwise be inundating their servers with an inefficiently lossless format from 1989. Content delivery networks reformat JPEG images into WebP files. Our handheld devices continuously monitor their own orientation in space and diligently turn images from portrait to landscape for us. It is a very contemporary brand of vexation and anger to be fighting with a phone over the format of a photograph whose "orientation," stored in EXIF format, contradicts what human observers

12   See also Jacob Burckhardt on Baroque formats quoted in Niehaus 2018, 30.

might consider natural. Unruly—we might even say queer—formats, indeed. Many of us have by now surely also encountered television sets that refuse to play video files because of a particular format: the file system format of a storage medium, an unlicensed audio stream format or even a nominally supported video format in the wrong container or with a quirk like an incompatible bit depth. Such irritations of modern life, in turn, sustain the online cottage industry of format converter software and services.

[Figure 3] Screenshot from a trailer for *The Hitchhiker's Guide to the Galaxy* (2005) circulated on YouTube, showing traces of multiple reformattings. The image originated with an anamorphic widescreen aspect ratio of 1:2.39. My brief examination suggests that this trailer may have been digitized into DV NTSC format, erroneously captured without correcting for DV's narrow pixel aspect ratio of 0.91 (thus stretching in width) and letterboxed into a 3:2 frame, subsequently letterboxed again into a 4:3 frame and finally pillarboxed for YouTube into a 16:9 frame.

[Figure 4] The same frame from the 2007 Touchstone Home Entertainment Blu-ray release of the film.

All of these reformattings leave their own folds. Trimming the edges of a scanned book's pages is a subtractive reformatting, like the lossy amputation of paintings that art historian Jacob Burckhardt pleaded against in 1886 (Müller 2014; Niehaus 2018). At times, reformatting can even induce a complete effacement of media objects: Paolo Cherchi Usai (2000, 61) once recalled a fulminant anecdote in which a print of Hans-Jürgen Syberberg's *Parsifal* (1982) was hacked to pieces by a furious projectionist who was unable to correctly adjust its aspect ratio. But format changes are also generative. The black slabs of letterboxed films on television or the blurry aureoles that "correct" vertical videos to make them suitable for YouTube—these prostheses we graft onto things in order to make them "have" a certain format (figs. 3–4) are not simply empty or redundant spaces. They are evidence of procedural frictions across aesthetic, technological, and economic registers that sometimes, dramatically, escalate into format wars.

Importantly, this is not only a matter of "poor images" (Steyerl 2009) or "small formats" (Niehaus 2018) that want to circulate quickly and therefore shift and shed their shape recklessly and often. It can also happen to films during their transition from the formalized film industry into the film archive. As one of the examples known to me, the EYE Film Institute in the Netherlands, as is common in countries with state-subsidized film industries, asks digital film productions to bestow copies as Digital Cinema Distribution Masters (DCDMs) to the archive. This master copy contains the picture, sound, subtitles, and metadata of a film in lossless formats. Filming in HDTV resolution (with a width of 1920 pixels) is still not uncommon, for example, in non-fiction filmmaking, and for such material, EYE Film Institute asks that the image be padded to a width of 1998 pixels to ensure full compliance with standard DCDM resolutions.[13] Given a height of 1080 pixels, this translates to 1:1.85—a historical aspect ratio from the analog film era commonly called flat widescreen.

Replicating an analog format by adding 39 empty pixels on both sides of the image might seem insignificant (and in the grand scheme of things it very well is) but it also shows that formats have a mind of their own and a way of asserting themselves. They sometimes mutate vigorously within the same carrier, and at other times remain tenaciously persistent across generations of media. Formats tend to remain the same because of standardization, but they also change in nontransparent ways, folding into each

---

13   Mention of this resolution has been removed in the new Digital Cinema Initiatives 1.3
      DCDM specification published in 2018.

other and stratifying internal difference as versioning: U-matic becomes U-matic SP, 8mm becomes Super 8, HDCAM becomes HDCAM SR. Nitrate film shrinks and thus changes its format, becoming incompatible with projection hardware. Incompatible video formats turn into clumsy compromises like the 14:9 aspect ratio sometimes used in television production. Besides the public document that describes it, TIFF has private, non-standard, undisclosed, or unreliably circulated implementations that can impinge upon archival efforts. The discrepancy between format as a virtual, ideal standard and format as actualized form is why newer standardization initiatives like PREFORMA not only develop format *specifications* but also provide their *implementations* for reference. These paradoxical tendencies explain why some theories of formats commit to their mutability (Bucher, Gloning, and Lehnen 2010), while others insist precisely on their fundamental permanence (Niehaus 2018). I take this as an indication that format theory has yet to find a model of temporality that can account for formats' apparently contradictory propensities in a satisfactory way.

Conclusion: A Geology of Culture

At the risk of overindulging in semantics, let us remember that a fold is also a geological event, a bend in the sedimented strata of the soil. As the installation and video artist Annett Zinsmeister (2004) notes, the fold is a phase transition, a sudden change of orientation. One of the greatest folds in the history of Europe has been not only a format transition around 1480, when portable book formats began replacing the large folios (Füssel 2005). It was also an ideological reorientation—a reset, a formatting of the religious operating system, a *reformation*. The Reformation could take place because of a change of direction in the technological substrate of culture in the form of movable type but also, as Johannes Burkhardt and others have pointed out, the invention and rapid circulation of formats like the mass-printed pamphlet and daily report (Burkhardt in Schulze et al. 2005).

Formats thus engrave not only "old infrastructural context" (Sterne 2012, 15) but also the cultural, epistemic, political and even religious torsions of an age into concrete objects. They can be placeholders for class differences and social hierarchies (see Genette 1997, 17–22; Bucher, Gloning, and Lehnen 2010, 20). Entire value systems and cultures of taste are encapsulated in the way one unfolds a "tabloid" differently from a "broadsheet." Some formats are ascribed truth value, others are made out to be inherently untrustworthy—recall Reuters' 2015 ban on the use of the RAW format by photojournalists. The New York Public Library's massive collection of comic books is a testament to the cultural mechanisms of appraisal that delimit the set of archivable and archive-worthy formats: the "books" are, as a matter of fact, microfilms. In 2017, the Gerrit Rietveld Art Academy in Amsterdam inaugurated a new master's program in "film, design and propaganda." Its catchy slogan announced: "HD is the new A4." Here, HD, the parvenu format, metonymically serves as a proxy for a power transfer between media whose intricate gradations cannot be fully articulated with the totalizing term *medium* alone. This power transfer is also a reversal of direction: a retrograde motion from Hippasus back to Pythagoras, from the irrational beauty of $\sqrt{2}$ that governs ISO 216 paper sizes to the integer beauty of 2^n that digital screens like so much.

Formats and media are thus interlinked in nonlinear ways that we do not yet fully understand. They each follow idiosyncratic and multidirectional temporalities that slip against and attrit each other but, confoundingly, also undulate in tandem. Formats have far-reaching consequences for the experience of media, for the accessibility and reproducibility of scientific data, and for private and collective memory. The format of archival records has a significant impact on not only who is able and willing to access them (Capell 2010) but also their perceived authenticity and veracity (e.g., Hedstrom et al. 2006). That is why the "losslessness" of the TIFF format used in the forensic analysis of the *desaparecidos* files is so instrumental: it helps to discursively anchor the horrific losses of a volatile past in a technological promise of immutability.

In the archive—whether the dispersed archives of repression, the established institutional repositories of objects and knowledge like EYE, or their messy present-day online counterparts like YouTube—history can be traced as an unfolding of formats. Reformatting has become one of the chief activities that archives perform on the objects in their custody, alongside or as part of preservation. What format theory can contribute to historical research is an awareness that such reformatting actively inscribes histories in the margins and in the folds. To the historiographical question "what does this object say?" format theory adds: "why is it in this format?"

Even without looking inside the vessel at the content of an archival object, a close look at its format can reveal a great deal about the circumstances of its existence, and about the archive that contains it. Understanding format as a process draws attention to not only "the catacombs under the conceptual, practical, and institutional edifices of media" (Sterne 2012, 16) but also the politics suffusing those catacombs, and in some cases the bodies buried within. Format changes might perhaps be the preliminary tremors of large tectonic shifts in cultural and political systems. The reformatting of the *desaparecidos* paper files was an inflection point: the microfilming was a signal that mechanisms of institutional forgetting were being set into motion. The same mechanisms would later also make possible the past's coming into language. The transition from silver halide microfilm to TIFF file also marks an event that has been slowly taking place since the 1990s: the subduction of a tectonic formation known as analog media under the large stratum of digital data. To study media formats is therefore not just a good way to understand *media* history (Müller 2014; Sterne 2012), it might be a good way to understand the history of the world.

Acknowledgements
I thank Pamela Gionco for her helpful information concerning the history of microfilm use in Argentina. I also wish to thank Anne Gant and Ivo Noorlander for the generous and illuminating insights into the preservation practices and procedures at EYE Film Institute Netherlands.

References

Ares, Carlos. 1999. "Un ex general argentino afirma que hay un archivo de desaparecidos." *El País*, January 16, Online edition, sec. Internacional. https://elpais.com/diario/1999/01/16/internacional/916441210_850215.html.

Bergermann, Ulrike. 2016. "Digitus – Der letzte Finger." *Zeitschrift für Medienwissenschaft*, September 26. http://www.zfmedienwissenschaft.de/online/digitus.

Bickford, Louis. 1999. "The Archival Imperative: Human Rights and Historical Memory in Latin America's Southern Cone." *Human Rights Quarterly* 21 (4): 1097–122.

Bonnefoy, Pascale. 2017. "Cómo los archivos en microfilme de la dictadura de Pinochet se hicieron humo." *The New York Times*, October 30, sec. América Latina. https://www.nytimes.com/es/2017/10/30/chile-archivos-pinochet-dictadura/.

Bucher, Hans-Jürgen, Thomas Gloning, and Katrin Lehnen. 2010. *Neue Medien – Neue Formate: Ausdifferenzierung und Konvergenz in der Medienkommunikation*. Frankfurt am Main: Campus Verlag.

Capell, Laura. 2010. "Digitization as a Preservation Method for Damaged Acetate Negatives: A Case Study." *The American Archivist* 73 (1): 235–49. doi:10.17723/aarc.73.1.x381802g137421h3.

Cherchi Usai, Paolo. 2000. "The Ethics of Film Preservation." In *Silent Cinema: An Introduction*, 2nd edition, 44–71. London: British Film Institute.

Chun, Wendy Hui Kyong. 2008. "The Enduring Ephemeral, or the Future Is a Memory." *Critical Inquiry*, no. 35 (Autumn): 148–71.

Clarín. 1997a. "En Suiza no encuentran archivos de la represión." *Clarín*, June 13, Online edition, sec. Política. https://www.clarin.com/politica/suiza-encuentran-archivos-represion_0_H1lN_Z-AFe.html.

———. 1997b. "Archivos de la represión: pedido de ayuda a Suiza." *Clarín*, June 23, Online edition, sec. Política. https://www.clarin.com/politica/archivos-represion-pedido-ayuda-suiza_0_HyabOL-bRFx.html.

Decherney, Peter. 2013. *Hollywood's Copyright Wars*. Reprint. New York: University Press Group Ltd.

Deleuze, Gilles. 2006. *The Fold*. Translated by Tom Conley. London: Continuum.

Ernst, Wolfgang. 2002. *Das Rumoren der Archive: Ordnung aus Unordnung*. Berlin: Merve Verlag.

Friedman, Michael. 2018. *A History of Folding in Mathematics: Mathematizing the Margins*. New York: Birkhäuser.

Friedman, Michael, and Wolfgang Schäffner, eds. 2016. *On Folding: Towards a New Field of Interdisciplinary Research*. Bielefeld: transcript.

Galloway, Alexander R., and Jason R. LaRivière. 2017. "Compression in Philosophy." *Boundary 2* 44 (1): 125–47. doi:10.1215/01903659-3725905.

Genette, Gerard. 1997. *Paratexts: Thresholds of Interpretation*. Cambridge: Cambridge University Press.

Geoghegan, Bernard Dionysius. 2013. "After Kittler: On the Cultural Techniques of Recent German Media Theory." *Theory, Culture & Society* 30 (6): 66–82. doi:10.1177/0263276413488962.

Ginzburg, Carlo. 1989. "Clues: The Roots of an Evidential Paradigm." In *Clues, Myths, and the Historical Method*, translated by John Tedeschi and Anne C. Tedeschi, 96–125. Baltimore, MD: Johns Hopkins University Press.

Gionco, Pamela. 2016. "Usable / Non-Usable / Reusable: Present Continuous of Microfilms." presented at the 14th NECS Graduate Workshop: Return of the living-dead media: Media Cultures of Persistence, Resistance and Residue, Potsdam, July 27.

Graham, Peter S. 1994. *Intellectual Preservation: Electronic Preservation of the Third Kind*. Washington, DC: Commission on Preservation and Access.

Hanson, M. 2000. "Fingerprint-Based Forensics Identify Argentina's Desaparecidos." *IEEE Computer Graphics and Applications* 20 (5): 7–10. doi:10.1109/38.865872.

Haraway, Donna J. 2007. *When Species Meet*. Minneapolis: University of Minnesota Press.

Hedstrom, Margaret, Christopher Lee, Judith Olson, and Clifford Lampe. 2006. "'The Old Version Flickers More': Digital Preservation from the User's Perspective." *The American Archivist* 69 (1): 159–87. doi:10.17723/aarc.69.1.1765364485n41800.

Jancovic, Marek. 2017. "Lossless Compression and the Future of Memory." *Interactions: Studies in Communication & Culture* 8 (1): 43–59. doi:10.1386/iscc.8.1.45_1.

Kahan, Emmanuel Nicolás. 2007. "¿Qué represión, qué memoria? El 'archivo de la represión' de la DIPBA: problemas y perspectivas." *Question* 1 (16): 1–10.

Keenan, Thomas. 2014. "Counter-Forensics and Photography." *Grey Room* 55 (April): 58–77. doi:10.1162/GREY_a_00141.

Kinross, Robin. 2009. *A4 and Before: Towards a Long History of Paper Sizes*. KB Lecture 6. Wassenaar: NIAS.

Kirschenbaum, Matthew. 2012. *Mechanisms: New Media and the Forensic Imagination*. Cambridge, MA: MIT Press.

Kitaeff, V. V., A. Cannon, A. Wicenec, and D. Taubman. 2015. "Astronomical Imagery: Considerations for a Contemporary Approach with JPEG2000." *Astronomy and Computing* 12 (September): 229–39. doi:10.1016/j.ascom.2014.06.002.

Krajewski, Markus. 2006. *Restlosigkeit: Weltprojekte um 1900*. Frankfurt am Main: Fischer Taschenbuch.

Krämer, Sybille, and Horst Bredekamp. 2008. "Kultur, Technik, Kulturtechnik: Wider die Diskursivierung der Kultur." In *Bild Schrift Zahl*, edited by Sybille Krämer and Horst Bredekamp, 2nd edition, 11–21. Munich: Wilhelm Fink.

La Nación. 1997a. "Habría microfilms de listas de desaparecidos." *La Nación*, April 4, Online edition. https://www.lanacion.com.ar/66398-habria-microfilms-de-listas-de-desaparecidos.

————. 1997b. "Desaparecidos: confirman la existencia de documentos,"
May 5, Online edition, sec. Política. https://www.lanacion.com.ar/politica/
desaparecidos-confirman-la-existencia-de-documentos-nid68320.

Larobina, Michele, and Loredana Murino. 2014. "Medical Image File Formats." *Journal of Digital Imaging* 27 (2): 200–206. doi:10.1007/s10278-013-9657-9.

Latour, Bruno. 1999. *Pandora's Hope: Essays on the Reality of Science Studies*. Cambridge, MA: Harvard University Press.

Lesk, Michael. 1992. "Preservation of New Technology. A Report of the Technology Assessment Advisory Committee to the Commission on Preservation and Access." Commission on Preservation and Access.

Manovich, Lev. 2001. *The Language of New Media*. Cambridge, MA: MIT Press.

Maye, Harun. 2010. "Was ist eine Kulturtechnik?" *Zeitschrift für Medien- und Kulturforschung* 1 (1): 121–36.

Mazzucelli, Colette G., and Dylan Heyden. 2015. "Unearthing Truth: Forensic Anthropology, Translocal Memory, and 'Provention' in Guatemala." *Politics and Governance* 3 (3): 42–52. doi:10.17645/pag.v3i3.451.

Müller, Susanne. 2014. "Formatieren." In *Historisches Wörterbuch des Mediengebrauchs*, edited by Heiko Christians, Matthias Bickenbach, and Nikolaus Wegmann. Cologne: Böhlau.

Needham, Paul. 1988. "The Study of Paper from an Archival Point of View." *IPH Yearbook* 7: 122–36.

————. 1994. "Res papirea: Sizes and Formats of the Late Medieval Book." In *Rationalisierung der Buchherstellung im Mittelalter und in der frühen Neuzeit: Ergebnisse eines buchgeschichtlichen Seminars, Wolfenbüttel, 12.–14.* November 1990, edited by Peter Rück, 123–45. Marburg: Institut für Historische Hilfswissenschaften.

Niehaus, Michael. 2018. *Was ist ein Format?* Hannover: Wehrhahn Verlag.

O'Sullivan, Simon. 2012. *On the Production of Subjectivity: Five Diagrams of the Finite-Infinite Relation*. Houndmills: Palgrave Macmillan.

Schubin, Mark. 1996. "Searching for the Perfect Aspect Ratio." *SMPTE Journal* 105 (8): 460–78. doi:10.5594/J09548.

Schulze, Winfried, Werner Faulstich, Michael Giesecke, Johannes Burkhardt, and Gudrun Gersmann. 2005. "Begann die Neuzeit mit dem Buchdruck? Ist die Ära der Typographie im Zeitalter der digitalen Medien endgültig vorbei? Podiumsdiskussion unter der Leitung von Winlried Schulze." In *Kommunikation und Medien in der Frühen Neuzeit*, edited by Johannes Burkhardt and Christine Werkstetter, 11–38. Munich: De Gruyter Oldenbourg.

Sebok, Bryan. 2009. "Convergent Consortia: Format Battles in High Definition." *The Velvet Light Trap* 64 (1): 34–49. doi:10.1353/vlt.0.0040.

Seppi, Angelika. 2016. "Simply Complicated: Thinking in Folds." In *On Folding: Towards a New Field of Interdisciplinary Research*, edited by Michael Friedman and Wolfgang Schäffner, 49–76. Science Studies. Bielefeld: transcript.

Siegert, Bernhard. 1993. *Relais: Geschicke der Literatur als Epoche der Post, 1751–1913*. Berlin: Brinkmann & Bose.

————. 2010. "Türen. Zur Materialität des Symbolischen." *Zeitschrift für Medien- und Kulturforschung* 1 (1): 151–70.

————. 2013. "Cultural Techniques: Or the End of the Intellectual Postwar Era in German Media Theory." *Theory, Culture & Society* 30 (6): 48–65. doi:10.1177/0263276413488963.

————. 2015. *Cultural Techniques: Grids, Filters, Doors, and Other Articulations of the Real*. Translated by Geoffrey Winthrop-Young. New York: Fordham University Press.

Smither, Roger. 1987. "Formats and Standards: A Film Archive Perspective on Exchanging Computerized Data." *The American Archivist* 50 (3): 324–37. doi:10.17723/aarc.50.3.5802724670213420.

Sterne, Jonathan. 2012. *MP3: The Meaning of a Format*. Durham, NC: Duke University Press.

Steyerl, Hito. 2009. "In Defense of the Poor Image." *E-Flux*, no. 10 (November): 1–9.

Tanselle, G. Thomas. 1971. "The Bibliographical Description of Paper." *Studies in Bibliography* 24: 27–67. doi:10.2307/40371526.

———. 2000. "The Concept of Format." *Studies in Bibliography* 53: 67–115. doi:10.2307/40372094.

Vales, Laura. 1999. "Detrás de una puerta gris estaba la verdad." *Página/12*, November 25.

Walters, Tyler. 1995. "Thinking About Archival Preservation in the '90s and Beyond: Some Recent Publications and Their Implications for Archivists." *The American Archivist* 58 (4): 476–93. doi:10.17723/aarc.58.4.t05414u2q067767g.

Wehry, Matthias. 2017. "Digitale Rekonstruktion von historischem Bibliotheksgut: Projektvorstellung Leibniz-Fragmente und Massendigitalisierung von Flachware." *O-bib: Das offene Bibliotheksjournal* 4 (4): 189–98. doi:10.5282/o-bib/2017H4S189-198.

Wiedemeyer, Nina. 2014. "Buchfalten: Material Technik Gefüge der Künstlerbücher." Doctoral dissertation, Weimar: Bauhaus University Weimar.

Winthrop-Young, Geoffrey. 2014. "The Kultur of Cultural Techniques: Conceptual Inertia and the Parasitic Materialities of Ontologization." *Cultural Politics* 10 (3): 376–88. doi:10.1215/17432197-2795741.

Wolfe, Charles. 2009. "From Failure: On Prepositions and History." *The Velvet Light Trap* 64 (1): 98–99. doi:10.1353/vlt.0.0043.

Young, Liam Cole. 2015. "Cultural Techniques and Logistical Media: Tuning German and Anglo-American Media Studies." *M/C Journal* 18 (2). http://journal.media-culture.org.au/index.php/mcjournal/article/view/961.

Zinsmeister, Annett. 2004. "Transformation und Faltung." In *Digitale Transformationen: Medienkunst als Schnittstelle von Kunst, Wissenschaft, Wirtschaft und Gesellschaft*, edited by Monika Fleischmann and Ulrike Reinhard, 164–69. Heidelberg: whois.

The Screen as "Battleground": Eisenstein's "Dynamic Square" and the Plasticity of the Projection Format

Antonio Somaini

The question of the relations between the three concepts of format, medium, and *dispositif* is raised by different, pre- and post-digital ways of understanding the term "format." If we focus in particular on the history of cinema, we can study the relation between these three terms by referring to at least three different meanings of "format," indicating, respectively, the size of the photosensitive area of a frame within a celluloid film (8mm, 16mm, 35mm, 70mm, etc.), the aspect ratio of a projected image, and the way in which a digital moving image file is encoded for storage, processing, transmission and display, often through some kind of compression. In all three cases, what emerges is the close link between the concepts of "format" and "form": more precisely, between "format" and the process of "giving a standardized form" (in the sense of "formatting") to visual phenomena by capturing, storing, and organizing them through specific material supports, procedures, and techniques that will condition the way they will become visible again through some kind of visual or audiovisual *dispositif*.

Jonathan Sterne's (2012, 8) definition of the format as "what specifies the protocols by which a medium will operate", originally formulated in the context of a study on the history of the audio MP3 format, may also apply to the three meanings of format we just mentioned. The size of the photosensitive area of a frame within a celluloid film, the aspect ratio of a projected image, and the encoding of a digital image file define indeed some of the "protocols" according to which the medium of cinema operates, by conditioning its storage, processing, transmission, and display possibilities. Interpreted in this sense, the term format does not coincide with and may not be subsumed under the older notions of medium and *dispositif*. The three terms indicate three different levels that interact and intersect with one another without ever coinciding, and their history, etymology, and connotations are significantly different. The notion of "medium," for example, has a history within which different meanings and different genealogical lines interweave and intersect with one another. In it, we find not only the meanings of "medium" that emerged during the 1920s and 1930s—the medium as a means of mass communication (as in the expression "mass media") or as a set of supports, techniques, and procedures defining the specificity of some artistic practice (as in the expression "the medium of painting")—but also older understandings of "medium," such as the medium as a person or object acting as an intermediary between the realms of the living and the dead, as in the tradition of Spiritism or as a sensible environment, atmosphere, *milieu*, or *Umwelt* defining the conditions of sensory perception: a meaning that reaches back to Aristotle's notion of *metaxy* in his treatise *De Anima* and that reappears again in a series of contemporary studies on the material, environmental, and elemental dimensions of media.[1]

In this essay, I will study the relations between format, medium, and *dispositif* taking as a reference point a text that tackles the question of format (both in the sense of the photosensitive area of the frame within a celluloid film and in the sense of the aspect ratio of a projected image) from a point of view that is at the same time figurative, perceptual, psychological, anthropological, art-historical, and, we could say today, media-archaeological. The text, well known within the field of film studies, is entitled "The Dynamic Square," and was written by a film director, Sergei Eisenstein, who throughout his artistic and intellectual trajectory never ceased to explore the potential of the new techniques, formats, and *dispositifs* that were transforming the cinematic medium, such as sound, color, widescreen, and stereoscopic cinema. Eisenstein did not have the possibility to experiment with this last technology but nevertheless took it as the object of a long essay, "On Stereocinema," written in 1947 at the end of his life (Eisenstein 2013).

---

1   For a brief history of the concept of "medium" interpreted as sensible environment, atmosphere, *milieu*, or *Umwelt*, with a focus on Walter Benjamin's writings, see Somaini 2016. An example of the current relevance of this tradition for contemporary media theory can be found in Peters 2015.

"The Dynamic Square" is the title of a lecture given by Eisenstein at a meeting organized by the Technicians Branch of the Academy of Motion Pictures Arts and Sciences in Hollywood on September 17, 1930. After having left the Soviet Union in the summer of 1929 and travelled across Europe—visiting cities such as Berlin, Zürich, London, and Paris, where he entered into contact with film directors such as Jean Painlévé and the group of "dissident" Surrealists who had distanced themselves from André Breton in order to join Georges Bataille and his journal *Documents*[2]—Eisenstein arrived in the United States in the month of May 1930 together with his two close collaborators, the assistant Grigori Aleksandrov and the camera operator Eduard Tisse. Aleksandrov and Tisse had worked with him on all the films realized during the 1920s—*Strike* (1924-25), *Battleship Potemkin* (1925), *October* (1927-28), and *The General Line* (1926-29)—and would accompany him across Mexico, between December 1930 and March 1932, to work on another film project destined to remain unfinished, *Que viva Mexico!*.

After a few weeks spent on the East Coast, during the summer of 1930 Eisenstein settled in California, where, thanks to the mediation of the producer Jesse L. Lasky, he signed a contract with Paramount Pictures. None of the film projects Eisenstein worked on while under contract—*An American Tragedy*, from a 1925 novel by Theodore Dreiser; *Glass House*, a dystopian film set in an entirely transparent building reminiscent of the most ambitious projects of glass architecture developed during the 1920s;[3] *Sutter's Gold*, based on the novel *L'Or: La merveilleuse histoire du général Johann August Suter* (1925) by Blaise Cendrars—was developed beyond the stage of a script accompanied by drawings, and the contract itself was ceased by mutual consent in October 1930.

Even though the collaboration with Paramount didn't lead to any actual film being realized, the encounter with the Hollywood studio system led Eisenstein to face a number of technical transformations which were taking place at the end of the 1920s, such as the introduction of various wide-screen formats, the competition between them, and the drive towards standardization. Since the second half of the 1920s, a number of wide-screen formats (based either on wide film or on wide-projection formats, sometimes using anamorphic distortions) had been gradually introduced. Natural Vision, developed by George K. Spoor and P. John Berggren, was a

2   On Eisenstein's six months in Paris between November 1929 and May 1930, see Rebecchi 2018.

3   Eisenstein's notes and drawings for the unrealized film project *Glass House* have been published in French translation in Eisenstein 2009. On *Glass House*, see Somaini 2017.

process using 63.5mm film, a 1.84 negative aspect ratio, and a 2:1 projection aspect ratio (a/r, from now on), which was used for the first time in 1926 for a film on the Niagara Falls and then in 1927 for J. Stuart Blackton's film *The American*, also known as *The Flag Maker*. Fox Grandeur, developed by Fox Film Corporation in 1929, used 70mm film, a 2.07:1 negative a/r, and a 2:1 projection a/r. Vitascope, developed by United Artists in 1930, used 65mm film, a 2:1 negative a/r, and a 2.05:1 projection a/r. And Magnafilm, developed by United Artists, used 70mm film. In 1930, RKO Radio Pictures developed another kind of Natural Vision, this time using 65mm film. Finally, if we limit ourselves to the main widescreen formats developed before Eisenstein's lecture, there was Realife, developed by MGM, which used 70mm film, a 2.07:1 negative a/r, and a 1.75:1 projection a/r.

The memorandum distributed before the meeting organized by the Technicians Branch of the Academy of Motion Pictures Arts and Sciences did not mention specifically any of these widescreen formats, but rather a broader idea of "Wide Film and Wide Screen formats" with aspect ratios of 3:4, 3:5, and 3:6 (Eisenstein 2010b, 206). The aim of the meeting was to evaluate these different horizontal formats, both in aesthetic and in technical terms, in the effort to reach some kind of consensus among technicians and producers leading eventually to some kind of standardization. One of the authors mentioned in the memorandum, Loyd A. Jones, pleaded in favor of wide, horizontal formats based on what he considered to be a prevalence of the horizontal format in the history of painting: his contribution was accompanied by a series of statistical considerations, mainly based on pre-Impressionist landscape paintings, according to which the dominant ratio of base to altitude in the history of painting was 1:1.5 (Jones 1930).

In opening section of his lecture, Eisenstein positions himself immediately against any form of standardized, normative approach to projection formats, stating that "by not devoting enough attention to this problem, and by permitting the standardisation of a new screen shape without the thorough weighing of all the pros and cons of the question, we risk paralysing once more, for years and years to come, our compositional efforts in new shapes as unfortunately chosen as those from which the practical realisation of the Wide Film and the Wide Screen now seems to give us the opportunity of freeing ourselves" (Eisenstein 2010b, 206). His plea in favor of the widest freedom in spatial frame composition is followed by the concrete proposal of a "dynamic square," a square film format that would be *dynamic* in the sense that it could produce different projection formats at any stage during the screening of a film, exploring—through manipulations during filming or editing that would mask "a part of the shape of the film square, the frame" (Eisenstein 2010b, 209)—the whole range of smaller squares and vertical or horizontal rectangles that are contained within the initial, basic square.

The plasticity of this square film format, according to Eisenstein, would allow the medium of cinema to adapt to the multiple spaces, objects, and shapes that could be represented within a film, opening up a maximum degree of freedom in spatial and figurative composition, without privileging either the horizontal dimension or the vertical one. Following a conflictual and dialectical approach to film form that he had developed at the end of the 1920s (in particular in "The Dramaturgy of Film Form," written in 1929 and meant to be published in the catalogue of the exhibition *Film und Foto* in Stuttgart[4]), Eisenstein sees in the "dynamic square" a flexible screen shape capable of visualizing the contrasts between "vertical and horizontal tendencies" that can be found in the visible world and that—through a kind of empathic experience of space that had been theorized in the field of art history by figures such as August Schmarsow and Heinrich Wölf-flin[5]—become psychological contrasts in the spectator. As we read in "The Dynamic Square":

> In the forms of nature as in the forms of industry, and in the mutual encounter between these forms, we find the struggle, the conflict between both tendencies. And the screen—as a faithful mirror, not only of conflicts emotional and tragic, but equally of conflicts psychological and optically spatial—must be an appropriate battleground for the skirmishes of both these optical-by-view, but profoundly psychological-by-meaning, spatial tendencies on the part of the spectator. (Eisenstein 2010b, 208)

The only screen shape that can allow these horizontal and vertical tendencies to unleash all their expressive and dialectic potential, according to Eisenstein, is the square, the "dynamic square":

> The battlefield for such a struggle is easily found—*it is the square.* . . . The one and only form that is equally fit, by alternately suppressing right and left or up and down, to embrace all the multitude of

4   An English translation of this text, originally written by Eisenstein in German, can be found in Eisenstein 2010a.

5   On the presence of the question of empathy in German theories of architecture between the end of the 19th and the beginning of the 20th century, see Mallgrave and Ikonomou 1994 (which contains also an English translation of August Schmarsow's "Das Wesen der architektonischen Schöpfung," 1894).

expressive rectangles in the world. Or used as a whole to engrave itself by the 'cosmic' imperturbability of its *squareness* in the psychology of the audience.

And this specially in a *dynamic* succession of *dimensions* from a tiny square in the center to the all-embracing full-sized square of the whole screen!

The dynamic square screen, that is to say one providing in its dimensions the opportunity of impressing, in projection, with absolute grandeur every geometrically conceivable form of the picture limit. (Eisenstein 2010b, 208–209)

In *Battleship Potemkin*, Eisenstein had experimented with such a possibility in the scenes of the mass pilgrimage, across the city and the port of Odessa, toward the little tent on the dock hosting the body of the deceased sailor Vakulinchuk, one of the protagonists of the mutiny (fig. 1).

[Figure 1] Still from *Battleship Potemkin* (1925).

This experiment, as Eisenstein recalls in "The Dynamic Square," had been limited and insufficient, since the masking of the two lateral portions of the horizontal frame had produced indeed "an upright standing strip" but had not broken really with the dominant, horizontal format. "The *vertical spirit*," writes Eisenstein, "can never be attained in this way: first, because the occupied space comparative to the horizontal masked space will never be interpreted as something *axially opposed to it*, but always *as a part* of the latter, and, second, because in *never surpassing the height* that is bound to the horizontal dominant, it will never impress as an opposite space axis, the one of uprightness" (Eisenstein 2010b, 209). In one of the sections of his unfinished book *Nonindifferent Nature* (1939–45), Eisenstein recalls how for the premiere of the film in Moscow he had imagined a more daring solution, which would have emphasized even more the plasticity of the screen. At the end of the projection, as the gigantic stern of the battleship comes closer and closer to the spectators sitting in the movie theater (fig. 2), the screen was supposed to be suddenly torn by a real stern, onto which some of the real sailors of the Battleship Potemkin in 1905 would have stood in front of the audience, a sudden breach out of the space of representation into the space of the spectator.[6] Eisenstein had found numerous examples of this in Kabuki theater, where a long, raised platform called *hanamichi* cuts across the space of the audience and is used for the main character's entrances and exits (fig. 3).

[Figure 2] Still from *Battleship Potemkin* (1925).

6   A description of this idea, which was not carried out, can be found in Eisenstein 1987, 33–34.

[Figure 3] *Hanamichi* stage at National Theatre of Japan. Source: Nesnad / Wikimedia Commons (CC BY 4.0 license).

One of the unrealized projects Eisenstein worked on first in Berlin in 1926 and then while under contract with Paramount in 1930, *Glass House*, was specifically conceived as an experiment in spatial frame composition. Meant to be staged and filmed within a completely transparent space, *Glass House* was characterized by a camera that could see through glass walls, ceilings, and pavements (fig. 4). Initially unaware of this transparency, the protagonists of *Glass House* would have suddenly perceived it, turning the space of the house into a dystopian environment of relentless optical surveillance. In this way, the film staged a double, aesthetic and political experiment, exploring the figurative potential of glass as a transparent material and analyzing the consequences of a social life unfolding in a condition of total transparency.

During the 1920s, the widespread use of the technique of masking (including the particular cases of the iris shot, the counter matte or *cache/contre-cache*, and the split-screen) are the sign of a shared need to overcome the rigidity of the standardized 1:1.33 aspect ratio of silent films in order to explore a whole new range of expressive possibilities. The different types of masking allowed film directors to reframe the image, for example by giving it a circular or oval form surrounded by a black halo, thereby evoking the opening of the eye or the view through a hole or

[Figure 4] Eisenstein's sketch for *Glass House*. Source: Eisenstein 2009.

[Figure 5 a–d] Stills from *Der müde Tod* (1921) with masking in various shapes and formats.

[Figure 6] Still from *Der müde Tod* (1921)

through a lens, with all the aesthetic and psychological connotations that this reframing of vision might entail.

Among the many examples we could mention within the cinema of the 1920s, Fritz Lang's *Der müde Tod* [*Destiny*] (1921) shows us how the technique of masking could be used for different kinds of circular, oval, rectangular, or even triangular reframing (fig. 5). Lang introduced a reframing that architectural forms, such as ogival arches and circular openings (fig. 6), often create with their dark walls producing the effects of masking. In the film, these various kinds of reframing end up *compressing* the visible space, by surrounding it with areas of shade and black which seem to symbolize the haunting presence of death, the central theme of the film.[7]

Many other examples of variable projection formats might be mentioned, such as the triple-screen projection (later renamed "Polyvision") with which Abel Gance experimented in the final section of his monumental *Napoléon* (1927). At the moment in the narrative when the film shows Napoleon's invasion of Italy, the single-screen projection, with its 1:1.33 aspect ratio, suddenly turns into a tryptich with an astounding aspect ratio of 1:4.00: a wide projection format that allows Gance to explore a

7   For an interesting analysis of Fritz Lang's use of different kind of maskings in *Der müde Tod*, see Kuo 2018, 286-291.

[Figure 7] Three stills from *Napoléon* (1927).

whole series variations in frame composition (fig. 7). László Moholy-Nagy mentions Gance's *Napoléon* in the second edition of his *Malerei Fotografie Film* (*Painting Photography Film*), published in 1927, in which he dedicates a chapter to what he calls, in German, "Das simultane oder Polykino," the "simultaneous cinema" or "polycinema," a new cinematic *dispositif* consisting in a semi-spherical, concave screen onto which several films could be projected at the same time. In his book Moholy-Nagy presents a diagram (fig. 8) of what he considered to be an example of how one could approach the cinematic *dispositif* in a "productive" way, "productive" in the sense of creative, unconventional, unprecedented, and according to a general vision of artistic practice as a "productive," sensory-enhancing approach to media such as painting, photography, film, typography, and radio that Moholy-Nagy theorizes throughout his book. The diagram is accompanied by a concrete demonstration of how three films could be projected at the same time, overlapping onto one another within the semi-spherical screen of the Polykino:

> From left to right runs the film of Mister A: birth, life story. From bottom to top runs the film of Madam B: birth, life story. The projection surfaces of the two films intersect one another: love, marriage, etc. The two films can then either intersect each other, through overlapping sequences of events, or run parallel to one another; or, a new, common

Um recht deutlich zu werden, teile ich eine schematische **Skizze** mit

Von links nach rechts läuft der Film des Herrn **A**: Geburt, Lebenslauf. Von unten nach oben läuft der Film der Dame **B**: Geburt, Lebenslauf. Die Projektions⸗ flächen der beiden Filme schneiden sich: Liebe, Ehe usw. Die beiden Filme können dann entweder sich kreuzend, in durchscheinenden Geschehnisfolgen oder parallel nebeneinander weiterlaufen; oder es kann ein neuer gemeinsamer Film der beiden Personen an die Stelle der beiden ersten treten. Als dritter bzw. vierter Film könnte der Film des Herrn **C** gleichzeitig mit den Vorgängen **A** und **B** von oben nach unten oder von rechts nach links oder auch in anderer Richtung laufen, bis er die anderen Filme sinngemäß schneiden bzw. decken kann, usw.

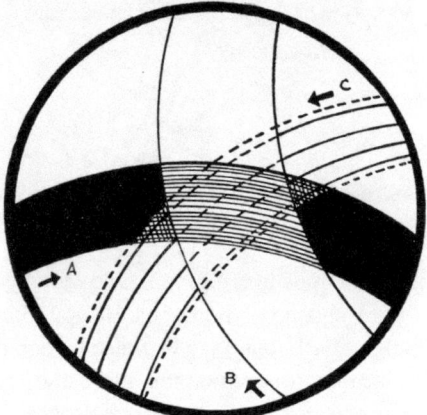

Ein solches **Schema** wird natürlich für ungegenständliche Lichtprojektionen in der Art der Fotogramme ebenso geeignet, wenn nicht geeigneter sein. Mit Ein⸗

40

[Figure 8] "Polycinema" projection diagram. Source: Moholy-Nagy 1927.

film of the two persons might step in and replace the two previous ones. As a third or fourth film there could be the film of Mister C, which could run at the same time as the events unfolding in the films A and B, moving from top to bottom or from right to left, or in any other direction, until it would cross paths in a meaningful way with the other films, by intersecting them, being superimposed onto them, etc. (Moholy-Nagy 1927, 40, our translation)

Eisenstein's lecture on the "dynamic square" comes, therefore, at the end of a decade that had seen many experiments on the format of image projection: through masking, multi-screen dispositives, and variations on the shape and size of the screen itself. Well aware of all these experiments, Eisenstein presents us with a unique example of how the question of the projection format and of its relationship with cinema as a medium and a *dispositif* might be tackled from a series of different points of view: figurative, perceptual, psychological, anthropological, art-historical, and media-archaeological.

Figurative, to begin with, because Eisenstein emphasizes the fact that only a dynamic projection format may enhance "the figurative potential of the screen" and therefore allow a reconsideration of "the whole aesthetic of figurative composition in cinema which for thirty years has been rendered inflexible by the inflexibility of the proportions of a screen frame determined inflexibly once and for all" (Eisenstein 2010b, 206). The "dynamic square" may in fact adapt to the wide variety of horizontal and vertical forms that can be found in the profilmic space, both in natural landscapes and in man-made, built environments. Many of these forms, he writes, "have been banished from the screen until today" (Eisenstein 2010b, 209). Among them we find vertical forms: "Glimpses along winding medieval streets or of huge Gothic cathedrals overwhelming them. Or these replaced by minarets if the town portrayed should happen to be oriental. Decent shots of totem poles, the Paramount building in New York, Primo Carnera, or the profound and abysmal canyons of Wall Street in all their expressiveness" (Eisenstein 2010b, 209). We also find horizontal forms, such as the infinite horizons, fields, plains and deserts of "the Death Valley" (Eisenstein 2010b, 208), a landscape that Eisenstein would soon find again in Mexico, in the wide open fields of agave that we see in the images shot for the episode "Maguey" of *Que viva Mexico!*.

Perceptual, then, because only the "dynamic square" projection format seems to respond, according to Eisenstein, to both the *horizontal* and *vertical* dimensions of human visual experience, without privileging exclusively the lateral vision through a kind of "passive horizontalism" (Eisenstein 2010b, 207).

Psychological, since the "dynamic square," with its unstable format, may become "a gigantic new agent of impression" onto the mind and the body of the spectator, opening up, through "the rhythmic assemblage of varied screen shapes" (Eisenstein 2010b, 218), new possibilities within that constant search for expressive means capable of influencing the spectator that characterizes Eisenstein's entire theoretical reflection: from the early essays on the "expressive movement" of the actor and on the "montage of attractions" to the late writings on "pathos," "ecstasy," and the "regression" toward "pre-logical," "sensorial," "archaic" forms of thought and expression that we find in unfinished book projects such as *Nonindifferent Nature* (1939–45) and *Method* (1932–48).[8]

Anthropological, since the to-and-fro between vertical and horizontal views allowed by the "dynamic square" leads the spectator to reexperience the transition from horizontal to vertical life forms that, according to Eisenstein, characterizes both the development of the single human individual and the development of entire societies, according to a vision of history based on the parallelism between ontogenesis and phylogenesis, which appears throughout Eisenstein's late writings. As he writes in "The Dynamic Square,"

> We started as worms creeping on our stomachs. Then we ran horizontally for hundreds of years on our four legs. But we only became something like mankind from the moment when we hoisted ourselves on to our hind legs and assumed the vertical position. Repeating the same process locally in the verticalisation of our facial angle too. (Eisenstein 2010b, 207)

This gradual drive towards the vertical dimension, though, did not lead for him to a disappearance of the previous, horizontal forms of perception, both at the individual and at the societal level:

> In the heart of the super-industrialised American, or the busily self-industrialising Russian, there still remains a nostalgia for infinite horizons, fields, plains, and deserts. . . . An individual nation achieves the height of mechanisation yet marries it to our peasant and farmer of yesteryear. The nostalgia of "big trails," "fighting caravans," "covered wagons" and the endless breadth of "old man rivers." . . . This nostalgia cries out for horizontal space. (Eisenstein 2010b, 208)

Art-historical, since the "dynamic square" allows cinema to refer to the various horizontal and vertical composition formats that can be found throughout the history of the arts, not only in the West but also in the East. In his text Eisenstein mentions—referring once more to that Japanese cultural and artistic tradition he had been interested in since the early

---

8   For a partial translation of the texts that Eisenstein had written for the book project entitled *Method*, see Eisenstein 2017. On the idea of "sensorial thinking", one of the core idea of Eisenstein's unfinished book, see Vogman 2018.

1920s—the *makimono* and *kakemono*, the horizontal and vertical scroll paintings produced within a figurative culture that did not adopt any kind of rigid framing nor privilege the horizontal format, as one could see, for example, in the variable shapes of the *ukiyo-e* woodblock prints of Hokusai's series *One Hundred Views of Mount Fuji*, for example *Mount Fuji Seen Through a Spider Web* (fig. 9).

[Figure 9] *Mount Fuji Seen Through a Spider Web*, woodblock print by Hokusai (ca. 1849).

Source: Smithsonian Libraries.

Media-archaeological, finally, because the plastic, malleable, unstable projection format that Eisenstein suggests with his "dynamic square" is a way of acknowledging the fact that cinema, rather than having any kind of medium-specificity that isolates it from other moving-image and projected-image media, is firmly rooted within the *longue durée* of a whole series of forms of light and image projection, each of which produced different kinds of formats. In his notes for a "general history of cinema"—an unfinished book project that Eisenstein developed during the last two years of his life, between 1946 and 1948[9]—the media-archaological dimension that pervades much of Eisenstein's writings of the 1930s and 1940s comes to the foreground, and it is here that we find the idea that filmic projections are part of a history to which belong the light filtered through the stained-glass windows of the Gothic cathedrals and producing different color light plays through the space of the nave and onto the interior walls, the light projections of magic lanterns and phantasmagorias, the various traditions of shadow theater and shadow projections (the Javanese *Wayang* and the Turkish *karagöz*), the projected light of the Dioramas, Loïe Fuller's light shows, the revolving lighthouse on the Palais de l'Industrie in 1889 and the centuries-long tradition of fireworks. According to Eisenstein, in the projection of a film into a movie theater, one can feel the echo of these various traditions of image projection, thereby refusing to accept any standardized, normative projection format.

This media-archaeological dimension of Eisenstein's essay leads us to draw a series of conclusions concerning how the relation between format, medium, and *dispositif* emerges from his idea of the screen as a "dynamic square." Rather than being confined within the perimeter of some kind of medium specificity, cinema is for him a medium that is firmly located within a wide network of media that constantly remediate each other, interweaving with one another throughout the course of history. Cinema's *dispositif* is not a fixed set of elements deployed in space according to a stable configuration, but rather a *dispositif* that never stops transforming in time. The first experiments of stereoscopic cinema carried out during the 1940s in the United States and the Soviet Union, for example, were considered by Eisenstein as a form of extending the process of montage from the flat space of the screen to the entire volume of the movie theater, impacting much more directly the bodies and the senses of the spectators. The idea of a malleable, flexible projection format that is synthesized with the expression "dynamic square" is fully coherent with such an open vision of the cinematic medium and the cinematic *dispositif*, and directly linked

9   See Eisenstein 2016.

to Eisenstein's belief in the limitless potential of montage. His idea of the "dynamic square" envisioned the screen as a "battleground" through which "the magic force that is montage" could open up "an entirely new era of constructive possibilities" (Eisenstein 2010b, 215).

References

Eisenstein, Sergei. 1987. *Nonindifferent Nature*. Translated by Herbert Marshall. Cambridge: Cambridge University Press.

———. 2009. *Glass House*. Edited by Alexandre Laumonier. Dijon: Les Presses du Réel.

———. 2010a. "The Dramaturgy of Film Form (The Dialectical Approach to Film Form)" [1929]. In Sergei Eisenstein, *Writings, 1922–1934. Selected Works Volume 1*, edited and translated by Richard Taylor, 161–80. London: I.B. Tauris.

———. 2010b. "The Dynamic Square" [1930]. In Sergei Eisenstein, *Writings, 1922–1934. Selected Works Volume 1*, edited and translated by Richard Taylor, 206–18. London: I.B. Tauris.

———. 2013. "On Stereocinema" [1947]. In *3D Cinema and Beyond*, edited by Dan Adler, Janine Marchessault, and Sanja Obradovic, 20-59. Toronto: Public Books and Intellect.

———. 2016. *Notes for a General History of Cinema*. Edited by Naum Kleiman and Antonio Somaini. Amsterdam: Amsterdam University Press.

———. 2017. *The Primal Phenomenon: Art*. Edited by Oksana Bulgakowa and Dietmar Hochmuth. Translated by Dustin Condren. Berlin: PotemkinPress.

Jones, Loyd A. 1930. "Rectangle Proportions in Pictorial Composition." *Journal of the Society of Motion Picture Engineers* 14 (1): 32–49.

Kuo, Li-chen. 2018. *Le noir comme invention du cinéma: matière, forme, dispositif*. PhD dissertation. Paris: Université Sorbonne Nouvelle Paris 3.

Mallgrave, Harry Francis, and Ikonomou, Eleftherios, eds. 1994. *Empathy, Form, and Space: Problems in German Aesthetics, 1873–1893*. Santa Monica: The Getty Center for the History of Art and the Humanities.

Moholy-Nagy, László. 1927. *Malerei Fotografie Film*. Munich: Albert Langen.

Peters, John Durham. 2015. *The Marvelous Clouds: Toward a Philosophy of Elemental Media*. Chicago: The University of Chicago Press.

Rebecchi, Marie. 2018. *Paris 1929: Eisenstein, Bataille, Buñuel*. Milan: Mimésis.

Somaini, Antonio. 2016. "Walter Benjamin's Media Theory: The *Medium* and the *Apparat*." *Grey Room* 62 (Winter 2016): 6–41.

———. 2017. *La Glass House de Sergueï Eisenstein*. Paris: Éditions B2.

Sterne, Jonathan. 2012. *MP3: The Meaning of a Format*. Durham, NC: Duke University Press.

Vogman, Elena. 2018. *Sinnliches Denken: Eisensteins exzentrische Methode*. Berlin: Diaphanes.

HD's Invention of Continuity and SD's Resistance? A Historiography of Cinema and Film to (Be)come and Formats to Overcome

Oliver Fahle and Elisa Linseisen

In our paper, we propose the necessity of implementing the concept "format" to reflect on the correlation between cinema, film, and the digital, which currently finds its film-theoretical condensation in the notion "post-cinema" and the (problematic) interdependence of "the analog" and "the digital." We want neither to deepen the historiographic ditch by talking about "revolution" or "paradigmatic changes" nor to overcome the threshold by seeking continuity between the analog and digital. Rather, we would like to explore cinematic development in terms of its change and modification, or, in other words, its *becoming*, which is, after all, a genuinely cinematic category. Therefore, we will proceed in the three following steps: First, we want to outline that, from a film-philosophical perspective, a development from analog to digital would count not as problematic but rather as a genuine cinematic form of modernization. Second, we would like to use the current post-cinematic debate and Francesco Casetti's model, his "seven keywords for the cinema to come" (2015), on the subject to expose two interconnected historiographic tendencies of cinematic persistence and resistance. We would like to cut them down to the notions "medium" and "format." Taking David Joselit's efforts into account, we understand formats and formatting in the context of motion pictures as "image-power." The latter, we would like to argue, would offer a historiography that does not claim paradigmatic changes or inventions of continuity. Third, we would like to exemplify this using the case of high-definition (HD) digital imagery, in correlation with and in contrast to other digital formats, here recognized through standard definition (SD). At this intersection of two digital formats, we recognize generation loss, the loss of quality when copying digital data, as a form of historiographical resistance that continues to write a history of cinema and film to come, but also of formats to overcome.

I.

The historiography of film can be showcased through its own discussion with other media, by integrating the latter into film's techno-aesthetic configurations. These inclusions can be named as an increase in complexity of what can be defined as cinema or film. Complexity then would not only put a distinct ontological status at stake but also take this signifying fragility as a recursive "offer" to develop even further. That is what we call cinematic becoming. The questions "What is cinema?" and "What is film?" reoccur as film-philosophical questions, posed by the medium itself. Film answers with new aesthetic forms, namely breaking with existing norms and perpetually reinventing itself under the strain of other media influences. We identify a development in cinema and film that occurs exactly at the moment when cinema is challenged by other media. But we understand this "collision" as necessity for film and cinema to evolve further (Fahle 2011). What we infer is that cinema and film only reflect their own mediality if they are able to reflect about other media or problematize their relation with them. By establishing these relationships, cinema and film refer to what cinema and film are not. But we cannot understand this mode of differentiation as a distinct media threshold. On the contrary, defining what cinema and film are not is an inherent part of cinema and film itself (Fahle 2015).

With the help of Gilles Deleuze, we can detect the dynamic of cinematic becoming. Deleuze describes a setting that reveals itself in a highly medialized form as cinema and film rival with the whole world: it is a "world which looks to us like a bad film" (1989, 172). In a letter to Serge Daney, Deleuze specifies his disfavor: "that's just what television amounts to, the whole world turning to film" (1995, 78). When "the world itself is turning cinematic, becoming 'just an act' directly controlled and immediately processed by a television," then cinema and film have to take "the battle to the heart of cinema, making cinema see it as *its* problem" (Deleuze 1995, 76, 75). For Deleuze, therefore, cinema and film are *"pure immanence"* (2005); they are what they are and what they are not at the same time. Deleuze expresses this paradox as a demand: "Cinema ought to stop 'being cinematic,' stop playacting, and set up specific relationships with video, with electronic and digital images, in order to develop a new form of resistance" (1995, 76).

Malte Hagener uses Deleuze's idea of immanence for his concept "media-immanence" (2011, 51; Medienimmanenz)[1] to describe current media constellations under digital influence. Here, we observe the same situation that Deleuze describes as "bad film": media do not simply represent a world; instead, the world is made by media. Hagener points out that no distinction can be drawn between cinema, film, and reality because cinema and film have interwoven deeply into the texture of daily life (2011, 52). In a time of media-immanence, there should no longer be any doubt that audiovisual media have become ubiquitous, or, as Hagener argues, that "our perception and our thinking have become cinematographic" (2011, 52).[2] Whatever we experience is always already mediated, "so that we are, in a certain way, in the cinema, even if this is (physically) not the case" (Hagener 2011, 52).[3] Media-immanence describes a state of dereferentialization that makes it hard to distinguish already fragile media identities such as video, electronic, and digital images and therefore disperses not only cinema and film but also the term "media." As we have pointed out, in film philosophy and film theory, this state of media-immanence is not seen as a problem for film and cinema in that they vary, modify, and readjust, thereby describing an infinite state of becoming.

II.

Suddenly, this story of discontinuous continuity seems to be convulsed by another "rhythm." With the millennium, a media-historiographical, allegedly insurmountable classification enters cinema and film's becoming: digitality. The phenomena that can instantly be summarized under this notion were endowed with the great promise of modernization and development: there were so-called *"new"* media (Manovich 2002, most prominently), and all analog media, such as cinema and film, were downgraded as "old," despite their capacity to modernize. This disfavor addresses analog cinema and film, which prompts a number of theoreticians to proclaim that cinema and film have to be something different now, but not in an immanent but dissociative, deconstructive way (Rodowick 2007, most prominently).

1   All translations by Elisa Linseisen.
2   "sind selbst unsere Wahrnehmung und unser Denken kinematographisch geworden."
3   "so dass wir in gewisser Weise im Kino sind, selbst wenn dies (physisch) nicht der Fall ist."

Post-cinema is a reaction to a particular form of media historiography, one that considers the introduction of "the digital" as a paradigmatic shift, shattered by the ontological uncertainty of what cinema and film actually *are*. To distinguish itself from these first euphemisms, a still ongoing discourse about the latest state of cinema and film has run underneath this notion for nearly a decade. Post-cinematic film theory tries to adjust and match the indicated capacity of cinematic becoming and the capacity of a specific form of digital modulation (Linseisen 2018). As an important position in the post-cinematic discourse, Francesco Casetti's book *The Lumière Galaxy* shall be named here. Proposing seven key concepts for a cinema to come—"relocation," "relics/icons," "assemblage," "expansion," "hypertopia," "display," "performance"—Casetti outlines a way to think of cinema and film's transformation and by doing so reaffirms our suggested film-philosophical understanding. Casetti points out that under digital circumstances cinema relocates itself within media-immanence but does not dissolve. Several cinematic characteristics are saved, even when cinema and film show up in formerly "uncinematic" environments. His post-cinematic statement is to think about the continuity of cinema in the interplay of media persistence, which would not be a fixed "dispositive" named cinema, but rather multiple cinematic configurations enabling a cinematic *experience* across various media and formats.

His concept of relocation allows Casetti to abstract from a media-technical fixation on film and cinema. To do so, Casetti uses Walter Benjamin's idea of "thin media" (Benjamin 1991, 126).[4] Here the characteristics of mediality lie not in an ontological density but in its potential to *effect*. These effects or impacts come into being when the medium liberates itself from its historical confinement. Some characteristics of mediality shine brighter as a "thin layer" and help to specify what a medium actually is far away from its original context, object, and related "topological ballast." What does that mean for the identity of film and cinema? As an answer, Casetti reveals his heuristics:

> The relocation of cinema triggers a discursive strategy aimed at rendering the past and the present instrumentally compatible. In reading current situations in light of what cinema has been, we interpret in a somewhat forced way not only what we find before us, but also our point of comparison itself. In this manner, we seem to "invent" continuity. (Casetti 2015, 210–211)

---

4   Benjamin writes: "Immer aber ist dieses Medium verhältnismäßig dünner als dasjenige auf das diese Werke zur Entstehungszeit auf ihre Zeitgenossen wirkten" (1991, 126).

Cinema and film in Casetti's post-cinematic approach aren't historical, nor material or concrete results, but discursive strategies of "thin media." They have to lose their "ontological density" to live on as a media ideal. Why is this necessary? Post-cinematic media-immanence seems to depend to a certain degree on media idealization to develop in line with a historical continuity. And this is related to what we would like to implement as cinema and film's formats. To catch up with Casetti's dynamic of expanding cinema, some stable ideas of cinema and film have to remain. Otherwise, their identity would fade into the plurality of its formatted existences through relocation. If, for example, William Wyler's *Ben-Hur* (1959), shot with an MGM Camera 65 using 65mm film stock with an aspect ratio of 2.76:1, were to be relocated to television, then it would be necessary to think about the serious stylistic interventions involved, such as pan-and-scan procedures and letter- and pillar-boxing, which reframe the image to fit either PAL or NTSC frames. Image formats constitute the link between material individuality in shape, size, and proportion and its infrastructural adaptability. Formats stand for distributed conspicuity, which in the case of *Ben-Hur* meant hazarding film aesthetic consequences.

How do these aesthetic changes, which are brought up by the relocation of film and cinema, have an impact on what can be understood as their identity? Do these moments of reformatting comply with cinematic becoming? First, we note that in times of media-immanence forms of reformatting increase, as cinema and film relocate across a widening range of media and platforms. Müller (2015) identifies the introduction of digital computers as the moment when formats and formatting become ubiquitous. Here, formats describe not only the physical materiality of storage media but also the cultural techniques involved in the digital practices that make media readable and accessible and its content organizable. The notions "format" and "formatting" therefore seem to develop, first of all, specifically in relation to digital phenomena and, second, display this relation as widespread mediality, or, in our words, a form of media-immanence.

Post-cinematic digital media-immanence seems to be highly influenced by steady processes of reformatting.[5] From that point of view, a certain amount of idealization seems necessary to think about mediality. The

5   Florian Krautkrämer extends Malter Hagener's concept of media-immanence into "post-cinematic media-immanence" (2014, 124; Postkinematographische Medienimmanenz). He creates a setting that allows one to watch audiovisual material from different sources on different screens and to de-locate media from their context as well as relocate them.

cinematic way of becoming therefore cannot be thought in combination with an excessive way of reformatting. The identity of cinema and film had to be stabilized. This could be done, as Casetti suggests, with the help of discursive strategies, that invent continuity and think about cinema and film as an overexposed idea of the medium's present and past. Furthermore, as we would like to suggest, the plurality of formats also supplies a solution. Formats do not feature characteristics of historical persistence and invented continuity; rather, they resist development. This means that formats are not easily transferable from one historical context to another. They would not appear as "thin formats" in Benjamin's sense. Formats rely to a certain extent on the media-technical surrounding in which they circulate. If this network is left out, incompatibilities have to be taken into account. The resistance of the format also can be understood as a supportive facility to stabilize the invented continuity of media historiography. It does so by setting up historical push-backs and media-technological confines that prevent thin media from fading into oblivion.

The resistance of the format also enables a new perspective on the idea of media-immanence. In the following, we branch off into art theory to explain how this could work. David Joselit seems to have listened to Deleuze's demand to look for a new form of resistance by amplifying the range of avant-gardism with what he calls "image-power," a new wave of "modernization" in art that is "devoted to seizing circulation as a technology of power" (2011, 94). Joselit's idea of image-power centers on the concept "format," as distinct from the notion "medium," because of its "capacity to configure data in multiple possible ways." For Joselit, format "is a more useful term than 'medium,' which, all heroic efforts to the contrary, can seldom shed its intimate connection to matter (paint, wood, lead, paper, chalk, video, etc.)" (2011, 82). In art theory the correlation between medium and matter is strongly in place in Clement Greenberg's ([1939] 1989) classical-modernistic understanding of "medium" as the material specificity of art, particularly of painting, and Rosalind Krauss's (1999, 2000) postmodern understanding of mediality. Krauss (2000, 5) emphasizes the ideas of modernization and dereferentialization that we sketched above in discarding the notion of medium, which is so bound up in Greenberg's restriction of media essence based on materiality.

Joselit denies the notion "medium" *explicitly* because of its connotation of materiality by using the notion "format." "Format" then could not, as we recognized in the case of *Ben-Hur*, be understood as the pure material property of mediality. Joselit develops his idea on formats, first, by taking the high potential of *circulation* into account, "where value is purposely diminished as opposed to accumulated through the dissemination of images" (2011, 84). Arriving at meaning not from a fertile act of production but in its aftermath, Joselit labels image-power as *effects*, an "almost pure transitivity in the absence of a direct object" (93). As "consequences that cannot be fully anticipated during the phase of aesthetic production" (93), derivations are possible and introduce counter-distributions that won't follow the predefined path of circulation and attest the potential that "any quantum of data might lend itself to several, possible contradictory, formats" (82). The solution to facing this erratic aggregation of definitions is to find tools to encounter a vast form of medialization, or, with Hagener, we might say, a media-immanent world.

This "shift from producing to formatting" is what Joselit calls the "epistemology of search," "where knowledge is produced by discovering and/or constructing meaningful patterns—formats—from vast reserves of raw data" (2011, 82). Resistance with the help of formats can be seen in their unpredictability. Variety and modification would lie, then, not so much in media materiality or its aesthetic contouring as in its handling and processing. These "vast reserves of raw data" seek and ask for a critical handling, which would demonstrate how patterns of links generate formats. What Joselit seeks with his idea of formats is overcoming the commonplace to understand art as object:

> In mediums a material substrate (such as paint or canvas) converges with an aesthetic tradition (such as painting). Ultimately, mediums lead to objects, and thus reification, but formats are nodal connections and differential fields; they channel an unpredictable array of ephemeral currents and charges. They are configurations of force rather than discrete objects. In short, formats establish a pattern of links or connections. (2013, 55)

Taking Joselit's understanding of format and putting it into relation with post-cinema, we see that media-immanence shows an excessive dynamic that, in our opinion, perpetuates cinematic becoming and the effects of thin media. It seems that some sort of divergence is needed to stop a supposedly boundless expansion, an exponentiated effect and an undifferentiated form of development. This can be realized by the understanding that there is a difference between formats and media grounded in their modes of processing and handling. Formats also include thinking about a wide range of loss—of falling into oblivion and into the media-technical cleft of incompatibilities. From a format perspective, generation loss is always already taken into account. Every digital action demands a reconciliation of formats and their incompatibilities. This specific media setting would ask for different correlations of a cinematic historiography of derivation and modulation. A new resistance through image-power, therefore, could be regarded as similar to what Deleuze wants when he asks for cinema "to stop 'being cinematic'" (1995, 76): there is a specific form of loss to consider. In the case of the format, this would imply not merely a reflection based on a structural idea of boycotting certain media-specific qualities of aesthetic forms. Rather, it would imply relying on the potential to circulate, redistribute, and counter-distribute them. We will understand the above by taking an in-depth look at the moment when cinema, film, and digitality first met.

III.

According to Simon Rothöhler (2013), digital cinema begins with "digital rollout," the moment when all cinematic phases, from production to distribution, occur without having any photographic exposure as an intermediate stage, such as projecting film in the cinema. For Rothöhler, from that moment on, digital cinema can be understood as an aesthetic and media identity. Therefore, what can be called digital cinema would not start with the "dawn" but with the "high noon" of digital image quality and the corresponding media-technical "network" that is in most of its parts defined by the initialism "HD." High definition, which phenomenologically stands for supposedly super-sharp and detailed imagery, describes pixel proportions, for example, 1280 x 720 pixels, but does not name an accurate technical specification. Yet it is used as an umbrella term for different aspects of digital mediality. Rothöhler speaks of HD as a "meta-label" that could be attached to a range of digital audio and image formats, such as the 2K and 4K standards for the digital image package DCP, the HDMI transmission interface, and the grid of CCD sensors, as well as the formats for iPad screens, smartphone displays, monitors, television screens, and digital light projectors. In the case of digital cinema, HD therefore not only outlines the dispositive in the movie theatre but also constitutes a "career" of film in a technical way that leaves out the dark rooms of the cinema and introduces, in Casettis words, its relocation. The term stands for a decentralized image network in which the digital image circulates and therefore displays some conditions of media-immanence.

It seems that HD brings the digital and cinema into a mutual agreement and even makes a historiographical promise: it offers "continuity" as we came to identify in Casetti's heuristics. This theoretical implementation can be recognized through aesthetic reflections in cinema and film that playfully show the material idiosyncrasies of analog film reels through reframing and combining different aspect ratios, as in *Mommy* (2014, dir. Xavier Dolan) and *The Grand Budapest Hotel* (2014, dir. Wes Anderson), or taking up their signature scratches, fuzziness, and color grades with the help of digital filters, as prominently applied in *La La Land* (2016 , dir. Damien Chazelle). HD places *Ben-Hur*'s nine galloping chariot-race horses horizontally in one single widescreen. Offering a brilliant restoration, with praise for being the first format to present *Ben-Hur* as it was shown in movie theaters and thus assumedly satisfying all aesthetic and formative demands of the film shot in 1959, HD suggests a smooth continuity between the analog version of the original and the 8K-restored version on Blu-Ray released 2011.

If HD enables a consistency of cinema between analog and digital, then, we argue, there is a blind spot, respectively a gap, in this linear narration: this post-cinematic reflection may be confident about cinema and film's analog past but not at all about its digital history, so it seems. Considering digital cinema and film starting with HD implies denying the whole phase of experiments that came before HD. What we can see here is that post-cinema's invention of continuity presupposes the a-historicity and idealization of "the digital." Inversing the focus, we look not so much at the relation between the analog and digital as at another, apparently insurmountable, threshold, the one between SD, the standard-definition digital video format, and HD, or the distinction between two digital formats.

SD, in comparison to HD, stands in for analog PAL and NTSC signals but also describes the first digital transmission rates and digital video formats beyond television, which, as we may soon recognize, cannot be as easily converted into HD as it seems when dealing with not yet digitized pictorial material, such as *Ben-Hur* showed. Manuals on video technology determine SD as a pixel proportion of digital imagery that by definition would not be HD (see, e.g., Schmidt 2013, 15). Both SD and HD describe resolution capacities that can also describe analog signals. They subsume a plurality of different technical specifications and formats but in the end tend to be utilized to underline the difference between "the analog" and "the digital," even in Schmidt's manual for video technology. Here he writes that, although HD can be analog and SD can be digital, SD is explained in the chapter on analog signals and HD is discussed in relation to digital video formats. One way to feign a "clear cut" between "the analog" and "the digital," at least through numbers, is to draw a line between the highest digital SD signals and the lowest HD resolution, the aspect ratio 4:3 (SD) vs 16:9 (42:32), in pixels: 960 x 720 vs. 1280 x 720.

What we can see through the history of digital video formats is that in the moment of its obsolescence, SD is defined as "standard," when actually HD should be established as the prevalent resolution. SD therefore can be described as a retronym specification that is provided with an identity after its existence. In this way, the constructive nature of standardization, as "any set of agreed-upon rules for the production of (textual or material) objects" (Bowker and Star 1999, 13) is easily laid open. The relation between HD and SD points to the problems that arise when media-ontological clas-sifications (What "is" digital cinema and film in contrast to analog cinema and film?) attempt to set "clear cuts." To overcome them, we expect to trace down two tendencies of film historiography that nonetheless depend on each other. We would like to differentiate between a history that tries to eliminate these clear cuts by "inventing continuity" and a history that looks at what falls victim to those cuts, in other words, what "resists" an idea of further development. We would like to break these two histories down to the notions of "medium" and "format." Digital cinema's media historiography starts with HD and the relation between "the analog" and "the digital" and its post-cinematic tendency to invent continuity. Digital cinema's format historiography starts with SD and the problem of where to draw the line between different digital formats. Here, the pursuit of continuity is replaced by questions of in/compatibility, which we identify as a resistance to develop. On the one hand, film and cinema as medium seek historiographical *persistence* that, on the other hand, is kept running by the historiographical *resistance* of the format.

What is compatible and was is not? On a media-technical level, the format resists the historical flow of continuity. In the case of the SD format, this means that great efforts have to be taken in order to liberate it from a specific media-historical context—to relocate it. The resistance of the format represents a historical incompatibility that can be found when we return to the origin of the technology: The allegedly first fully digital produced film, and therefore coming fairly close to the "digital rollout," *Windhorse* (1998), directed by Paul Wagner, had to be photographically exposed to be shown in theatres. Yet this pioneering status didn't provide it with an outstanding position in cinema's historiography. *Windhorse* used digital technology for one reason specifically: it was shot in parts on location in Tibet, where, due to heavy political restrictions, the film team had to mime tourists using cameras that looked like small amateur recording devices. Those eventually did offer a sufficient quality to show the images on the big screen. The digital footage furthermore was cut and post-produced with digital equipment.

This initiation of a "digital cinema to come" wasn't meant to be a paradigmatic change. In the same year, however, an aesthetical rethinking, triggered by the same technical features at the basis of *Windhorse*, took hold: the films of the Dogme 95 movement used digital cameras to express their lasting critique of the film industry and Hollywood imagery. Lars von Trier's film *The Idiots* (1998) was shot using the same camera used for Wagner's *Windhorse*: the Sony DCR-VX1000, the first digital camera that combined the MiniDV format with a CCD chip. In this specific case, the reason for its use wasn't the delivered quality, which far exceeded analog video. On the contrary, having a shaky hand for transforming their jittery video image into a political statement and adhere to their "vow of chastity," Lars von Trier and the Dogme 95 movement initiated a persistent way to voice criticism. They used heavy pixilation, overcharged auto-focus, intentionally blurred images from excessive whip pans, noise from poor lighting conditions, and overexposures from too fast light changes. Here, and unlike the aspiration for using digital cameras in the *Windhorse* production, the creators used digital techniques purposefully to create low-resolution images, with poor quality not being something to overcome.

Additionally, we can identify this by having a look at the archival procedure conducted at Zentropa, Lars von Trier's film company. The DV format of the VX1000 is a master format, meaning that all information collected during shooting is stored there. Rather than using this master DV format for restoration, Zentropa is using a 35mm negative that the film was transferred to. The restorer of *The Idiots*, Cecilie Rui, explains that the detour through film is necessary to provide a sufficient quality for distribution and preservation:

> In the case of *The Idiots*, it was originally shot on DVcam. A very bad starting point for restoration. All of Zentropa's final films have been transferred to 35mm original negative. We used that material as a starting point for this film. We can extract much more information in the picture from a 35mm negative. We do an *Arriscan* from 35mm to files. In this case, since it was shot on DVcam, scanning any higher than 3K is a waste of time and money—since we will not get any more information from the picture. (Email to Elisa Linseisen, November 11, 2017)

To store and restore a specific form of digital film, which is based on the technical specification of digital SD, the genuine material is transferred to 35mm so that it can then be transferred back to the digital, this time in HD. What we can see here is that continuity is only reached through the integration of film stock, the integration of the analog, to preserve the aesthetic feature of the SD image. To add continuity to cinema and film's historiography, SD has to be detached from its existence as a format to circulate further as an aesthetic feature. The latter can easily be set in a specific tradition of style, related to the handheld cameras of the new waves in the 1960s and, from our perspective, now could easily be provided with a successor of pixelated digital images. Moreover, what we can infer is that cinematic continuity and the resistance of formats are both recognizable through forms of "bad quality," such as aesthetic or technical loss or media-aesthetic disruptions. But we think it is important to differentiate between a media-aesthetic idea of "low" and a media-technical "low" definition of digital formats.

Here we would stray from the path of invented film-historiographical continuity and suggest a differentiation between high and low formats, drawing on HD vs. SD. Two stories can be told. On the one hand, SD pixels saved on 35mm film, as in the blurred imagery of Dogme 95, should be identified as a *media-aesthetic form* of low definition. The latter would go along with what Marshal McLuhan describes in *Understanding Media* as "cold media" in contrast to "hot media," with the difference drawn explicitly in terms of "resolution," a difference between high and low definition. McLuhan differentiates the two on a phenomenological level. High-definition media offer their content sharp and noise free, while low-definition media appear blurry and pixelated. The breaking point the aesthetic would offer, its low definition, happens in perfect alignment with cinematic continuity, so much so, in fact, that the material base of the noisiness is discarded to save the phenomenological effect. It is lost from that point when the SD aesthetic is transferred onto the 35mm film stock. If SD had tried to catch up with the high quality of HD, not only would continuity have had to be invented but also pixels. With the help of upscaling, pixels can be doubled, repeated, or be blown up, meaning, in the case of Dogme 95, that the requested aesthetic specification would be lost if the format, in terms of continuity, were saved. Archival practice takes the detour through 35mm film solely because the quality of the SD image should not get better. SD on 35mm digitized in 2K therefore would in McLuhan's notion describe the paradox of *high low-definition imagery*.

On the other hand, SD pixels are saved as a *digital format* because of its supposedly good quality. For this story, we have to leave the path of cinema's continuity. If we follow the career of the Sony DCR-VX1000 and its MiniDV format, we see what a format derived from cinematic persistence could look like. Its irrelevance for production in digital cinema can be countered by its importance apart from cinema's narrative of continuity:

the SD aesthetic offered by the VX1000 and its MiniDV cassettes had an important heyday in a success story that continues to this day in the skateboard community. Right now, every recorded trick by the VX1000 is a question of format compatibility. SD stands for a specific form of digitality that is not at present set up for circulation. We could identify the technical context the SD image acts in using Haidee Wasson's idea of "networked cinema," which is an important step in the direction of a decentered form of image movement. The networked state of cinema relates low-definition imagery not to its compression, on account of excessive circulation, but to a specific infrastructural dependence, a relation between the image and a unique network where the aesthetic of the image and its content can be derived from the infrastructural requirements: "the exhibition of moving images is intimately tied to the material specifications of the networks through which they travel, their particular technological form, and the specific screens on which they appear" (Wasson 2008, 78).

If we consider where the SD images of the DCR-VX1000 appear nowadays, this tight relation between an integrated network and the quality of the image is torn apart. The internet delivers its content decentralized. Here, digital imagery heavily depends on its capacity to be compatible and flexible. This often leads to peculiarities of bad resolution, which can be described with what Hito Steyerl calls "poor images." Poor images are formatted images, being "uploaded, downloaded, shared, reformatted, and reedited" and offer a "digital uncertainty" (Steyerl 2009). SD images, as we have recognized through the example of Dogme 95, are clearly differentiable from poor images, as the "poor image is a copy in motion . . . it accelerates, it deteriorates. It is a ghost of an image . . . distributed for free, squeezed through slow digital connections, compressed, reproduced, ripped, remixed, as well as copied and pasted into other channels of distribution" (Steyerl 2009).

Poor images, the "Lumpenproletariat" (Steyerl 2009), within the class system of digital imagery, can be described more by the loss of compression than by their information density. Poor images are based on the high-standard requirements of an HD-spacious network. Their low definition results from moving in a not-even-remotely-comprehensible web, and its bad quality is the result of unpredictability and contingency, caused by incompatibilities and compression. How do the SD images of the DCR-VX1000, recorded by the skateboard community, fit into this scenario?

On YouTube we can find a certain number of carefully designated SD videos delivered by the VX. What we can also find on the video-sharing platform are many videos concerned with the question of how to transfer the recorded data from a camera having no USB output or memory card. In this specific subcultural context there is no division between SD as format and SD as aesthetics. With Dogme 95's *The Idiots*, bad quality should be saved for the sake of cinematic continuity. For the skateboard community however, the format should be saved for the sake of, in their opinion, so-called good quality. On YouTube numerous influencer videos discuss why the VX1000 still has the best quality for its purpose, emphasizing the fish-eye-lens effect or the clear sound of the uncompressed audio that portrays the collision of skateboard and pavement like no other camera. Whether it is true or not, what we can see is the effort to guarantee the compatibility of the recorded data, *just because* the format's incompatibility is at stake. With every image production, the incompatibility of the format has to be kept in mind.

What we can see here is that technology is expected to disappear. This effect takes the shape of format incompatibilities in terms of the digital, which can be seen only when we cast aside those mixed feelings that arise from worrying about the stability of cinema's continuity (and those concerns about "ontological threats"). The possibility of loss, however, even appends "ontological density" to the format by designating it as "good quality." In the case of formats, relocation does not produce media ideals or self-reflexive modes in order to develop those any further, as a film-philosophical approach suggests. Rather, the format needs to be at stake to find new (qualitative) ways of existence, like the revaluation of the VX1000 MiniDV format. Here, one can find, in Joselit's sense, a form of image-power.

*

Moving back to our opening statement about the post-cinematic, ques-tioning cinematic becoming in digital times, we could say that, by holding up the persistence of cinematic continuity, the new resistance of formats, their image-power, is lost. Formats show a media-historical attachment. Sometimes formats overcome these ties and start to move in time and space, and sometimes they do not. If media-technological hurdles are passed, such as MiniDV videos on YouTube, and the format proves its compatibility, we would like to claim a specific form of potential that is different from cinema's idea of continuity and becoming. Hence, we want to ascribe it to the relation of mediality and its specific surrounding, where, in the case of the digital image, it leads to the question of resolution. Therefore, we would like to differentiate imagery not by its perceivable, phenomenological quality but by its relation to the surrounding network. HD then can be described as an image made to circulate in a decentralized context, whereas SD is bound to a specific technical and even hardware-based surrounding. The potential of the format is distinct from forms of cinematic becoming. The difference lies in the idea of historicity. Cinema, as a medium, is capable of auto-surveying itself and its relation to other media and using this intermedia feedback loop to develop itself even further. The development of formats means a generation loss. Formats in a media-immanent condition are already and permanently at stake. They do not build up facets of complex interrelations over their history to develop further; rather, they exist to be forgotten. And if that is not the case, it is because somebody cares. Subcultural examples, such as the tender concern of the skateboard community of how to save their format, show how counter-narratives can appear when modernization starts by reformatting the existing imagery, extracting meaning by post-productive interventions and media-technical detours. A new form of resistance built up by the format might not be as recognizable from what the images show but from what they do, according to Joselit. Digital cinema and film would then not offer as much to look but instead invite us to look after images.

References

Benjamin, Walter. 1991. "Fragmente vermischten Inhalts: Zur Ästhetik." In *Walter Benjamin: Gesammelte Schriften*, vol. 6, edited by Rolf Tiedemann and Hermann Schweppenhäuser, 109–130. Frankfurt: Suhrkamp.

Bowker, Geoffrey C., and Susan Leigh Star. 1999. *Sorting Things Out: Classification and Its Consequences*. Cambridge, MA: MIT Press.

Deleuze, Gilles. 1989. *Cinema 2: The Time-Image*. Minneapolis: University of Minnesota Press.

———. 1995. "Letter to Serge Daney: Optimism, Pessimism, and Travel." In *Negotiations, 1972–1990*, 68–81. New York: Columbia University Press.

———. 2005. *Pure Immanence: Essays on a Life*. Translated by Anne Boyman. New York: Zone Books.

Fahle, Oliver. 2011. "Der Film der zweiten Moderne oder Filmtheorie nach Deleuze." In *Philosophie und Nicht-Philosophie: Gilles Deleuze – Aktuelle Diskussionen*, edited by Friedrich Balke, 115–129. Bielefeld: transcript.

———. 2015. "Außen." In *Essays zur Film-Philosophie*, edited by Lorenz Engell, Oliver Fahle, Christiane Voss, and Vincenz Hediger, 117–168. Paderborn: Fink.

Greenberg, Clement. 1989. "Avant-Garde and Kitsch." In *Art and Culture: Critical Essays*, 3–21. Boston: Beacon Press.

Hagener, Malte. 2011. "Wo ist Film (heute)? Film/ Kino im Zeitalter der Medienimmanenz." In *Orte filmischen Wissens: Filmkultur und Filmvermittlung im Zeitalter digitaler Netzwerke*, edited by Gudrun Sommer, Oliver Fahle, and Vinzenz Hediger, 45–59. Marburg: Schüren.

Joselit, David. 2011. "What to Do with Pictures." *October* 138: 81–94.

———. 2013. *After Art*. Princeton: Princeton University Press.

Krautkrämer, Florian. 2013. "Revolution Uploaded: Un/Sichtbares im Handy-Dokumentar-film." In *Zeitschrift für Medienwissenschaft* 11: 113–126.

Krauss, Rosalind. 1999. "Reinventing the Medium." *Critical Inquiry* 25 (2): 289–305.

———. 2000. *A Voyage on the North Sea: Art in the Age of the Post-medium Condition*. New York: Thames & Hudson.

Linseisen, Elisa. 2018. "Werden/Weiter/Denken: Rekapitulation eines Post-Cinema-Diskurses." *Zeitschrift für Medienwissenschaft* 18: 203–209.

Manovich, Lev. 2002. *The Language of New Media*. Cambridge, MA: MIT Press.

McLuhan, Marshall. 2001. *Understanding Media: The Extensions of Man*. Cambridge, MA: MIT Press.

Müller, Susanne. 2015. "Formatieren." In *Historisches Wörterbuch des Mediengebrauchs*, edited by Heiko Christians, Matthias Bickenbach, and Nikolaus Wegmann, 253–267. Cologne: Böhlau.

Rodowick, D. N. 2007. *The Virtual Life of Film*. Cambridge, MA: Harvard University Press.

Rothöhler, Simon. 2013. *High Definition: Digitale Filmästhetik*. Cologne: August.

Schmidt, Ulrich. 2013. *Professionelle Videotechnik: Grundlagen, Filmtechnik, Fernsehtechnik, Geräte- und Studiotechnik in SD, HD, DI, 3D*. Berlin: Springer.

Steyerl, Hito. 2009. "In Defense of the Poor Image." *e-flux* 10. http://www.e-flux.com/journal/10/61362/in-defense-of-the-poor-image.

Wasson, Haidee. 2008. "The Networked Screen: Moving Images, Materiality, and the Aesthetics of Size." In *Fluid Screens, Expanded Cinema,* edited Janine Marchessault and Susan Lord, 74–95. Toronto: University of Toronto Press.

Pod Fictions

Kalani Michell

The discussion of how to expand *Cinema Journal*, the official, peer-reviewed, scholarly publication of the Society for Cinema and Media Studies (SCMS), was not only about different formats but took place in different formats. In Twitter discussions in 2012 and 2013, Christine Becker, author of *It's the Pictures That Got Small* (2008), then the newly-named *Cinema Journal* online editor, noticed a desire in the field for a more expansive format to cover the even more expansive field of media studies. "I grew very intrigued at this idea and then I created a Google Doc to drum up ideas. Maybe ten people were chiming in then and they had ten different ideas for formats" (Becker and Kackman 2013a). Out of the Google-Doc-10 came the preference for a podcast, *Aca-Media*, which would offer "an academic perspective on film, television and other media formats" (Becker in Becker and Kackman 2013a, fig. 1). Its website header reflected its sponsorship and, by extension, the institutions it serves: "SCMS & *Cinema Journal* present: *Aca-Media*." By giving the podcast a name of its own, the novelty of this enterprise is emphasized. Something different, yet related, is to happen here. Something new, hip, trendy, digital. Something broader than cinema, but supposedly present, if not explicit, in our old familiar cinema journal. SCMS & *Cinema Journal* present: A.k.a. Media. It was about finding media in cinema, and about finding media in academia, which structured its production. Hosted by Becker, together with Michael Kackman, co-editor of *Flow TV,* it was initially conceived as a monthly podcast, eventually aligning with the ebbs and flows of the US-American semester schedule. Episodes were to last between 30 and 40 minutes in the beginning and soon ran for about an hour, consisting, as described in the inaugural episode, "of interviews with media studies academics, topic segments about everything from media news, to pedagogy to professional development, and essentially . . . [will] take you behind the scenes of media studies academia, the life, the research, the knowledge, the crippling insecurities and stresses, but also the joys of the life we lead" (Becker in Becker and Kackman 2013a).

ACA-MEDIA

A podcast offering an academic perspective on media, from SCMS & Cinema Journal

Home   Episodes   Subscribe   **About Us**   Contact   Social   Sponsors & Partners   Not-Kackman Gallery

ABOUT THE PODCAST

SUBSCRIBE in iTunes **(also available via** RSS, Stitcher, and SoundCloud)

Aca-Media is a monthly podcast that presents an academic perspective on media. Hosts Christine Becker and Michael Kackman explore current scholarship, issues in the media industries, questions in pedagogy and professional development, and events in the world of media studies. Aca-Media is sponsored by *Cinema Journal*, the official journal of the Society for Cinema and Media Studies, and has been funded in part by the Institute for Scholarship in the Liberal Arts at the University of Notre Dame. You can contact the show at info@aca-media.org, join our Facebook group, and follow us on Twitter at @aca_media.

[Figure 1] "About Us," *Aca-Media* website. http://www.aca-media.org/about/.

Interviews with academics: How exciting. You do not have to just read their work. Now you can even hear their original voices in an official, sanctioned venue if your institution doesn't have the money to bring them to campus. Will they tell you anything different from what they say in their articles? Will listeners be lured in by the authorial voice, the belief that, through it, they can be initiated "to their way of being, their joy or their pain, their condition; [that] it bears an image of their body, and beyond, a whole psychology" (Barthes 1985, 254–55)? Is this voice behind the curtain supposedly unscripted? What truth, supplement or secret is the audience about to uncover and embrace in this section? *Media news, pedagogy, professional development*: Don't worry. You don't have to feel outdated in your research (or) in front of students. You can now talk with your class about the new Facebook update. Impress superiors with the latest critique of student evaluations and inferiors by dropping the current job market statistics. Paste a timely, "real life" media example at the beginning of your historical case study to show "what is at stake"/"why this matters." *Behind the scenes of academia—the life, the research, the knowledge, the stresses, but also the joys of the life we lead*: No. We academics are not dead. We have a life. Believe it. We'll pull back the curtain and show you. Two lives, in fact: a first life with research, knowledge, insecurities, and stresses, and a second life full of joy. And they go together. Here is a section of an organization's journal that seeks to revive the belief in academia as a harmonious, indispensable cohabitation of glorified knowledge, as work and as pleasure. We are not ancient or stale. We are not statues. We live, breathe, are vivid.

Taking the heterograph and anagrams in "Aca-Media" seriously makes it more complex than a medial expansion of *Cinema Journal* run by academics. "Anagrammatical interventions within a word can be justified, on one level, on the grounds that one cannot finally decide between what is original context and distorted or derived context, what is 'proper' and improper, what is serious or not serious, or what is correct and what is a gimmick. . . . The anagram is never completely arbitrary in its manipulation of the sign" (Brunette and Wills 1989, 88). "Academia" in "Aca-Media," yes, this is most obvious, but other linguistic devices and their problems are kept in play as well. "Aca-Media" is searching for a place for our two lives, for an academic's work and joy, to cohabitate and enrich each other, a safe harbor where we can "self-proclaim . . . our allegiances as 'aca-fans,' a hybrid of academic and fan critics that acknowledges and interweaves both intellectual and emotional cultural engagements" (Mittell 2010).[1] It's a place to celebrate ourselves, a site of self-aca-fandom, where we can exoticize our scholarly love and applaud our bravery for writing about media that bring us not just pain, but also so much joy: *Star Wars*, *Twilight*, and *Stargate Atlantis*.[2] "Aca-Media" is simultaneously searching for what is also known as ("a.k.a.") "media," an abbreviation used for objects that disguise themselves, for aliases, and used figuratively to critique objects and proper nouns quickly, a means of descriptive compression. "Aca-Media" searches for ways to designate, characterize, and distinguish "media" in "academia" and for ways to reassure life in "academia" if it is not, in this present format, original or intact, but hyphenated and divided.

After eight episodes of the podcast, the hosts decide they are done with mere supplements, with merely expanding upon the print logic of their organization's publication. They are still bound, however, to the logic of an anniversary to decide *Aca-Media*'s focus, not yet at the point of independent

---

1   Cf. Bogost (2010) and Stein (2011a; 2011b).
2   See Stein (2011c).

topic proposals. This ninth episode, devoted to the 75th anniversary of the radio broadcast of *War of the Worlds*, deviates from the standard format of program elements (fig. 2). Becker interviews Neil Verma, author of *Theater of the Mind* (2012), about how the infamous public panic in response to *War of the Worlds* issued from an inability to orient oneself around a familiar voice, place, or time and a lack of location markers for where or when the action takes place. One-third of the listening audience tuned into the show after switching channels due to a format change.[3] Having listened to the familiar disembodied voice of ventriloquist Edgar Bergen as Charlie McCarthy on *The Chase and Sanborn Hour*, they channel surfed when the musical break began. Listeners couldn't see the dummy, but knew who he was, trusted how he worked, and knew the dummy could always be reversed.[4] It was a disorientation with which listeners felt safe, liked even. *War of the Worlds* was different. "No voice speaks in all scenes, no place contains all effects, and no person frames the horizon of the fiction. If intimacy is like a tracking camera shot, 'War [of the Worlds]' is a montage, a world that we teleport around instead of moving through" (Verma 2012, 66). It was a lack of intimacy with the trusted radio voice, whose role is to guide the listener by providing location and perspective, that made this broadcast so unnerving. It led to the aliens seeming somewhere visually unlocatable, constantly lurking in the aural background. The listener couldn't find their position because she didn't know her own. The broadcast played with its own format rules to unsettle the sense of presence, and present time. As Verma (2012) explains, "Its rhythm lies not in . . . steadying increments, comforting us that time is indeed marching on, but rather in a series of interruptions as one format intrudes on another with a sudden cut, suggesting that the structure of time is devolving" (71). The *Aca-Media* podcast might be closely tied to cinema—serving as its sponsor and prominent in its iconography—but it's striving, in this episode, to think about its format. What does it mean to change the channel and find oneself in the middle of an unknown program, one which is uncertain, threatening, disorienting?

3   See Hagen (2005, 244).

4   "Charlie was such a perfect ventriloquist dummy in radio because he constantly said that he wasn't, in fact, a dummy. This switch makes it clear that, in reality, he knows everything about Bergen, that he knows all his secrets, everything hidden and desired inside him, and that he was in no way prepared to keep all of this to himself. So Bergen, the one who started all this, always ends up being the dummy" (Hagen 2005, 235; my translation).

October 10, 2013

In Episode 9 we celebrate the 75th anniversary of the famous "War of the Worlds" broadcast by talking with Neil Verma about the program, its use of radio aesthetics, the panic that ensued, and the relevance of "War of the Worlds" today. There might be one or two other things going on in this episode as well … just saying.

DOWNLOAD THIS EPISODE

OR CLICK BELOW TO PLAY:

[Figure 2] *Aca-Media* Episode 9: "I'm Sure It's Nothing." *Aca-Media* website. http://www.aca-media.org/episode9.

[Transcript of *Aca-Media* episode 9, interview with Neil Verma by Christine Becker, interrupted by a report from Bill Kirkpatrick with Herman Gray, 20:35–23:00]

Neil Verma: What I think is important for media studies people to think about is . . . we should avoid the humorlessness that I think could creep into our own tactic of aggrandizing the event. Like, I think [Orson] Welles thought it was funny. I think a lot of people kind of did a bit of a facepalm and were like "Oh, you got me." And that was a big part of the overall effect of it. . . . It ultimately was a great event in radio. [sound of a tape being changed, switched out, indicating a channel change, a broadcast or format interruption]

Michael Kackman: Chris, I'm really sorry to interrupt again, but I wanted to bring in this report from Bill Kirkpatrick from Santa Cruz.

Bill Kirkpatrick: Hi, this is Bill Kirkpatrick on the campus of UC Santa Cruz talking to Professor Herman Gray about the issue of race in *War of the Worlds* and in general about the contested space of radio and television, television in particular, as a space for contesting racial meanings. Professor Herman Gray.

Herman Gray: You know . . . I . . . um . . . I've been studying . . . um . . . what is race? Um . . . I don't ever recall . . . I don't know a thing about race or television, where . . . the images of black people or brown people exist . . . um . . . uh . . . I don't know anything about that. [aural feedback]

Kirkpatrick: Um . . . Michael and Chris . . . I'm going to send it back to the
   studio . . . from Santa Cruz, California . . . uh . . . This has been Bill
   Kirkpatrick with Professor Hermann Gray? [sound of a tape being
   switched out]

Christine Becker: Uh . . . so maybe it's not just at Notre Dame? Is there
   something . . .

Kackman: We're going, we're going to have to explore this further. But . . .

Becker: This is . . . I'm starting to freak out a little bit. This is . . .

Kackman: I'm sure . . . I'm sure . . . I'm sure it's nothing. Let's just get back to
   your interview. (Becker and Kackman 2013b)

A corny media studies joke, yes, but one that forces a coming-together
of two referenced time periods—staged in the podcast as a disruption,
an interference, and an intervention—that leads to a series of other
problematic and perhaps productive situations now put into proximity.
The podcast moves from the dramatization of radio news that led to the
gradual building up of public panic in 1938 to the dramatization of academic
podcast news that will certainly not lead to a gradual building up of public
panic in 2013. It speculates on listening attitudes now, for podcasts, versus
those that were possible back then, in radio. It positions simulated news
that matters (the end of the world) next to simulated news that doesn't
(established professors doing an about-face, denying their reputations).
It assumes a familiarity with academic standards (that race, radio, television, and popular culture, for example, matter) and authorities (that
Herman Gray is the author of *Watching Race* [2004]), and it justifies and
reinforces these standards by staging their dissolution into right-wing and/
or scare-tactic journalism (into statements like, "I'm colorblind"). It parallels
the dissemination of information via radio in the 1930s with the dissemination of information from one campus to another via broadcast networks,
social media, and its own medial form as a podcast. It's about how to talk
about radio of the past in a podcast of today that can accommodate and
anticipate media, and their respective institutions, of the future.

Although, in relation to podcasts, one is likely to first think of format in
terms of file types, such as the MP3, exploring format problems here
entails more than an analysis of material medial qualities, such as film
gauges or flexi-discs, and goes beyond internal technical specifications,
such as file extensions. Formats are a means of organizing, categorizing,
and creating hierarchies within and between medial forms, and, within
radio studies, the term is frequently evoked to refer to "the arrangement

of program elements, often musical recordings, into a sequence that will attract and hold the audience segment a station is seeking" (Hausman et al. 2012, 8).[5] This includes the advice, comedy, and variety formats in the early years of radio and the DJ, top-40, soul, and classical formats in the later years. Thus, format becomes, in radio scholarship, a term designating genre, programming decisions, and serialization schedules. The format of one medium also affects, and can carry into, another. While radio, in its early years in the United States, was envisioned as a medium that could potentially educate the broader public on good aesthetic taste, bringing classical music to network radio, for instance, it was precisely the conditions of radio's format with the rise of commercialization that led to a change in this perception.

> Because daytime programing was addressed at women audiences, advertisers could see themselves as helping the homemaker care for her home and family, as well as her own appearance, and they thereby justified using harder sales tactics there than in evening programs. . . . Daytime radio—in particular the serial dramas that soon dominated it—eventually gave all of network radio the taint of feminized commercialism, an association that would carry over to television. Perhaps as a result, TV never carried the discursive potential to be a site of cultural elevation that radio did in its early years. (Newman and Levine 2011, 20)

This echoes the understanding of format as

> denot[ing] a whole range of decisions that affect the look, feel, experience, and workings of a medium. It also names a set of rules according to which a technology can operate. . . . Most crucial dimensions of format are codified in some way—sometimes through policy, sometimes through the technology's construction, and sometimes through sedimented habit. (Sterne 2012, 7–8)

Taking this podcast as an object of investigation requires a consideration of format on various levels. One must think about what it means to have access to this scholarly information and knowledge via MP3s online and

---

5   On the relationship between format and the packaging of generic arrangements, see also Volmar, Jancovic, and Schneider in this volume, specifically the reference to Gilbert Seldes: "To make individual programs forgettable, yet hold the audience, means that the format must be the link between one program and another. . . . Drama and the big popular comedy programs are in the upper reaches of radio; lower down, format is purely a matter of packaging, wrapping other people's goods in new paper" (Seldes quoted in Volmar, Jancovic, and Schneider in this volume).

available for subscription and download instead of via similar programs on terrestrial radio, and how this file extension organizes and categorizes this knowledge differently. It asks that one pay attention to the relationship between medial forms that this format implies and upon which it functions, and assess how the format of this particular podcast is codified in various ways—through SCMS policies, conventions, and stated objectives; through the technologies to which it has access and those it seeks to embrace; and through the habits of those in positions of power versus those who remain on the fringes of the network. And it requires one to examine the relationship between various medial forms within which this podcast is situated—not only the interest in new medial forms and their possibilities for expanding an academic audience and network, but also the material task of expanding *Cinema Journal*, of opening it up to new formats, exploring the relationship between writing and listening that this constructs in a journal and in a podcast with cinema in its title and visual branding. Key to this brand is the clichéd icon of analog film, the filmstrip, serving as the carrier for other media (fig. 3). And it's not just any medium—any radio—that is allowed to be carried by, or featured in, cinema, but quality radio (fig. 4).

[Figure 3] *Aca-Media* website header.

ACA-MEDIA EPISODE 9:

I'M SURE IT'S NOTHING

(OCTOBER, 2013)

[Figure 4] "Aca-Media_Ep9_Filmstrip_V2.jpg"[6] and screenshot. http://www.aca-media.org/episode9/.

If "podcast" derives, in part, from broadcast, then carriers and the mode of carrying remain of key concern to this format.[7] Broadcasting in the

6   This is the name of the image file on the website.

7   "broadcast, *v.* 1813, formed from English *broad* wide across + *cast*, v. on the basis of earlier *broadcast*, adj. (of seeds) scattered (1767), itself formed from *broad*, adj. + *cast*, past participle" (Barnhart 1988, 118).

agricultural, historical sense denotes dissemination, as expansively as possible, of the same seed from a central point. In the context of radio, it's the transmission of the same signal from a central point. Podcasting can accommodate transmissions from multiple points, undermining the idea of a hub. The relationship between the center and the periphery is more complex than it once seemed. It's a threat to centrality that is carried in the metaphor of the pod (fig. 5–6).

[Figures. 5–6] *Invasion of the Body Snatchers* (1978). Dir. Philip Kaufman.

"Lobós: a pod. . . . Look how quickly it roots. . . . Indeed, some of these plants may thrive on devastated ground" (Elizabeth Driscoll in *Invasion of the Body Snatchers*). If you get too close to one, you are emptied of meaning, of your subjectivity, sovereignty, and substance. The dissemination of pods, in this horror scenario, sheds light on what hatches and grows when you stop being vigilant. The pod packages, carries within it, something conspiring to replace you. And you can so easily be replaced, almost nobody will notice. The process looks revolting, like a festering wound, but it's not this. It's not destruction that immediately scares you, but life outside your own, threatening your own.

[Transcript of *Invasion of the Body Snatchers*: 1:31:45–1:33:42]

Geoffrey Howell (pod person): Nothing changes. . . .

David Kibner (pod person): You will be born again . . . Free of anxiety, fear
. . . .

Jack Bellicec (pod person): Your minds and memories will be totally
absorbed. Everything remains intact. . . .

Kibner (pod person): Don't be trapped by old concepts. . . . You're evolving
into a new life form. Come and watch. (Invasion of the Body Snatchers)

To the outside world, they look the same as you, but you know the
difference. They don't share your values. They don't want to continue your
way of life. They can promise that you, and your legacy, will remain intact,
that nothing will change, but you know better. After pods are cast, their
only chance of survival is to creep up on their hosts and supplant them
when they are most vulnerable.

In this podcast, the cinematic visual branding seeks to invalidate and
suppress this threat right away. After all, cinema has a history, in SCMS,
of feeling threatened. Institutional history chronicles how, over 15 years
ago, the "m" crept in on SCS, the Society for Cinema Studies, signaling a
more permanent acceptance of television studies, sound studies, and
nontheatrical film and, later, of digital media and the growing number of
so-called intermedial and interdisciplinary subfields.[8] This proliferation
of media has continued, evident in the initiative to expand *Cinema Journal*
when Will Brooker, author of *Using the Force* (2002), began his tenure
as editor in 2013. The publication of SCMS has opened up its pages and
lent its name to not only this podcast but also web-only features such as
pedagogical dossiers, online additions to its printed format, and now a
section of peer-reviewed video essays.[9] Within this discourse on the need
to "expand" academic publishing are various visions for the institution—to
be seen as fresh, up-to-date, open to new ideas and formats—as well as
the hopes and fears about what the so-called "ivory tower" is and how to
get out of it. What kind of "knowledge" do academics want to bring to the
broader or even "outside" world at a time when the institution of higher
education, and the humanities in particular, is in a state of financial crisis
repeatedly proclaimed, and at a time when SCMS can still boast, in contrast
to other humanities organizations, about its increasing membership?[10]

8   See "Organizational History."
9   See "Cinema Journal: Mission Statement."
10   See Simpson (2015, 5).

Where are the boundaries of the "outside" world for this academic podcast whose audience cannot be considered as preexisting, but rather, based on the discourse observed in its inaugural episode, seems to consist of a vague mix of advanced undergraduate and graduate students, early-career scholars, avid public listeners and fans of film scholarship, and some *Cinema Journal* subscribers?[11] One can understand this anxiety surrounding the ivory tower by thinking it along the lines of a radio tower, stressing accessibility, equality, and limitlessness, while knowing that this centralized structure for broadcasting messages and ideas opens itself up to the pos-sibility of appropriation and threatening foreign transmissions from the outside.[12] Lodged in this discourse are the specters of other media creeping in, media forms that are both coded as no-longer as well as not-yet, as it is "a proper characteristic of the specter, if there is any, that no one can be sure if by returning it testifies to a living past or to a living future" (Derrida 2006, 123).[13]

In Brooker's concept for *Aca-Media* and the other online outgrowths of *Cinema Journal*, there wasn't supposed to be this kind of slippage. Other media had a specific place of cohabitation next to the journal or, in his words, surrounding it (fig. 7).

11   On the latest demographics of U.S. podcast listeners, see Edison Research (2019). For earlier demographic reports, see, for example, Edison Research (2012). "Podcast listeners are loyal, affluent and educated [and] 80% listen to *all or most* of each podcast episode" (Winn 2019). Given this apparent commitment of podcast listeners to the episodes on their devices, recent scholarship stresses the need to pay closer attention to the broader medial interface in which podcasts are embedded and to the non-aural material toward which they guide their listeners. See Hancock and McMurtry (2018, 91) as well as Hilmes (2013). The various audiovisual materials compiled under each podcast episode on the *Aca-Media* website should also be thought of as an integral part of, rather than an addendum to, the audience's experience.

12   On the relationship between the architectural forms of early radio towers and their utopian promises of limitlessness and universality, see Buck-Morss (2002, 137).

13   On the discourse of ghostly presence in early amateur radio transmissions and of alien presence in centralized broadcast radio, see Sconce (2000, 93–94).

January 27, 2013

In this inaugural episode of Aca-Media, we interview incoming editor of *Cinema Journal* and Batman scholar Will Brooker, discuss the recent Flow Conference in Austin, TX (featuring a screening of the new Fox drama *The Following*), and report on the tribute to the late Alexander Doty held last fall in Bloomington, IN.

DOWNLOAD THIS EPISODE
OR CLICK BELOW TO PLAY:

 Ep. 1: Ceci N'est Pas Un Podcast
Cinema Journal Presents Aca-Media

[Figure 7] *Aca-Media* Episode 1: "Ceci N'est Pas Un Podcast." *Aca-Media* website. http://www.aca-media.org/episode1.

[Transcript of *Aca-Media* episode 1, interview with Will Brooker by Christine Becker, 14:35–15:55]

Christine Becker: How do you see those online initiatives, then, tied to those goals of dialogue, expansion, and so forth?

Will Brooker: The way I see that is, we're in an interesting situation here because *Cinema Journal* is a slow-moving, prestigious, literally a shiny black vehicle, and it is slow, and it's high status, and it carries privilege, and it should remain high value, because we wouldn't be doing anyone any favors if we kind of lowered the currency of what it means to be published in *Cinema Journal*, because that actually helps people to get jobs and to get tenure and so on, to get promotion. So, although I want to make the journal more accessible, I want to do that without devaluing the journal at all. So, the way of doing that I think is, really again I think it's through my approach to popular culture, which is similar to Jonathan Gray's idea about paratexts really. You have the text and then you have the surrounding satellites or the system of circulating texts. He borrows it from Gérard Genette in his work on literature. But the idea is that *Cinema Journal* will be the kind of key text, the core text, and will remain the core text, and is slow-moving like the sun or whatever. And around it we have all these faster-moving satellites which engage with each other, and they are easier for other people to engage with, and they're easier for other people to reach than getting right through to the main, the main hub. (Becker and Kackman 2013a)

Cinema Journal: slow, prestigious, the core text, the sun. In the horror podcasting scenario, the origins of the pods are shown right away, in the title sequence (fig. 8).[14] The dissemination of the pods is caused by the solar winds. By the sun, creeping in on the scene.

[Figure 8] *Invasion of the Body Snatchers* (1978). Dir. Philip Kaufman.

The dream of being able to assume the vantage point of the sun, the dream of omnipotent vision secured by this position, is an old one.[15] "The sun is the condition of all seeing. It is a medium: we do not see it, but we see everything by way of it. . . . If the eye is the light of the body, then the great star—the sun— . . . is the light of the intelligence" (Peters 2010, 16). Trying to see this medium that sees and positions everything else, however, presents a particular problem, namely blindness.[16] To see and know the sun, one has to look around it, or at what surrounds it. But as soon as one acknowledges the things on the side, the anxiously-desired structure of center and periphery—*Cinema Journal* as central (traditional, prestigious, legitimate, shiny black) and podcasts, video essays, and other online media as para-objects (experimental, more temporally responsive, and/or immediate)—is no longer stable. "Paratexts have the effect of promoting the unity of a text, but they can only accomplish this without hindrance when they are not

14   This is later confirmed by the pod people: "We drift through the universe from planet to planet, pushed on by the solar winds. We adapt, and we survive" (David Kibner [pod person] in *Invasion of the Body Snatchers*).
15   "Leonardo da Vinci . . . : 'Il sole non vide mai nessuna ombra—The sun never sees a shadow'" (Kittler 2010, 19).
16   See Kittler (2010, 51).

read in the strict sense of the word as such, that is, when no questions are asked about details, when there are no inquiries into how they function, how they make references to circumstances of production or distribution or to other aspects" (Stanitzek 2005, 34). If acknowledging and reading the pods unfixes their presumed relationship to the central text, this means, in this case, that doing so allows the claims made about cinema here, about the primacy and stability of its ontology, to be seen as such, and to see the placement of media surrounding it as equally unstable, "a habitation without proper inhabiting, call it a haunting" (Derrida 2006, 20). This horror episode of *Aca-Media* simulating the return of radio history is called "I'm sure it's nothing," because that's what the hosts, those bodies subjected to parasites, must tell themselves over and over, both when they fear the coming of the new and the death of old.

[Transcript of *Aca-Media* episode 9, interview with Neil Verma by Christine Becker, interrupted by a follow-up report from Bill Kirkpatrick with Michele Hilmes, 32:51–33:54]

Bill Kirkpatrick: . . . I was wondering if I could ask you about your latest research on radio. . . .

Michele Hilmes: On what?

Kirkpatrick: On . . . uh . . . radio. Your work on radio studies.

Hilmes: *Radio*? That medium went out with TV. Seriously, who would waste their time on something without pictures?

Kirkpatrick: Uh . . . Professor Hilmes, I'm . . . surprised to hear you say that. I thought that you thought that radio was an important medium? Isn't that . . .

Hilmes: Meh. If you're stuck in your car in traffic, you might punch a few buttons in your dash, I suppose, but you know, only if you forgot your iPod or there's nobody to text to kill the time. Who wants to listen to somebody drone on and on without pictures, graphics, *something*? Radio is *over*. Didn't you see my Facebook post about this?

Kirkpatrick: Uhhhh, no . . . I guess I must have missed that . . . well, uh . . . that's uh . . . I guess that's an interesting new . . . uh . . . perspective from Professor Hilmes. I guess . . . um . . . [*smacks lips*] . . . Christine and Michael, I'm going to [*interference with the transmission: voice distorted, tone descending, voice fading out*] throw it back to you in the studio.

[sound of a tape being switched out, long flatline beep]

Kackman: Bill, can you, can you offer further explanation of that? . . . Bill?
(Becker and Kackman 2013b)

It's a version of a familiar story. The first tales of pod-people manipulating human minds through wireless audio transmissions occurred in the 1920s, when radio in the United States was undergoing a major transformation during the institutionalization of broadcasting.[17] "In these new tales, radio became a marker of an unknown alien presence, extraterrestrial or otherwise, and a harbinger of potential subjugation. With the growth of broadcasting, authors skeptical of the new medium's social implications reimagined wireless as invisible puppet strings with the potential to manipulate the earth's docile population" (Sconce 2000, 94). Now, as radio is undergoing another transformation, one hears how something from the outside has possessed and displaced not only the trusted authorities but also one's sense of time. Audiences are listening to an illusion of liveness in this episode, to what sounds like a real-time radio broadcast experiencing interference in a format in which such noise is usually edited out in post-production, as if it were haunted by radio's physical, material past at the same time that it is alienated by the podcast's uncertain material presence.

> Hovering behind so much sonic hauntology is the difference between analogue and the digital: so many hauntological tracks have been about revisiting the physicality of analogue media in the era of the digital ether. MP3 files remain material, of course, but their materiality is occulted from us, by contrast with the tactile materiality of vinyl records and even compact discs. (Fisher 2014, 21)

As with alienation, the rhetoric of spiritualism and mysticism—longing, loss, and haunting—pervaded an array of early popular, scientific, and technical discourses on radio. It was motivated by "the way that receivers reel in distant voices out of that incomprehensible dimension called spectrum and effortlessly bring them straight to us, linking us, through the air, to unseen others. The fact that radio waves are invisible, emanating from 'the sky,' carry disembodied voices and scan signals deep into the cosmos links us to a much larger, more mysterious order" (Douglas 2004, 41).[18] This podcast retrieves the voices of radio's advocates to tell listeners that the medium is *over*, and that new media confirms it, while the sonic manipulation at the end of the interview and the subsequent radio silence confuses it. But I tell myself that I'm sure it's nothing.

---

17   On the different trajectories of US and European radio histories, see Hagen (2005; 2008).

18   See also Sconce (2000, pp. 59–91, 92–123).

As with radio, the scholarly discourse on podcasts has oscillated between alienating and haunting, between the occupation and replacement of radio through a new form and the revival and reanimation of radio in a new form. This is, in part, because secondary sources on podcasting often recycle terms and concepts from industry discourse, which tends to want to market its products as radically new (and thus radically different from what came before, namely radio).[19] In the earliest writings on the format, podcasts were often fantasized as the antidote to radio, which, while rarely defined, was presumed to mean for-profit, corporate, mainstream broadcast radio.[20] In later texts, podcasts were often imagined to be a means of extending the life of radio currently under threat from other media and digitization. These texts also had a tendency to elide the complex history of radio, from early variety shows to amateur productions to underground and experimental programming.[21] Either radio was dead and podcasts represented the more democratic, immersive, personal, intimate, utopian future of audio culture, or radio was still living, now just in a different format, an approach that called for finding the utopian old in the utopian new. Both arguments reiterated what were assumed to be the unique qualities of podcasting: presumably freed from broadcasting schedules, podcasts were described as a time-shifting technology, creating a community of listeners that was believed to be liberated from standardized episodic and broadcasting schedules. In contrast to radio programs, podcasts could be long or short, produced and released at will, according to their own timetables, and therefore were believed to be more experimental in terms of what content was included in their programs and how this content was arranged. Such analyses praised the changes to playback and reception in podcasts, namely the ability to listen "anywhere," releasing an audio production from its presumed restriction to the space of the home, car, or personal computer.

19   See Bottomley (2016, 50–51). For examples of the emphasis placed on the novelty and participatory, amateur, or DIY qualities of podcasts, see a range of case studies: Santo and Lucas (2009), Meserko (2015a; 2015b), Salvati (2015), Hancock and McMurtry (2017), and McCracken (2017).
20   See, for example, Berry (2006). On the early journalistic employment of "podcast" to describe the emergence of new amateur online radio formats, as well as the corporate branding of the term (a combination of branded device and the means of delivery), see Sterne et al. (2008): "Despite Apple's fervent desire to control all things pod, the term podcast was primarily the product of a disorganised exchange carried out amongst technology journalists and online computer enthusiasts in the early 2000s" (n.p.).
21   See, for example, Hilmes (2013) and Edmond (2015).

These texts also characterized the podcast audience as exhibiting different listening habits and expectations than radio listeners. Changes to dissemination techniques, such as Really Simple Syndication (RSS) feeds, offered listeners the ability to subscribe to podcasts they liked, receiving automatic downloads from sites. Software scripts allowed for the transfer of these files to their personal devices, such as smartphones, and to apps, such as iTunes, that enabled listeners to build collections. And since they were no longer encountering programs by chance, as they presumably did with radio, these were listeners who were imagined to be more committed.[22] Podcast listeners choose to subscribe, opt in, and press play. They have their favorite hosts whom they know and trust. They are fans. The wide reach of the internet collects them, rendering programs financially viable that would have otherwise been too specialized for a broadcast audience and at the same time giving listeners the feeling that they can finally get the in-depth coverage and analysis of the micro topics they care about. A podcast host can take her listeners on a lengthy, windy introduction into a certain story, for example, without the immediate concern that they will change the dial.[23] Podcasts are channeled through headphones directly into the listener's ears, and they are presumed to have some exceptional qualities. They are characterized as intimate and conversational, detailed and uncompromising, and, in some cases, exhibiting a certain sense of liveness between program segments, an unexpectedness as to what will come next: from bizarre sound effects to chummy conversations to lengthy found audio footage.[24] They often emphasize the conditionality of ideas, presenting arguments in draft form, with hosts and guests raising a selection of points and then moving on without the need for a dramatic conclusion or a sense of closure.[25] It was presumed that, for these reasons, podcasts have a tendency to focus on certain themes and genres that benefit from these styles and conventions, such as nonfiction in-depth storytelling, advice programs, personal profiles, longform journalism, and current cultural, political and site-specific events.

Emerging scholarship on podcasts is seeking to complicate such techno-democratic arguments, pointing out that one must not only take into account the complex history of radio (as something more than mainstream

---

22 Apple's podcast analytics, which launched on December 14, 2017, supports the assumption, to some extent, that podcast audiences are composed of committed listeners (see "Access Podcast Analytics" 2018 and Katz 2018). Cf. Quah (2018) and Goers (2018).
23 See Ragusea (2015) and Llinares et al. (2018).
24 See Bottomley (2016, 71–77).
25 See Llinares (2018, 134).

broadcasting) but also differentiate between podcasting as a distribution channel for existing radio content and podcasting as an emerging programming and formatting vehicle for different, sometimes new content.[26] This most recent literature also calls attention to the features that radio broadcasting and podcasting nevertheless seem to have in common, namely the use of specific auditory forms and arrangements that emphasize their liveness and ability to authenticate and help shape social structures and environments in ways that seems intimate, immediate, and responsive. "After all, the 'intimacy' of podcasting is one of its most remarked upon characteristics. And intimacy implies immediacy, closeness, presentness, sharedness: all attributes that are vital to radio's sociability" (Bottomley 2016, 71).

Intimacy is a concept that not only characterizes podcasts but also applies to broader distinctions in Western thought between hearing and seeing, what can be described as the long-held dichotomy between vision objectifying and sound personifying:

> Vision, since it is untainted by the subjective experience of light, yields a knowledge of the outside world that is rational, detached, analytical and atomistic. Hearing, on the other hand, since it rests on the immediate experience of sound, is said to draw the world into the perceiver, yielding a kind of knowledge that is intuitive, engaged, synthetic and holistic. [And] while we can never be certain of what we see, there is no doubt about what we hear. . . . We do not suffer from aural as we do from optical illusions. In short, when it comes to affairs of the soul, of emotion and feeling, or of the 'inwardness' of life, hearing surpasses seeing. (Ingold 2000, 245)

Such assumptions about the promise of oral communication were underlying the relationship that Brooker sought to construct between *Cinema Journal* and *Aca-Media*, between a printed text and an audio file. One can hear it in the style of communication between the hosts, reminiscent of the "chumcast," "in which two or more hosts riff off each other, chatting in a casual or rambunctious manner around a theme, making the listener feel included in a private no-holds-barred conversation" (McHugh 2016, 12). And one hears this promise to reveal the "inwardness of life" in how the podcast pads its interviews with *Cinema Journal* authors. In between questions about the topic, argument, methodology, and scholarly contribution of their texts, guests are asked about where they're from, how

---

26   See Markman and Sawyer (2014, 21), as well as Heise (2016, 1–2) and Llinares (2018, 125–26).

they got here, what problems they encountered in their research, what fascinated them about their topics. These are things you wouldn't necessarily read in *Cinema Journal*, fulfilling the promises of intimacy described in the inaugural episode, "to take you behind the scenes of media studies academia," and showing you the research, knowledge, insecurities, and stresses, as well as the great joy (Becker and Kackman 2013a). When *Cinema Journal* leaves its pages and passes through your ears, it refashions itself as a little insider tip from those who have been solidified in the shining black beacon-vehicle of hope for attaining tenure, in its main text. It offers information from those who know for those who seek to know, those on the fringes striving for acceptance in the academy, responding to what Erhard Schüttpelz notes is the continual complaint of first-year students: they are not given enough information, not enough canonical texts and prescriptions for methodological approaches that could help them stop feeling like dilettantes. "Man will sich in der Institution mehr *zuhause* fühlen dürfen" (Schüttpelz 1995, 47). One wants to feel more *at home* in the institution.

October 30, 2014

It's a spooky, mystery-filled Halloween for the Aca-Media team. Chris has just moved into a new house, only to discover that it might be haunted. While she and Michael investigate (luckily our SCMS grant enabled us to afford a deflux modulator!), we bring you a "*Cinema Journal* Classics" interview with Jennifer Hyland Wang about her 2000 *CJ* piece on *Forrest Gump*. Then we give you a tour of last year's SCMS Undergraduate Conference and a preview of what you can expect from next year's ... if the ghost doesn't get you first!

DOWNLOAD THIS EPISODE
OR CLICK BELOW TO PLAY:

Ep. 18: You're Gonna Scare Him Again
Cinema Journal Presents Aca-Media   3:25 / 52:48

[Figure 9] *Aca-Media* Episode 18: "You're Gonna Scare Him Again." *Aca-Media* website. http://www.aca-media.org/episode18.

Schüttpelz suggests that you never really arrive in the institution, you're never at home, never safe, and that can be productive. Just before Halloween in 2014, Becker and Kackman played around with the idea of coming home and not feeling safe. This episode has a great idea. This time, it revisits an earlier *Cinema Journal* contribution rather than a contemporary one, and Becker describes this as "a key thing in academia, the revisiting of things from previous years," in this case a classic essay on *Forrest Gump* (Becker and Kackman 2014, fig. 9). The podcast can't get started, however, because she claims that something is lurking around in her new house.

[Transcript of *Aca-Media* episode 18, introduction sequence with Christine Becker and Michael Kackman, 3:25–4:02]

Christine Becker: Just before the Coffin's moved in . . . um . . . in 1979, the previous owner died here.

Michael Kackman: [*anxious*] Oh gaaaawd.

Becker: And the previous owner was a professor.

Kackman: [long sigh, disgusted, creeped out] Ughhhhh.

Becker: And so . . .

Kackman: Was his *office* down here?!

Becker: That could very well be.

[a tool booting up, getting ready to scan something]

Kackman: I'm getting some flux bits here. . . .

[the tool powered up, scanning, moving around to detect something]

Becker: So . . . A couple times when I've come down here, I've . . . I've heard things. And I swear, they sound like words . . . [*things being moved around in a large, confined space, lids opening and shutting, surfaces being tapped*] They sound like words about academia. [*something ripping or being torn off*] Someone saying something. Scary things. About academia.

[things being pushed around, knocked over]

Kackman: Well, there are a lot of scary things about academia.

[tapping on something wooden]

Kackman: Do you think we can reach out to this guy? (Becker and Kackman 2014).

An academia of the past, of the 1950s or 1960s, is haunting her, and the hosts must exploit their sonic space—ringing bells, tripping over things, dropping the mic—to perform the proper rituals to ease the ghost's concerns about the state of academia today. Don't mention Twitter, Kackman says—you might scare him.

While this episode is haunted by the ghosts no-longer, the one sampled previously, also thematizing the podcast's relationship with other media, attests to its cohabitation, its uncertain tension, with those specters that are not-yet. In the 2013 academic *War of the Worlds* podcast drama, the professor replaces the operator in this sign-off rather than returning to console listeners.[27]

[Transcript of *Aca-Media* episode 9, closing sequence with Bill Kirkpatrick, 49:50–51:19]

[whooshing or winding up of an incoming transmission, as if from or into outer space]

Kirkpatrick: This may be the last podcast. [atmospheric, ambient sounds, as if transmitting from a hollow, desolate space] But I'll stay here 'til the end. The collective knowledge of . . . decades of cinema studies . . . media studies . . . radio . . . TV . . . cultural studies . . . it's gone. [sporadic, metallic whooshes of transmissions in the background] The, the MOOCS have taken it all. . . . This is the end now. . . .[28] [short, metallic whooshes] 2X2L calling! . . . 2X2L calling! [short, metallic whooshes] Isn't there anyone in media studies?! . . . Isn't there anyone in . . . academia?!" [louder atmospheric, ambient outer space sounds] "Isn't there . . . " [higher-pitched incoming transmission with static or interference, quickly increasing in volume, as if approaching] " . . . anyone?!" [ten seconds of effects indicating a cutting off or interruption of transmission: high-pitch, harsh whooshing in; alarm steadily beeping in two tones, back and forth, indicating warning or error; quickly descending tone of static hiss; other sounds fading out, beeps isolated, intense, descending in tone; abrupt silence] (Becker and Kackman 2013b).

In the 1938 broadcast, it's an alien, and in the 2013 broadcast, it's something alien, the unknown future of media studies coming from outside, making us academics ask ourselves what happens if we believe our discipline has broken down—what happens if there's nobody left, no reigning authorities, in what we know to be cinema and media studies. Radio silence often connotes avoidance, but at other times, paradoxically, a response.[29] When it

27   Cf. Operator ("2X2L calling CQ . . . 2X2L calling CQ . . . 2X2L calling CQ New York . . . Isn't there anyone on the air? . . . Isn't there anyone on the air? . . . Isn't there . . . anyone? . . . 2X2L") and Professor Pierson ("As I set down these notes on paper, I'm obsessed by the thought that I may be the last living man on earth") in *War of the Worlds*.

28   MOOC is an acronym for a massive open online course. On the MOOC controversy around this time, see "What You Need to Know About MOOCs." For a more recent take, see Hill (2016).

29   "The second paradox of 'radio silence' bears precisely on the concept of silence to which it appeals, and is nowhere more concisely stated than in the French pro-words

was time for *Cinema Journal* to change editorial hands, in November 2017, SCMS members were invited to enter into a discussion about changing the name of the organization's premier journal. Fantasies about its new title and format ensued, but were ultimately overwhelmed by the frustrations and anxieties that set them in motion (fig. 10). Many felt that this was too little too late. Why did time seem so out of joint? Why was there such a disconnect between the organization, its journal, the efforts to expand this publication, and its diverse body of members, whose interests are already, but in no way sufficiently, represented in conference panels and scholarly interest groups? Faced with radio silence on what to do, some responded.

[Figure 10] Facebook screenshot. November 30, 2017.

'silence, silence, silence!' where something of a molecular articulation of a perfor-mative contradiction is to be heard. The phrase is its own override" (Mowitt 2015, 154).

Ghosts of the past return, both as fears and hopes for the future—for a time and situation when this can all be laughed at. A few months later, a public discussion about the name change, hosted by the new *Cinema Journal* editor, Caetlin Benson-Allott, author of *Killer Tapes and Shattered Screens* (2013), was streamed via Facebook Live. A platform on which academics can flaunt their two lives—work and joy—show they're not dead, but hip even, tech-savvy, using a feature that carries connotations of urgency, democracy, and activism. The stream tells the tale of the name debate in terms of a problematic divide: Surveying the last few years, Benson-Allott finds out that 47% of the papers delivered at the SCMS annual conference were exclusively about cinema, while cinema topics dominated 85% of feature articles in *Cinema Journal* (Cinema Journal 2018b). The media kids attend the conference and publish somewhere else, and the goal is to get their words into the pages of cinema's journal by expanding it, offering the same "m" which once crept in on SMCS to now invade the title of that "core text." The anxieties that surface in this exchange concern the pod problem of supplanting, decentering. It's a concern about the boundaries of formats, recalling the familiar MP3 problem of the limits of human hearing and the anxiety about what is sampled out of this format, how this is reconfigured for the listener and whether it's within her human abilities, both physically and conceptually, to notice it.[30] It's a problem of locating the boundaries of the human, and the humanities, in this format and, for this case, an issue of where one format ends and the other begins, ensuring that one is not decentered in the process. SCMS soon decides on a strategy for quelling this friction: "IT'S OFFICIAL! We tallied up more than 1,000 votes—78% were in favor of changing the name to the Journal of Cinema and Media Studies (JCMS)!" (Cinema Journal 2018a). Add a letter to the name, add media and international people to the editorial crew, add special interest groups to write shorter texts. Additive rather than generative, more reactionary than self-reflexive, and not uncommon in disciplinary paratexts. Take a departmental website, that place where people go "not just to obtain information about our programs, but also to get hints about the type of contexts that structure the work of the particular department" (Hueser 2009, 236). A film department website with famous filmmakers, stars, and filmstrips begs the question: Why do we academics stop working when it comes to our paratexts? How can we continue to do our work in the pods we cast, in the formats we employ to disseminate our discipline, and how can the complexity of these formats represent and

30   See Sterne (2012, 177–79).

perform the complexity of our work?[31] The interface is a site that draws attention to the interaction between formats, a methodological point of departure for investigating the limits of different formats and how they interact within a carrier.[32] At the moment, this pod remains a site of friction, and if "the interface is an 'agitation' or generative friction between different formats," then one can find here many levels of irritation, maybe some of them generative (Galloway 2013, 31). In the minds of many SCMS fan fiction media kids, their pod has not yet taken off. The live stream tells them not to be worried, their feet are still on the ground, their disciplines have not been radically reformatted, but remain, with cinema as the sun, as they believe to know them. Their pod was never really cast, a simple fiction, but maybe there is not only, in this case, a possibility for generative frictions, but also for generative fictions.

Acknowledgements

Many thanks to Kerim Doğruel, John Mowitt, and Verena Mund for their helpful comments on this paper.

References

"Access Podcast Analytics, Best Practices, and Secure RSS Feed." 2018. *iTunesPartner.Apple.com*, July 18. Accessed September 1, 2018. https://itunespartner.apple.com/en/podcasts/news/100002358.

Barnhart, Robert K., ed. 1988. *The Barnhart Dictionary of Etymology*, s.v. "broadcast, *v.*" Bronx, NY: The H. W. Wilson Company.

Barthes, Roland. 1985. "Listening." In *The Responsibility of Forms: Critical Essays on Music, Art, and Representation*, translated by Richard Howard, 245–60. New York: Hill and Wang.

Becker, Christine, and Michael Kackman. 2013a. "Ceci N'est Pas Un Podcast." *Aca-Media.org*. Accessed April 15, 2014. http://www.aca-media.org/episode1/.

———. 2013b. "I'm Sure It's Nothing." *Aca-Media.org*. Accessed April 15, 2014. http://www.aca-media.org/episode9/.

———. 2014. "You're Gonna Scare Him Again." *Aca-Media.org*. Accessed January 15, 2015. http://www.aca-media.org/episode18/.

Berry, Richard. 2006. "Will the iPod Kill the Radio Star?" *Convergence: The International Journal of Research into New Media Technologies* 12 (2): 143–62.

Bogost, Ian. 2010. "Against Aca-Fandom: On Jason Mittell on Mad Men." *Bogost.com*, July 29. Accessed November 15, 2017. http://bogost.com/writing/blog/against_aca-fandom/.

Bottomley, Andrew. 2016. "Internet Radio: A History of a Medium in Transition." Dissertation, University of Wisconsin-Madison.

Brunette, Peter and David Wills. 1989. *Screen/Play: Derrida and Film Theory*. Princeton: Princeton University Press.

Buck-Morss, Susan. 2002. *Dreamworld and Catastrophe: The Passing of Mass Utopia in East and West*. Cambridge, MA: MIT Press.

---

31   See also Mowitt (2011, 192–201).
32   See Galloway (2013, 30–33).

Cinema Journal. 2018a. "IT'S OFFICIAL!" *Facebook.com*, January 27. Accessed January 27, 2018. https://www.facebook.com/CinemaJournal/posts/1993391230674318.

———. 2018b. "Welcome to the live discussion of the Cinema Journal name change referendum. Please leave your comments below!" *Facebook.com*, January 8. Accessed January 8, 2018. https://www.facebook.com/CinemaJournal/videos/1969627549717353/.

"Cinema Journal: Mission Statement." *SCMS*. Accessed October 15, 2017. https://www.cmstudies.org/page/cinema_journal.

Derrida, Jacques. (1994) 2006. *Specters of Marx: The State of the Debt, the Work of Mourning, and the New International*, translated by Peggy Kamuf. New York: Routledge.

Douglas, Susan. 2004. *Listening In: Radio and the American Imagination*. Minneapolis: University of Minnesota Press.

Edison Research. 2012. "The Podcast Consumer 2012." *EdisonResearch.com*, May 29. Accessed April 11, 2019. https://www.edisonresearch.com/the-podcast-consumer-2012/.

———. 2019. "The Podcast Consumer 2019." *EdisonResearch.com*, April 5. Accessed April 11, 2019. https://www.edisonresearch.com/the-podcast-consumer-2019/.

Edmond, Maura. 2015. "All Platforms Considered: Contemporary Radio and Transmedia Engagement." *New Media & Society* 17 (9): 1566–82.

Fisher, Mark. 2014. *Ghosts of My Life: Writings on Depression, Hauntology and Lost Futures*. Winchester: Zero Books.

Galloway, Alexander. 2013. *The Interface Effect*. Cambridge: Polity Press.

Goers, Stacey. 2018. "Remote Audio Data Is Here." *NPR.org*, December 11. Accessed January 10, 2019. https://www.npr.org/sections/npr-extra/2018/12/11/675250553/remote-audio-data-is-here?t=1555594135307.

Hagen, Wolfgang. 2005. *Das Radio: Zur Geschichte und Theorie des Hörfunks—Deutschland/USA*. Munich: Wilhelm Fink Verlag.

———. 2008. "Alternating Currents and Ether: Two Paradigms of Radio Development: U.S. vs. Europe." In *Re-Inventing Radio: Aspects of Radio as Art*, edited by Heidi Grundmann, Elisabeth Zimmermann, Reinhard Braun, Dieter Daniels, Andreas Hirsch, and Anne Thurmann-Jajes, 53–62. Frankfurt am Main: Revolver.

Hancock, Danielle and Leslie McMurtry. 2017. "'Cycles upon Cycles, Stories upon Stories': Contemporary Audio Media and Podcast Horror's New Frights." *Palgrave Communications* 3. Article number: 17075. Accessed November 15, 2017. https://www.nature.com/articles/palcomms201775#data-availability.

———. 2018. "'I Know What a Podcast Is': Post-*Serial* Fiction and Podcast Media Identity." In *Podcasting: New Aural Culture and Digital Media*, edited by Dario Llinares, Neil Fox, and Richard Berry, 81–105. Basingstoke: Palgrave MacMillan.

Hausman, Carl, Frank Messere, Philip Benoit, and Lewis B. O'Donnell. 2012. *Modern Radio Production: Production, Programming, and Performance*. 9th edition. Belmont, CA: Wadsworth Publishing.

Heise, Nele. 2016. "On the Shoulders of Giants? How Audio Podcasters Adopt, Transform and Re-invent Radio Storytelling." *Transnational Radio Stories*, Online Radio Master of the Martin Luther University of Halle-Wittenberg, 1–6. Accessed October 15, 2018. https://hamburgergarnele.files.wordpress.com/2014/09/podcasts_heise_public.pdf.

Hill, Phil. 2016. "MOOCs Are Dead: Long Live Online Higher Education." *Chronicle.com*, August 26. Accessed November 15, 2017. https://www.chronicle.com/article/MOOCs-Are-Dead-Long-Live/237569.

Hilmes, Michele. 2013. "On a Screen Near You: The New Soundwork Industry." *Cinema Journal* 52 (3): 177–82.

Hueser, Rembert. 2009. "Looking Good with Kafka." In *The Meaning of Culture: German Studies in the 21st Century*, edited by Martin Kagel and Laura Tate Kagel, 225–54. Hannover: Wehrhahn Verlag.

Ingold, Tim. 2000. *The Perception of the Environment: Essays on Livelihood, Dwelling and Skill*. London and New York: Routledge.

Invasion of the Body Snatchers. 1978. Film. Directed by Philip Kaufman. Culver, CA: United Artists.

Katz, Miranda. 2018. "Podcast Listeners Really Are the Holy Grail Advertisers Hoped They'd Be." *Wired.com*, January 29. Accessed September 1, 2018. https://www.wired.com/story/apple-podcast-analytics-first-month/.

Kittler, Friedrich. 2010. *Optical Media: Berlin Lectures 1999*. Translated by Anthony Enns. Cambridge: Polity Press.

Llinares, Dario. 2018. "Podcasting as Liminal Practice: Aural Mediation, Sound Writing and Identity." In *Podcasting: New Aural Culture and Digital Media*, edited by Dario Llinares, Neil Fox, and Richard Berry, 123–45. Basingstoke: Palgrave MacMillan.

Llinares, Dario, Neil Fox, and Richard Berry. 2018. "Introduction: Podcasting and Podcasts—Parameters of a New Aural Culture." In *Podcasting: New Aural Culture and Digital Media*, edited by Dario Llinares, Neil Fox, and Richard Berry, 1–13. Basingstoke: Palgrave MacMillan.

Markman, Kris M. and Caroline E. Sawyer. 2014. "Why Pod? Further Explorations of the Motivations for Independent Podcasting." *Journal of Radio & Audio Media* 21: 20–35.

McCracken, Ellen. 2017. "The *Serial* Commodity: Rhetoric, Recombination, and Indeterminacy in the Digital Age." In *The* Serial *Podcast and Storytelling in the Digital Age*, edited by Ellen McCracken, 54–71. New York: Routledge.

McHugh, Siobhan. 2016. "How Podcasting Is Changing the Audio Storytelling Genre." *The Radio Journal: International Studies in Broadcast and Audio Media*, 14 (1): 65–82.

Meserko, Vincent M. 2015a. "Standing Upright: Podcasting, Performance, and Alternative Comedy." *Studies in American Humor* 1 (1): 20–40.

———. 2015b. "The Pursuit of Authenticity on Marc Maron's *WTF* Podcast." *Continuum* 29 (6): 796–810.

Mittell, Jason. 2010. "On Disliking Mad Men." *Just TV*, July 29. Accessed November 15, 2017. https://justtv.wordpress.com/2010/07/29/on-disliking-mad-men/.

Mowitt, John. 2011. *Radio: Essays in Bad Reception*. Berkeley: University of California Press.

———. 2015. "Radio Silence; or, on the Fritz." *Cultural Critique* 91: 150–63.

Newman, Michael Z. and Elana Levine. 2011. *Legitimating Television: Media Convergence and Cultural Status*. New York: Routledge.

"Organizational History." *SCMS*. Accessed October 15, 2017. https://www.cmstudies.org/page/org_history.

Peters, John Durham. 2010. "Introduction: Friedrich Kittler's Light Shows." *Optical Media: Berlin Lectures 1999*, by Friedrich Kittler, translated by Anthony Enns, 1–17. Cambridge: Polity Press.

Quah, Nicholas. 2018. "A Year In, Apple's Podcast Analytics Have Been an Evolution, Not a Revolution." *NiemanLab.org*, December 4. Accessed January 10, 2019. https://www.niemanlab.org/2018/12/a-year-in-apples-podcast-analytics-have-been-an-evolution-not-a-revolution/.

Ragusea, Adam. 2015. "Three Ways Podcasts and Radio Actually Aren't Quite the Same." *Current.org*, July 13. Accessed September 1, 2018. https://current.org/2015/07/three-ways-podcasts-and-radio-actually-arent-quite-the-same/.

Salvati, Andrew J. 2015. "Podcasting the Past: Hardcore History, Fandom, and DIY Histories." *Journal of Radio & Audio Media* 22 (2): 231–39.

Santo, Avi and Christopher Lucas. 2009. "Engaging Academic and Nonacademic Communities through Online Scholarly Work." *Cinema Journal* 48 (2): 129–38.

Schüttpelz, Erhard. 1995. "Die Akademie der Dilettanten (Back to D.)." In *Akademie*, edited by Stephan Dillemuth, 40–57. Cologne: Permanent Press.

Sconce, Jeffrey. 2000. *Haunted Media: Electronic Presence from Telegraphy to Television*. Durham, NC: Duke University Press.

Simpson, Jill. 2015. "Letter from the Executive Director." In *SCMS 2015 Conference Program*. *SCMS*. Accessed October 15, 2017. www.cmstudies.org/resource/resmgr/2015_Confere nce/SCMS2015_programNR.pdf.

Stanitzek, Georg. 2005. "Texts and Paratexts in Media." Translated by Ellen Klein. *Critical Inquiry* 32 (1): 27–42.

Stein, Louisa Ellen. 2011a. "On (Not) Hosting the Session that Killed the Term 'Acafan'." *Antenna*, March 18. Accessed November 15, 2017. http://blog.commarts.wisc. edu/2011/03/18/on-not-hosting-the-session-that-killed-the-term-acafan/.

———. 2011b. "Post-SCMS musings on the value of the word acafan." *Louisaellenstein. com*, March 17. Accessed November 15, 2017. https://louisaellenstein.com/2011/03/17/ why-the-term-acafan-matters-but-maybe-we-could-lose-the-dom-in-acafandom/.

———. 2011c. "SCMS 2011 Workshop: Acafandom and the Future of Fan Studies." *Louisaellenstein.com*, March 16. Accessed November 15, 2017. https://louisaellenstein.com/2011/03/16/ scms-2011-workshop-acafandom-and-the-future-of-fan-studies/.

Sterne, Jonathan. 2012. *MP3: The Meaning of a Format*. Durham, NC: Duke University Press.

Sterne, Jonathan, Jeremy Morris, Michael Brendan Baker, and Ariana Moscote Freire. 2008. "The Politics of Podcasting." *The Fibreculture Journal* 13 (FCJ-087). Accessed September 1, 2017. http://thirteen.fibreculturejournal.org/fcj-087-the-politics-of-podcasting/.

Verma, Neil. 2012. *Theater of the Mind: Imagination, Aesthetics, and American Radio Drama*. Chicago and London: University of Chicago Press.

War of the Worlds. 1938. Directed by Orson Welles. New York: CBS.

"What You Need to Know About MOOCs." 2012. *Chronicle.com,* August 8. Accessed November 15, 2017. https://www.chronicle.com/article/ What-You-Need-to-Know-About/133475#comments-anchor.

Winn, Ross. 2019. "2019 Podcast Stats & Facts (New Research From Apr 2019)." *PodcastInsights.com*, April 11. Accessed April 11, 2019. https://www.podcastinsights.com/ podcast-statistics/.

Authors

Erika Balsom is a senior lecturer in Film Studies at King's College London, specializing in experimental cinema, moving image art, documentary, and film and media theory. Her book, *After Uniqueness: A History of Film and Video in Circulation*, was published by Columbia University Press in 2017.

Oliver Fahle is Professor of Film Studies at Ruhr-University Bochum with a research focus on the aesthetics and theory of film and audiovisual media, and Deputy Speaker of the German Research Foundation graduate collective "Documentary Practices: Excess and Privation."

Florian Hoof is a research associate at MECS, Institute for Advanced Study on Media Cultures of Computer Simulation, Leuphana University Lüneburg. His fields of research include digital cultures, organizational media, film and media history, non-theatrical film, and media industries. His book *Angels of Efficiency: A Media History of Consulting* is forthcoming with Oxford University Press in 2020.

Marek Jancovic is a lecturer at the Institute of Film, Theater, Media and Cultural Studies at the University of Mainz and guest researcher at the Amsterdam School for Cultural Analysis. His doctoral dissertation *Misinscriptions: A Media Epigraphy of Video Compression* explores the value of decay and error for media-historical research.

Elisa Linseisen is a postdoctoral Assistant Researcher at the Institute of Media Studies at Paderborn University. Her doctoral dissertation engages with an aesthetic theory of high definition images with a media-philosophical focus.

Ramon Lobato is Senior Research Fellow in the School of Media and Communication at RMIT University, Melbourne. His research interests include video markets, piracy, and informal media economies.

Roland Meyer is a postdoctoral researcher and lecturer in art history at the Faculty for Architecture, Civil Engineering and City Planning of the Brandenburg University of Technology Cottbus-Senftenberg. His research focuses on the history and theory of technical images, the visual culture of modernity and the history of art, design and architecture after 1945. His latest book, *Operative Porträts: Eine Bildgeschichte der Identifizierbarkeit von Lavater bis Facebook*, was published by Konstanz University Press in 2019.

Kalani Michell is Assistant Professor of European Languages and Trans-cultural Studies at the University of California Los Angeles. Her primary research interests include film studies, media theory and historiography, installation and performance art, and print culture.

Alexandra Schneider is Professor of Film and Media Studies at the Johannes Gutenberg-University Mainz and Principal Investigator at the DFG-funded Research Training Group "Configurations of Cinema."

Antonio Somaini is Professor in Film, Media, and Visual Culture Theory at the Université Sorbonne Nouvelle Paris 3. His works deals with the history of film and media theories (W. Benjamin, S.M. Eisenstein, L. Moholy-Nagy, D. Vertov) and with key issues in contemporary visual and media culture, such as the implications of high and low definition, and the new forms of machine vision. He is currently working on a book entitled *Medium Archaeology* (University of Minnesota Press) and on an exhibition entitled *Time Machine. Cinematic Temporalities* (Parma, Italy, January-May 2020).

Markus Stauff works at the Media Studies department at the University of Amsterdam. His main research areas are television and digital media, governmentality studies, and media sports. For publications see: https://www.uva.nl/profiel/s/t/m.stauff/m.stauff.html

Wanda Strauven teaches Film and Media Studies at the Johannes Gutenberg-University Mainz. Her research focuses on early cinema, touch-based media and screen practices of post-cinema from interactive media installations to creative media hacking by today's children.

Julian Thomas is Professor of Media and Communication at RMIT University, Melbourne. He is interested in the histories of new communications technologies and informal media economies.

Axel Volmar is a Postdoctoral Research Fellow at the DFG-funded Collaborative Research Center "Media of Cooperation" (SFB 1187 Medien der Kooperation) at the University of Siegen. His research interests include the history and theory of digital media, infrastructures, and cultures, sound studies, digital temporalities and cooperative media.